PRAISE FOR
THE ICEMAN EXPERIENCE

"I had the privilege of coaching James at West Virginia State College and knew only bits and pieces of his background. After reading *The Iceman Experience*, my respect and admiration for his accomplishments on and off the court have only magnified. The journey of Iceman is masterly woven into memories that are at times unimaginable, which make them that much more inspirational. This is a great read for any basketball fan, especially those of the inner city, but more importantly, it's a great read for those looking to overcome obstacles in life."

—Bob Starkey, Women's Assistant Basketball Coach, Auburn Tigers

"*The Iceman Experience* is a sensitively told yet brutally honest reflection on life, the everyday struggles in 1970s Harlem, and how one of its own used the game of basketball to escape its ravages. The story is a triumph in what illuminates our country's ongoing struggles with the realities of racial strife, flaring emotions, determination, and heartache."

—Josie Olsvig, Author of *Gullah Tears*

"An incredible tribute to any inner-city athlete emerging from the desperately challenging, inspiring, and rewarding basketball era of the 1960s, '70s and '80s."

—Ron Moore, Second-Round NBA Draft Pick 1987, New York Knicks

The Iceman Experience: Memoir of a Harlem Playground Star

by James A. Washington

© Copyright 2021 James A. Washington

ISBN 978-1-64663-453-8

Published by

 köehlerbooks ™

3705 Shore Drive
Virginia Beach, VA 23455
800-435-4811
www.koehlerbooks.com

Memoir of a Harlem Playground Star

THE
ICEMAN
EXPERIENCE

JAMES A. WASHINGTON

VIRGINIA BEACH
CAPE CHARLES

*Dedicated to my loving mother, Evelyn Washington, without who's strength
and faith I may have never been able to achieve some
of my dreams.*

*And to my "Drew Crew", life long brothers and sister who helped me
discover an identity when I was still searching for one.
To you I am eternally grateful:*

*Mike Poole
Anthony (Quarterfield) Sanders
John (Jonny Mac) Easley
Warren (Big E) McDowell
Michael (Jelly) Richardson
Maurice (Mo Blind) White
Aaron (Ap) Allen
Anthony (Ant Ice) Poole
Daryle (Dee) White
Derrick (D Smooth) Matthews
Robert (Sputknik) James
Renee (Nay Nay) Brown RIP
Theodore (T-Gator) Jackson*

CONTENTS

INTRODUCTION
THE ICEMAN EXPERIENCE

GEORGE GERVIN IS THE original "Iceman" of professional basketball. Even though there has never been another Iceman at the NBA level, I'm sure there were thousands of other aspiring pro players such as myself answering to the "Ice" moniker during Gervin's NBA reign. Gervin came onto the scene playing in obscure basketball venues, first at Eastern Michigan, and then in the Eastern League, the precursor to the CBA, for the Pontiac Chaparrals. Gervin eventually made his way into the ABA and then the NBA where he would win four scoring titles in the latter 1970s and early '80s.

No guard in the modern era of basketball, pre-Michael Jordan and post-Jerry West/Oscar Robertson, has been a more prolific scorer than Gervin. Abnormally skinny, Ice was six foot seven and maybe 185 pounds when he began his pro career in 1974. He gave new meaning to the term "big guard," a trend that would only grow in basketball across America. Ice learned to play in Detroit, which, like NYC, Chicago, and many other big cities, was acclimated to a twenty-four-hour cycle of basketball. The original Ice knew what many of the boys I grew up with did: the only way to become great was to live the game. Basketball was life.

Gervin's gift, other than his length, was in his ability to score. He had a knack for scoring under almost any circumstance. It was the kind of gift you only discovered in a basketball-dominant culture. He scored from midrange, long range, one-on-one, one-on-two, or around the basket. After joining the NBA in 1976 after the ABA/NBA merger, Ice proved to everyone that he was legitimately un-guardable. He led the league in scoring for three consecutive years, from 1977 to 1980. The most memorable Iceman performance, to me, was his 1979 Eastern Conference Finals playoff battle with the Washington Bullets, who at the time had three Hall of Famers in Elvin Hayes, Bobby Dandridge, and Wes Unseld.

I was completely devoted to NBA basketball by this time and absorbed everything I could about the game. I read every issue of *Sports Illustrated* and *Basketball Digest* I could get my hands on. I watched NBA games on television, including basketball novelties like games of H-O-R-S-E played by NBA professionals on *Wide World of Sports*. I watched Red Auerbach's specials on fundamentals, and three-on-three and one-on-one competitions with players like Bob Lanier, Bob Dandridge, and Jo Jo White. To say I was into the game as a young teen was an understatement. Basketball literally defined who I was.

The Spurs lost the 1979 Eastern Conference Finals to the Bullets. It was a hard-fought seven-game series, with the Spurs losing the last and final game by two points. They would never get that close again during George Gervin's tenure. Unfortunately, Ice only had the talented Larry Kenon as his backup, who often played like an all-star but could also be inconsistent. Kenon, who was at least six foot eight, still holds the NBA record for most steals in a game: eleven.

Despite the on-and-off great play of Larry Kenon, the competitiveness of the series was exclusively due to Gervin's brilliance. Ice was three points away from almost single-handedly taking his team to the NBA championship, and a lot of people took notice. This gave me some insight: no matter how great a player you were, no one person could do it alone against the best players in the world—an important lesson to learn since I was already playing against some of the best fourteen and fifteen-year-olds in the world.

The first basketball player I emulated was Charlie Scott, a six-foot-six guard and fellow Harlem native. Charlie was the first Black scholarship player to play for UNC. I watched Scott play in the Rucker Tournament one hot Saturday afternoon and thought, *This guy has the game figured out.*

Soon after I saw Charlie play, another Harlem native and phenomenal street legend captured my imagination. Joe Hammond frequently battled Scott, Earl Monroe, and other future NBA Hall of Famers like "Tiny" Nate

Archibald in the summer leagues in Harlem in the early 1970s. I forgot about Charlie for a while after discovering Joe, until Scott wound up with the Boston Celtics in 1976 and I found myself rooting for him again. I also fell in love with the talents of Pete Maravich and David Thompson, two phenomenal NBA scorers at the off-guard spot. I liked a few small forwards in the NBA also, guys like Walter Davis, Bernard King, and Marques Johnson, especially after their epic battle for rookie of the year in 1978. I compared their stats every week. All of these guys influenced how I saw the game. I wanted to handle and shoot the ball like Pistol, score like Gervin, and stop on a dime and pull up for my jump shot like DT. I wanted it all.

People started calling me "Ice" around age thirteen, and the name stuck. It started in my block, but I wasn't quick to embrace the title since it came with a lot of unwanted pressure. In 1977, a lot of young boys were trying to be "Ice" and embellishing their skills by copping this popular nickname in basketball. Soon my nickname was being circulated around different neighborhoods where people didn't really know me, or my real name. Eventually, it was like playing to defend a title I didn't choose. People wanted to find out if my skills merited the label. As I got better, I realized I wanted my own signature and my own unique style of play. As Gervin's legacy grew larger and larger, there would be more and more imitation "Icemen" in almost every ghetto neighborhood where basketball was played. I didn't want to be just another one of them.

I hadn't found my loud game at thirteen or fourteen. A "loud game" meant not only that your skills and talent spoke for you, but also that you firmly believed in every loud word spoken on their behalf. Confidence and arrogance gave you a loud game. When people first called me "Ice," my game was quietly bubbling. As an introvert I didn't want the scrutiny the nickname came with. I just wanted to play basketball. Of course, eventually, as my "loud" game emerged, being an introvert or extrovert didn't matter as much. "Ice" would follow and define me everywhere basketball took me in the next ten years of my life.

The more I practiced and played, the more authentic my moniker became. My game appeared effortless to people watching from the sidelines, like it was a walk in the park.

That's what over 8,000 fans were thinking in February 1986 when I dropped fifty-eight points in a college conference tournament game at the West Virginia Civic Center in Charleston, West Virginia. It's a record that hasn't been broken in thirty-three years. I was twenty-two then, and had long ago stopped trying to escape the "Iceman experience" that followed my career and dominated my basketball life from 1977 until that night in the Charleston arena. Once I found my *loud* game, I enjoyed validating the nickname. When opponents doubted or questioned whether I was authentic, I got a high convincing them I was.

I wanted everyone to see that I was legitimately gifted. Even though people on the street and in basketball circles were calling me Ice as a sign of respect, I never wanted anyone thinking of me as a wannabe—the way many thought Kobe Bryant was a Michael Jordan wannabe. I never saw Kobe this way. Kobe Bryant came into the NBA as an eighteen-year-old rookie and was already a better shooter than Jordan even though he wasn't as impressive as a rookie. Jordan came into the league two years older and more experienced, but there were things Kobe did at eighteen that Jordan wasn't doing at twenty-two, even though Jordan was obviously a better player. If you compare twenty-two-year-old Kobe to twenty-two-year-old Jordan, that gap closes considerably.

I think Kobe's skills spoke well for his individual greatness but often wondered how he felt when people talked about him trying to be too much like Michael Jordan. Had I played in the NBA with any degree of success, the same thing could have happened in my situation. The last thing I wanted in my career was for people to think I was trying to be like George Gervin when I was trying to be *better* than George Gervin.

New York City ballplayers, the better ones, are known for our ball handling. If you watched any playground basketball in Harlem during the '70s and '80s, you would see exceptional ball-handling and play-making skills from a variety of guys. By my sixteenth birthday I was already thinking of ways to distinguish my talent from the original Iceman. Having an exceptional handle and increasing the range on my outside shot were skills I believed might help me get there, so I worked on these things obsessively.

Where I was trying to go with my game is exactly where Kevin Durant took his level of play more than twenty-five years later. Durant's taller, can shoot from longer range, has a better handle, and executes sharper and more dynamic change-of-direction moves to get space than the original Iceman did during his NBA career. Durant has perfected all of the things I worked on to try and supersede the original Iceman.

Today, Kevin Durant has taken the George Gervin Iceman experience to another galaxy. No one can say KD is trying to be *like* Gervin because he's accomplished more than anyone named Ice could ever think about doing offensively, not to mention he's three to four inches taller than Gervin. But Durant does play with the same unemotional demeanor and detached, cerebral approach.

I would have loved to bridge the gap between the original Iceman and the new-and-improved killer-Durant version of the Iceman, but that obviously wasn't in the cards. We've seen a lot of thin, prolific, high-scoring two guards between Gervin and Durant, but I don't think any other pro player has bridged the talent and style gap between these two exceptional wing scorers. Perhaps this book can shed some insight as to why I wasn't able to do it, and why I never, during my playing days, was able to shred the shadow of the original Iceman.

There were many titles and revisions for this book before I decided on *The Iceman Experience* as the title. I never kept a journal, but after reading Claude Brown's *Manchild in the Promised Land* in the sixth or seventh grade, I began writing about my own experiences in Harlem. As I accumulated nearly thirty years of old notebooks, record books, and stacks of papers, this book has taken various shapes, forms, and titles—such as *CREAM (Cash Rules Everything Around Me)*, *The Harlem Basketball Chronicles*, and *The Life and Times of a Harlem Streetball Player.* But none of them fit better than *The Iceman Experience* since my basketball career was encapsulated by the nickname "Iceman."

Being naturally quiet and intuitive, I was adept at observing things in others, especially things the average person simply missed or overlooked. These qualities enabled me to distinguish my talent amid the vibrant culture of basketball in Harlem in the '70s and '80s. But my basketball talent was always a double-edged sword. Even though my game was respected, my impersonal, laid-back, and cerebral persona made critics question my desire and heart for the game, much like Gervin and Durant's lack of passion has been questioned and periodically criticized by fans, writers, coaches, and sometimes other players. Making the game look easy and not getting excited can work for and against you in basketball. I learned to make this work for me, but not before a whole lot of heads had to be cracked.

In George Karl's book, *Furious George*, he talks about how hard it was for him to get a read on Gervin when both were playing for the Spurs in the late 1970s. Karl, who had played for Dean Smith, was a hard-nosed player from Pittsburgh whose style might fit in just as well in the NHL as it did the NBA. He played aggressively and passionately, showing how badly he wanted to win. On the flip side, George Gervin wasn't wired that way. Ice didn't get excited, and that perplexed Karl, who reportedly once said, "The way you beat Ice is you beat Ice up."

During my serious playing days, I didn't know any of this about Gervin or George Karl, but these stories could be describing pieces of my past basketball life. I was never manic, and never overly excited, but opposing coaches and players always felt they needed to deal with and neutralize me for their team to win.

If people can't match your talent, they're going to want to take the game to a place where your talent can be diminished or marginalized, especially when you weigh a buck eighty. If they can't outplay you, they try and "out physical" you. That's their only shot when dealing with super-talented guys able to score in a variety of ways.

I always viewed the "physical era" of basketball, something I believe grew wings out of the CBA into the NBA of the late '80s and '90s, as a means for players with no special or unique abilities or talents to keep up with exceptionally talented offensive players. If you really got something—I mean a real skill, talent, and mindset for being great—then no one player is going to stop you.

How can anyone keep up with Pete Maravich, David Thompson, or George Gervin? Clyde Frazier is known as one of the greatest guard defenders to play in the NBA, but that didn't help him the night Pete Maravich dropped sixty-eight points on the Knicks. If there had been a three-point line when "Pistol" scored sixty-eight, the score may have gotten into the eighties. Joe Dumars was a great individual defender. Do you think he ever really contained Jordan? The most dominant offensive players were always going to be too much for an individual defender, especially during the time I was coming up—when the combination of skill and imagination was at its apex.

During my playing days, people brought out "extras" when they couldn't handle what I was doing on the court, something that usually either backfired or was circumvented by my figuring out a workaround. Part of the Iceman experience was being, as they say on the streets, "light in the ass." Gervin, Durant, and I were all light-in-the-ass players. I was long and pretty good at blocking shots, so people learned to use their weight if they could. But when you're light in the ass, you learn to use what you have to anticipate and maneuver things to your advantage. This is a lifelong lesson. If your skills develop enough, you learn to use people's weight, strength, and aggression against them and in your favor.

Often, bigger, heavier, and more aggressive players who started out determined to dominant me were by the end of a game avoiding eye contact and looking to switch off. I've always believed you can't play basketball mentally or physically like a football player. In basketball, length often beats strength, and nuance or innate ability at the highest levels of the game cannot be deterred physically unless you remove or suspend the rules of the game. At least, that's been my experience.

Anyone great will tell you, if they've studied the game, that a lot of what basketball is has to do with nuance, and intangible and innate talent. The biggest and strongest guys will never dominate the landscape of basketball. Shaq did. So did Wilt and Moses. But they are not the rule or the natural progression for how basketball has evolved or is evolving. I recall the comment Kevin Durant made a few years ago when being compared to LeBron's physical stature: "Bron works on his body. I work on my game." And that's what I did as a skinny kid in Harlem. I worked on my game, perfecting every offensive shot and maneuver I could imagine until I was recognized everywhere as "Ice."

Many of my basketball coaches, similar to George Karl in his exchanges with George Gervin, never understood my personality, and I rarely cared or knew enough to provide them clarity on who or what I was on my way to becoming. I didn't receive what they were trying to give me, nor did I express my playing ability the way other guys did. I played for a lot of young and inexperienced coaches whose only reason for putting up with my aloof, nonchalant approach to the game was because of my talent. The one thing I always had working for me was managing to produce on the court, particularly when it counted most. With that kind of trade-off, most allowed me to be more of who I was.

Being aloof and at times seemingly disengaged and introverted is part of the reason why Kareem, the greatest scorer in the history of basketball, was never able to get an NBA coaching job once he was done playing. A lot of people never understood his personality or his political stances as an activist during his playing days, and it probably carried over into his post-basketball life.

Growing up in Harlem, if you were tuned in to what was happening around you, could shape you to question people and become more critical, nontraditional, and distrustful. This was definitely me inside and out. Coaches never questioned my ability to perform, but I wasn't much for deep, meaningful relationships with other people. I never had a coach I trusted to know what was best for me. I wanted to play and be the best player I could, and to whatever extent they could help me do that, fine. If I felt they weren't up to the task, then it was a different story. If I didn't know or trust them, all they got from me was my talent and ability—and not many of the extras and sacrifices conducive with allowing someone to help me become a greater player. This is a shortcoming of many athletes who fail to reach their ultimate potential.

Perhaps a John Thompson, John Chaney, or a Phil Jackson could have broken through and been the kind of mentor an athlete with my background needed most. Of course, I made do with what I had and was still able to learn from all my coaches and their experiences as I pursued my basketball dreams.

I believe now that to get to the pinnacle of their abilities, an athlete who discovers their gift requires a breakthrough somewhere, or an awareness that allows them to let someone in, someone they trust enough to sacrifice a part of themselves for. John Wooden did that for Kareem, and Phil Jackson was the same vehicle for alpha-male players like Michael Jordan and Kobe Bryant. But many athletes never reach their apex of talent and ability because they learned to only depend on themselves. It takes a lot more effort for a coach to gain the trust of athletes who have achieved a certain level of success on their own.

I learned to navigate—some would say survive—Harlem's streets from the 1960s to the '80s with little guidance, which may have been both fortunate and unfortunate. I had no father, older brother, or uncle to help me. What I learned, most of it, I learned on my own. I liked many of the Harlem coaches I played for in the community centers and summer leagues, but to say I trusted them with anything important would be a lie. It didn't help that I attended a specialized high school far removed from the basketball landscape I experienced in Harlem. As a result, I had no established coach/player relationship throughout my high school years the way the other players at my talent level I encountered in leagues around the city did. I learned to trust my talent. Any sacrifices I made were to improve my skill and ability, and that was where most of my emphasis was.

We live in a world of extroverted dominance. This ego-driven confidence is often associated with being a winner or a hard worker and having toughness and heart. The truth is, most of the world is introverted. Even people who exhibit extroverted tendencies aren't natural extroverts. A lot of the loudest and most out-front individuals are wearing masks because they falsely believe that introversion, and introspection, somehow makes you weaker. This leads people to say the wrong thing or play a role counterintuitive to their conscious self.

I saw a lot of this playing basketball. It's why super-talented introverts like Kevin Durant, Kareem, George Gervin, and many others are consistently misunderstood and mischaracterized. People still talk about how Barry Sanders, another example of an extreme introvert, walked away from football at the peak of his career. They couldn't understand how someone still in his prime and on the cusp of breaking the all-time NFL rushing record could just walk away from the game. Introverts are completely misunderstood in this world of what I believe is misguided extroversion.

My basketball life was a paradox. In a lot of ways, the way I played said things I didn't have the ability or confidence to verbalize in normal social settings or in life off the court. There was no social awkwardness for me on the basketball court. I became whoever I wanted to be out there. There was no fear, or trepidation—only new ground to conquer. As I became better and better at the game, people began assuming things. They figured no one who played the way I did could be shy, or awkward, or unsure about anything. They assumed my greatness on the basketball court extended to other areas of my life. And this was never the case.

Today, even though I'm long past my playing days, most of my childhood friends, college buddies, and former basketball associates still recognize and call me Ice. I'm certain there are thousands of other athletes answering to this homage to George Gervin, but I can't speak for them. I can only speak for my Iceman experience and what it meant to me. And so that's what I'm doing by writing this book. I can think of nothing more appropriate to describe my basketball experiences, from Harlem to Florida, to West Virginia, Hawaii, and eventually Europe, than naming this book *The Iceman Experience.*

• • •

Despite the pressure, being recognized as "Ice" was often a source of pride. I loved when unsuspecting opponents scoffed at the comparison. I'd light their asses up in a matter-of-fact manner and see a transformation come over them when they were confronted with reality—that I could really play. Suddenly they didn't fight through screens as hard. They switched off to guard someone else. Some loud talkers got quiet; others got even louder and tried to psychologically shift focus. I would remain quiet and become even more aggressive offensively to destroy any confidence they may have had. And then of course some guys would get extra physical, testing how much they could get away with, and this often ended in fights.

I learned to fight and retaliate when the situation called for it. There was always a guy out there like Kent Benson, a rookie center for the Milwaukee Bucks in 1978 who decided he could get away with flagrantly elbowing Kareem Abdul-Jabbar in the gut. Kareem, the introverted talent, squared up and knocked Benson down and nearly out with a single, jaw-breaking punch, leaving him cowering on the floor. It was the kind of thing a skinny introvert like me would eventually have to do when someone crossed the line. If you were talented, quiet, and not overtly physical, people were going to test you, especially when they got desperate and were being embarrassed. I occasionally had to fight my dearest friends and unfamiliar rivals for these reasons. It was par for the course in Harlem.

The Iceman Experience is as much about Harlem as it is about basketball. It's about how life in Harlem could be altered by the game and how I used the game to alter and shape my own reality. It is about how my basketball talents took me to the top of the basketball food chain in New York City without use of a road map or a path on the mainstream road.

I was never a high school all-American, yet I was recruited as if I was. I didn't attend Five-Star Nike camps or participate in the AAU farm system, yet by the time I was eighteen, I had received more than a hundred letters from Division I institutions. I talked to and had conversations with many high-profile college coaches trying to recruit me, like John Thompson, Bobby Cremins, Lefty Driesell, and Lou Carnesecca. I was an obscure talent who played in the shadows of the more popular high school all-Americans like Walter Berry, John Salley, Ed Pinckney, Kenny Hutchinson, and Pearl Washington, whose respect I had whenever I stepped onto the court with them. My journey was driven my own way, and so my subsequent shortcomings, missed opportunities, and failures in basketball ultimately reside with me.

Occasionally, I'll run across a guy from my past who can't help but ask me something like, "Damn, Ice, you were a bad mothafucka. What happened? Why didn't you go pro?"

I can only tell them the truth. I made too many bad decisions, acquired too many bad habits, and in some cases had absolute bad timing. It had nothing to do with my ability to play basketball, so what else can I say? This was my Iceman experience.

PART 1
1963–1968

CHAPTER 1
A CHANGE GONNA COME

LIFE BEGAN IN HARLEM. It was still famous Harlem, though poverty-stricken, run-down, and bad Harlem. Harlem in the 1960s was often portrayed in blaxploitation films like *Black Caesar, Across 110th Street,* and *Superfly.* This was the Harlem my generation would get credit for escaping or surviving. It wasn't the glamorous entertainment life you once saw on TV. World-famous venues like the Cotton Club, the Savoy, and Small's Paradise were gone. Great sports legends like Joe Louis and Sugar Ray Robinson left also, as did talented jazz musicians, and actresses like Eartha Kitt and Cicely Tyson. My Harlem was not a place you wanted to retire or live in too long. It was a place you left behind because, for too many people, it was easier to die in this Harlem than it was to live.

This was the case in 1963, the year I was born. I came into the world four years after great blues singer Billie Holiday died from a heroin overdose in 1959. Heroin ruled in Harlem. The biggest names in Harlem's preceding years were already legendary—names like James Baldwin, Adam Clayton Powell Jr., and Madam C. J. Walker. In my era, the rich and famous were Nicky Barnes, Pee Wee Kirkland, and Freddie Meyers, notable gangsters earning millions on Harlem's streets. Harlem from the 1960s to the 1980s was about drugs, poverty, and violence. There was always violence.

Like most of the world, Harlem was changing. Only, our changes were broadcast on television for the world to see. Changes in Harlem came with protest, discontent, and violence. Did I mention violence? Violence over Viet Nam. Violence on the streets, and violence in the hearts of people. This was the Harlem I inherited. The one I would eventually love, even though it seemed to hate me every now and then.

My parents were raised in rural South Carolina, sixty miles north of Charleston, the symbolic capitol of South Carolina. My father was nearly five years older than Ma and already living in Harlem when they met. Both were ready for a change of scenery, and neither wanted the farm life they were born into. Three motivations were driving people to migrate or immigrate all over the world: money, power, and respect. My parents wanted all three.

Black people who wanted to make money were leaving the South. Some moved north and returned driving Cadillacs they couldn't afford. Others wearing fancy clothes and hundred-dollar shoes left their Southern relatives and neighbors gaping in astonishment. The word would spread around their rural hometowns, giving people something to talk about. The message was received: money was the key to a new life, and north was where to go get it.

My parents also wanted the power of self-determination, to decide how they lived and were treated. That wasn't something Black people born in the 1940s believed they could get in the South, at least not to live and talk about it. Black people were being killed for being "too uppity" or being suspected of wrongdoing when their only real crime was having brown skin.

As for respect, both Ma and Pop had high respect for themselves, despite their restrictive Jim Crow environment. There were a lot of stories in the South about Black culture, but very few were of Black people having the money, power, or respect my parents came to Harlem looking for.

Harlem was the new world for people coming from the Carolinas, Georgia, or Florida. It was no different for Black people migrating from Mississippi, Louisiana, and Alabama to the south side of Chicago, St. Louis, Detroit, or Pittsburgh. Harlem had been home to Black culture's biggest personalities, and it was still a beacon for Black America despite declining conditions.

New York City seemed like a good place for two young people who thought a lot of themselves to take root. It was the biggest and most well known of all cities. Why not live in a place where the greatest heroes in Black culture had lived? It was a bold move, leaving the farms, dirt roads, and backwoods behind and venturing into the biggest metropolis on earth. Fortunately, both my parents had connections to New York City.

Pop's side of the family was already entrenched in New York by the time he and Ma met. He was an only son, and his family life was less structured. Pop's family had been moving north since the 1930s. His father, Wilbur, died before Pop started school. I learned little about my paternal grandfather, not even how he died. Not long after losing her husband, my paternal grandmother, who I called Nanna, followed her three sisters to New York City. Nanna was the third-oldest sister but the last to leave the South, looking for work, a new husband, and a better life. Her sisters took root in Boston, Connecticut, and Harlem.

Though Nanna initially came without Pop and Aunt Sister, the threat of violence increased her urgency for getting her children away from the South a soon as possible.

Pop's family was from Grover, SC, a twenty-to-thirty-minute drive from where Ma was raised. When Pop was eight or nine, he was playing in a school park next to one of the local food markets when a little White girl commented about his "pretty eyes." At some point in their exchange, she called Pop a nigger, though not necessarily intended to be an insult. It was not the first time someone White called him a nigger. He was called nigger by grown-up Whites as a matter of reference. It was normal.

But Pop must have been feeling differently that day. Initially, the little girl told Pop his eyes, which were a hazel green despite his dark skin, were pretty like a cat's. Pop would learn later he apparently had eyes like a White man. He retreated to a place behind the farmers market to avoid the girl, but she followed him, inviting a few other little White girls to observe Pop's eyes by saying, "Come look at this nigger with his cat eyes." Feeling ridiculed, Pop got angry and smacked the girl's face while waving her away. She cried. Pop was detained and admonished by one of the White farmers.

That night, the girl's father showed up at Great-Grandma Sue's house, demanding Pop be disciplined. He was a small man, a farmhand, but Pop was always quick to recount how the farmhand talked down to her, calling her everything but a child of God and threatening to whip Pop's nigger ass on the spot if she didn't. Great-Grandma Sue was not willing to witness a stranger beating her only grandson, and not knowing what else to do, she beat Pop a second time to appease the farmer. She said the first beating she gave him was for being stupid enough to hit the girl. The second was just one of those things he had to deal with since he was Black.

Life was never the same down south for Pop after that, not that it had been great before then. Pop eventually quit school and began his quest to follow his mother and other relatives to the big city.

Pop and Aunt Eleanor, who everyone called "Sister" because she looked more like her mother's youngest sister, Margaret, than her own mother, didn't make it to Harlem until 1955, the same year Emmett Till was murdered. Pop was thirteen or fourteen. Before moving permanently, they shuffled back and forth from the South to NYC as Nanna got established. Both spent considerable time with Aunt Margaret, who after marrying her husband, Uncle Preston, was a little better established. Throughout the 1950s, Pop and Aunt Sister witnessed card parties at Aunt Margaret's place where brown-bag corn liquor was poured from glass to glass and served with pigs' feet and cornbread.

It would be another seven years before Ma saw the big city, but like Pop, she had older relatives who had made the transition from rural South Carolina to Harlem, the Bronx, and Brooklyn.

Ma had the bigger family. Maybe it just looked bigger because it was more intact. I rarely knew who my father's relatives were outside his immediate family members. His mother, sister, and Aunt Margaret were the only family that seemed to matter to him. With Ma's family, I got to know my cousins and even second cousins because they were always around or congregating at some family event. On Pop's side we didn't have family events. When they got together, it was usually by chance.

Ma had four older siblings, three brothers and one sister, who were already living in New York City by the time she finished high school in 1962. Jim and Catherine found places in Harlem, and her other two brothers, Mayo (the oldest sibling) and Floyd, after living briefly in Harlem and the Bronx, had moved into public housing projects in Brooklyn. They were all married, had started families, and lived in tenements before moving into the projects. All made yearly pilgrimages back to the South.

Ma's sister Catherine was more secluded from our family. Her husband, James Mosley, was abrasive and kept her as remote as he could. He was a full-grown man when he met Aunt Cat, who was reportedly only fourteen. He was loud, aggressive, and abusive enough for my maternal grandfather to threaten to kill him, so Uncle Mosley's solution was to keep her isolated from the family.

Ma's family were church-tithing farmers who grew their own food and raised their own cattle. Grandma Katie, my maternal grandmother, canned fruits and vegetables year-round, and PaPa, my maternal grandfather, took care of the livestock and was a laborer on the railroad. A grocery store for them was a convenience, not a necessity. PaPa didn't talk much, so he was mysterious to me as a child. When we were down south during summer visits, I would catch him looking at me oddly, like he didn't know who I was. I found out later the only grandfather I would ever know didn't care for my father. Pop was just another James Mosley who snatched another one of his daughters. Ma was eighteen when she got married to Pop, and neither of my grandparents attended the wedding.

The Ravenells were considered well-off in Dorchester County because not a lot of people could do for themselves like they could. But the farm life for Ma's generation was dying quickly as most were leaving, headed to New York City, a place with little need for farming skills. Ma still had a strong connection to her family, but even though she was the last of five siblings to leave, she was more than willing to leave the farm lifestyle behind.

The differences between my mother and father's side of the family would play out for most of my life. Growing up, I often felt as if I was born to live two or more different lives than I was living. The strong traditions and rigid family structure of my mother's people stood in direct contrast to my father's looser, riskier, and less traditional family lifestyle. My father took risks—too many, some thought. Pop was wild in some ways. As a young Harlem migrant, he learned to gamble, smoke cigarettes, and peddle moonshine. Everyone thought he was a smart young cat, but he wasn't educated. Ma told me later in life how he marveled at how easily I read the Sunday paper cartoons out loud, especially the Blondie skits.

My mother was more pragmatic and traditional. Pop hated church, something I must have inherited, but my mother lived by the church and her faith. She used both to solidify her foundation in an environment she didn't completely understand or trust in New York City.

CHAPTER 2
THE HARLEM GHETTO
OF THE 1960S

HARLEM WAS VIEWED AS a wasteland by the rest of New York City. It was the world's most famous slum. Ma and Pop married, moved into their first tenement apartment in 1963, and started a new life. We lived in Spanish Harlem. Our building was on 117th Street between Madison and Park Avenues. It was a dilapidated structure and a health hazard. We were two blocks from Lexington Avenue, and in the heart of "the Barrio." Ma was new to the scene, so Pop tried to school her about life in the Barrio. He said Puerto Ricans ran the Barrio, since everyone else was outnumbered.

The truth was, East Harlem, like most bastions of vice in the city, including the police, was being managed and run by Italian and Jewish gangsters.

Our ravaged tenement was on the verge of being condemned, but no one seemed to care, not even the people living there. There was no landlord to complain to, and the super, Mr. Finch, a former number runner, was a drunk always on the lookout for his next bottle of Wild Irish Rose. According to Aunt Margaret, only the worst winos and drunks drank Wild Irish.

Some days there was no hot water in the building, and the wall paint was chipped in all the hallways. Squatters lived on the first floor, and entire families seemed to sleep all day only to come out in the late afternoons. One apartment ran an extension cord from the streetlamp post for power. The building was plagued by rats, and delinquent notices were posted in the lobby from the health department. Next to the building we called home was a vacant lot filled with rubble, bricks, rocks, broken wood, cans, bottles, and trash. It was normal for a truck to pull up and dump whatever junk or trash they wanted to discard into the lot. For the first five years of my life, 117th Street was home, where I learned to throw bottles against brick walls and play with alley cats.

In 1960, the census reported that only 51 percent of the housing in Harlem was of sound nature, as opposed to 85 percent in other areas of the city. We lived in the tenements from 1963 to '68, and by then the NYC buildings department was receiving 500 complaints a day from Harlem's tenements. People called about the rats, failing plaster, lead poisoning, lack of heat, unsanitary plumbing, and countless other inhibitors to a standard quality of life.

People were agitated and angry about their living conditions. Even the people minding their own business and going to work every day knew how fucked up things were. Revolution was brewing on streets of Harlem. The volume was turned up so high that we were all affected by it—right down to belligerent drunks, politicians like Adam Clayton Powell, or intelligent orators like Malcolm X. People were either getting high, getting angry, or getting out of Harlem.

The entire Black world was revolting around me. Halfway across the globe, Lumumba organized the discontented in the Congo as Malcolm organized on Lenox Avenue. Malcolm X in the early '60s was the most contentious Black voice not only in Harlem but everywhere he went to speak. People like Ma, fresh from the South, had never heard anyone talk about White people or society as openly defiant or as effectively as Malcolm X. My family didn't know how to take him, or the Muslims, but no one could ignore the effect he was having on the streets. The Muslim thing was new and foreign for my family. They steered away from getting into anything associated with it, but for those like me, just being born into this time, our perspective naturally evolved differently.

Harlem was more crowded but had less to offer than ever before. We were still the first stop for Black migrants from the South or the islands of Puerto Rico, Haiti, the Dominican Republic, and the West Indies. To many native Harlemites, people migrating from the South were easy marks. If you wanted to catch a mark (someone to get one over on), you hung out down at the Port Authority bus station on Forty-Second Street or down at Penn Station on Thirty-Fourth. You could catch a fresh sucker straight from the bushes. Another prime spot for fresh newbies was on 125th Street. People new to the scene for some reason always found their way to 125th Street because they read about it somewhere.

Some pimps said they caught their best hoes this way. If you were slick enough, a good hustler could make a living off the unsuspecting flocks arriving in New York City for the first time. Many came looking for well-paying jobs only to find lives of crime and obscure mediocrity, not the glamour and glitz they expected. On the other hand, migrants like Frank Matthews and Frank Lucas, two poor Southern boys from rural North Carolina, managed to become two of the richest narcotics distributors ever to hustle on the streets of New York City.

People most capable of escaping were moving out of Harlem by the 1960s. It was a contradictory time. Black people were still running north to escape the repressive South, but almost as soon as they arrived, they were trying to escape the violent, oppressive ghetto of the North. *The Jeffersons*, a TV show depicting a Harlem family moving to Queens to escape concentrated poverty, mimicked the reality of middle-class Blacks leaving behind two-thirds of a population living below the poverty line.

In some neighborhoods, living in the tenements was survival of the fittest. Some said Spanish Harlem was THE WORST area in Harlem. This was certainly how it was depicted in Alan Arkin's comedy film *Popi* in 1969. The father character in *Popi* is so desperate to save his two Puerto Rican sons from the perils of East Harlem life that he concocts a scheme to take them to Miami and have them pose as Cuban refugees. He figures if his sons are considered Cuban, they will be offered better opportunities in America than as Puerto Ricans. A desperate idea, it seemed to be a case of art imitating life. Puerto Ricans were dealing with their own hell in NYC.

It doesn't take a child long to learn about the predatory environment of the ghetto. Less resources and fewer guidelines—this is a reality that induces the rules of life. In these circumstances, neighbors took advantage of one another. Some self-destructively stripped or stole fixtures from their own buildings to sell, threw garbage in the alleyways, or participated in other common property damage and petty crime. The dilapidated housing situation did little to inspire a sense of ownership. Nearly everyone rented. Harlem was also overcrowded, saturated with people living check to check. A stickup, alcoholic, or drug addict lurked on every corner.

My education began around 117th Street. Nanna and Aunt Margaret lived two blocks away, on 119th Street, in a building on the corner of

Madison Avenue. Nanna took care of me during the day while Ma and Pop worked. I was around senior adults most of my early life but sometimes with Aunt Sister, who everyone said couldn't keep a job. Nanna wasn't married, but she lived with Willie, a man no one in my family had much respect for.

Willie walked on crutches, the result of a trucking accident that left one of his legs barely functional. If Willie went outside for anything, it was to wait for the mailman to bring his disability check. He usually smelled bad, either from drinking or not showering. Dragging his lame leg around didn't help, and my grandmother was no nurse. I don't remember anyone ever saying anything nice or positive about Willie, except that he got a disability check each month. Even Ma reviled Willie because he drooled over her right in front of my grandmother.

When I was eight or nine and no one else was around, I made fun of Willie. I don't remember exactly when I started calling him names and messing with him, but it had to be after a few years of seasoning and socialization in school and on the street. I was cussing pretty good by the age of nine. Willie liked to drink. He also stuttered, which was an invite to immediate ridicule. Nanna often called him "stupid ass" during his drinking binges. It didn't take long for me to follow suit. He would get drunk, start stuttering and trying to say something, and I would cut him off and say, "Shut up, stupid ass"—always from a safe distance.

Stupid ass was one of the first cuss words I tried out on Willie, but others followed. It was a perfect game, waiting for my grandmother to leave the room to try out new cuss words on an intoxicated, belligerent Willie. He would yell and tell Nanna I was cussing him out, but she routinely dismissed anything he said.

Pop probably hated Willie the most. He never wanted him around his mother. Some of the cuss words I used on Willie I picked up from Pop, especially words like *mothafucka*. When I called Willie a stupid mothafucka, it seemed to make him the angriest, so I always saved that one for last.

CHAPTER 3
THE DEATH OF AUNT SISTER

AUNT SISTER DIED SUDDENLY in 1967, the same year my little sister, Prissy, was born. Aunt Sister was twenty-three and had been a significant part of my early life in the Barrio. My younger days were spent running stoop to stoop and in and out of Miss Mable's candy store on 117th Street with Aunt Sister dragging me by the hand. She bought me my first record, "Shake," a Sam Cook hit that had her favorite song on the opposite side, "A Change Is Gonna Come."

It was my first real experience with death, even though death and funerals were constantly being talked about in my formative years— particularly at Aunt Margaret's, whose living room was a central meeting place for people in the neighborhood. Malcolm X was killed two years before Aunt Sister, and both King and Bobby Kennedy would die less than a year after. Death as an experience would repeat itself often in my childhood. By the time we lost Aunt Sister, I knew death wasn't good. When Ma told me Aunt Sister was going to have a funeral, I already had a frame of reference.

Aunt Sister, like Pop, was a heavy drinker and smoker. She started as a young teen. No one said that was what killed her, but like her father, she died suddenly amid controversy. People talked about how young Aunt Sister was. Being young and being dead were quite common by 1967. They said JFK was too young. So was Medgar Evers, Malcolm X, and four little girls in an Alabama church. Grown-ups said Dope-Fiend Danny from Lexington Avenue was too young to die, but he was dead. Danny hung around the block enough for me to remember him. He ran errands for older men and had even watched me playing on the stoop a few times when Pop asked him to. Danny OD'd on heroin the same year we lost Aunt Sister. He was fifteen. His body was found in an alley on 118th Street. Uncle Preston told everyone the rats had eaten so much of his face that his mother didn't want a viewing.

Some funerals were on television. Dope-Fiend Danny never made it to TV, but my memory of him was clearer than others. Sometimes Danny would be out on the stoop sleeping and slobbering on himself. I found out later he was nodding, something dope fiends did when they were high. Dope fiends would nod every now and then in parks, alleys, building stoops, and hallways. For kids like me, it was something to see.

No drug other than heroin was "dope" in NYC, something a lot of people never understood outside of New York. In some places, any illegal drug was considered dope, but to a New Yorker, especially one from the '60s, '70s and '80s, using dope means shooting or snorting heroin—or like my boy used to say, "her-ron."

It seemed like whenever grown-ups got together at Aunt Margaret's place, or out on the stoop, someone had either gotten shot or killed or had an overdose, and there was going to be a funeral. Aunt Sister's funeral impressed upon me that anyone could have a funeral at any moment, especially if they were young. But there was one death even more memorable than losing Aunt Sister.

Aunt Sister's viewing was in a funeral parlor not far from Nanna's building on Madison Avenue at 119th Street. Madison was a major street, with cars streaming uptown at lightning speed. I was told to stay away from it as soon as I was up on two feet. There was a school sitting catty-corner to my grandmother's building with a high, spiked, cast iron fence around it. The fence was bent inward on the corner, a large imprint on the otherwise formidable structure. Aunt Margaret said a little girl was hit by a car and killed on that corner, her body pinned where the huge dent was. Aunt Margaret said she would never forget the sound of that child's scream. Years passed, and the fence remained unrepaired and bent inward on the corner of 119th until one day it wasn't. Every time I looked at it, I thought about the dead little girl I had never seen or met. Another young person. Another Harlem funeral.

I didn't know much about how Aunt Sister died. No one explained in a way I understood. Drug use was the first rumor about Aunt Sister's early death. No one in the family said she OD'd, but for a young, pretty girl to die at twenty-three, a heroin OD was highly possible.

Some people never made it to the level of becoming drug addicts. Some died from their very first hit of heroin. When that happened, word went out on the streets, and junkies went crazy trying to get that "killer" heroin. They would say it was "the good shit," because it was more pure. Maybe Aunt Sister wasn't a full-fledged junkie but couldn't handle whatever she got on a first hit.

Junkies were a permanent part of the landscape in Harlem, especially around 117th Street. Ma and I were probably the only ones in my family afraid of them. Even Willie didn't seem to be afraid of junkies, and he could barely walk. When he was sober, he'd see a junkie near the building and tell them to get the fuck away from his stoop.

No one was safe with a junkie around unless the junkie was nodding. When a junkie was high, you could do anything around them, and they barely noticed. Their senses were dulled and their movements slow and uncoordinated. But a junkie was dangerous and had predatory senses when they were sick or on the hunt. A junkie like that could be supernatural. These were junkies you had to watch and stay away from.

Sometimes Ma and I had to walk through a throng of junkies on the corner of 116th Street and Madison Avenue. As soon as you got off the M116 at a certain time of day, they were milling everywhere. Some of them scratched and moved around like zombies. Ma would grab my hand tight and pull me toward 117th Street as I stared. Hands and wrists were eye level, so that's where my eyes focused. A junkie's hands weren't like regular people's hands. They were puffy, swollen, and often discolored. Their wrists and arms didn't show veins, and some had black spots and puncture holes. I started having nightmares about junkie hands touching and killing me. I thought so often about funerals and all the things that could take your life that I started dreaming of my own funeral.

I felt death the day of Aunt Sister's wake. I got chills as soon as I walked through the door of the funeral parlor. A morbid vacancy forced me to tighten up, especially in my stomach. As we approached the coffin, I was paralyzed with fear. Nanna was at my side, saying it was okay to touch Aunt Sister, but I felt like I was going to die. This was my first and earliest experience of holding back tears and deep feelings of anxiety. I wanted to break and run out of there, but Nanna was at my side, holding my arm, telling me it was okay to be there. I didn't think anyone living should be in that place, but she kept saying it was important to say goodbye. I wanted to. I really wanted to say goodbye to Aunt Sister, but I couldn't. I didn't see Aunt Sister lying there; I only saw a dead, stiff body.

When I reached the casket, I looked at her face. She looked pretty, like she was dressed to go out, but I knew it wasn't her. I was scared of dead Aunt Sister. Her hair was netted. Her face was light and powdered, without a mark or blemish on it. She looked like one of those stars from the old movies with chalky faces and red lipstick. The visual didn't stop me from being spooked. The smell of morbidity overcame me. Dampness lingered in the air, a nothingness I wouldn't be able to shake in my lifetime and perhaps the next. I looked at Aunt Sister's gloved hands to see if they were swollen.

With Nanna by my side, urging me not to be afraid, I touched Aunt Sister's stiff, hardened wrist, fearing her eyes were going to open and look right at me. What if she was a vampire and grabbed my hand? I dreamed about dead Aunt Sister many nights after seeing her in that funeral parlor. I got up at night and made sure the bathroom light was on. Many years afterwards, I wished Nanna had never taken me to see Aunt Sister that last time. That first experience with mortality would never leave me.

My little sister, Prissy, was born in March. It was an eerie paradox I couldn't grasp at the time—losing one family member and gaining another. The eerie feeling started when everyone began remarking on how much my new baby sister looked like Aunt Sister. And she did. People even said they could be the same baby, some kind of reincarnation thing. It was weird. But the comparisons didn't end there. As I grew older, more people commented on how much I looked like Pop, something nearly everyone agreed on. My younger sister and I seemed to be carbon copies of my father and Aunt Sister. The final uncanny similarity was that Pop and Aunt Sister were the same age distance apart as me and my little sister, four years. No one on Pop's side of the family believed it was coincidental.

Aunt Sister's death opened me up to a few things it took years to figure out. As I learned more about my father's side of the family, I formulated many questions in my mind, questions no one around me seemed qualified to answer. Nanna told me Aunt Sister went to heaven, but no one explained where heaven was. Could I send Aunt Sister a message? Could she send one back? As time went on, I began to realize just how little people knew about life and death.

One day while on the stoop, Aunt Margaret offered me my first explanation about where heaven was. She told me heaven was up in the sky.

She looked at me, pointed up, and said heaven was so far up there you couldn't see it from the ground, and I was amazed. Even though she said I couldn't see it, I tried anyway, as if I would be the first. Maybe I had special eyes. It was the first of many times I convinced myself that I would be the first to do or see something no one else could do or see. I wanted to see heaven.

When we moved into the big public housing project on 144th Street, we were twenty-one stories up from the ground floor. This was pretty high, and one of the first things I remember doing was looking up to see if I could see heaven and where Aunt Sister was. I couldn't. I fantasized about getting my own plane and flying high above the clouds, figuring the higher I got, the better chance I had of seeing where Aunt Sister was. But by the time I flew in an airplane for the first time, I no longer believed heaven was in the sky.

Everyone around me who talked about Aunt Sister or heaven said heaven was a better place—much better than where we were. They told me not to worry, that Aunt Sister was safe and happy in heaven. I believed them as long as I could. However, no one around me was happy about her going to heaven. They acted like she wasn't safe at all, and it was confusing. I felt duped, like everyone knew something I didn't, or maybe I knew something they didn't.

Almost a year after Aunt Sister's funeral, Martin Luther King was shot on April 4, 1968, by someone who wanted to send him to heaven. Another person everyone said was too young to die was gone, and everyone was sad all over again, crying even worse than when Aunt Sister died.

If heaven was so safe and good, why did everyone become so sad? It was the first time, but not the last, I began to question those closest to me—the first time I felt like they didn't have all the answers I wanted.

CHAPTER 4
APRIL 9, 1968

ON A TUESDAY MORNING April 9, 1968, I was sitting on our living room floor directly in front of our new TV. By this time we had moved out of the tenement on 117th Street and into the projects. Our new apartment was 21F, and it had a concrete, ice-cold floor. I sat anyway, daydreaming about the brand-new red bicycle I was going to get for my fifth birthday the following day.

I was also getting familiar with our new place. It was an adventure just reaching the twenty-first floor. Walking through the lobby, riding the elevator, and walking down long hallways was a lot different than living in the tenements. The windows were shut, but the wind still whistled outside.

Our television was the only thing in our living room, which I thought was the biggest room I'd ever been in. Pop brought home the new TV the week before, which was a pretty big deal as I remember it. It was a floor-model Motorola with wood paneling. Few people had floor models.

Like most days, Ma and Pop kicked off the morning with a disagreement. Their high-volume exchanges had become routine. As I sat on the concrete floor in front of the television, their ramblings resonated in the near distance.

This day felt different from the start. As a child, I couldn't explain it. My birthday was coming, but no one seemed happy about it. The first "wrong feeling" I had was everyone being home on a morning when no cartoons were on television. Ma wasn't at work, and neither was Pop, and this only happened on weekends. I adapted to routines quickly, and when they changed, I noticed. Today, something wasn't right.

I figured I was in the clear of Ma and Pop's disagreement since neither mentioned my name the entire morning. It was like I wasn't there. I kept an ear open for key words like *son, Butch,* or *James,* knowing they referred to me.

My parent's disagreements were so constant that they had degenerated to a level of unimportance to me. Every now and then, something got through that stuck, leaving me with questions I rarely asked but would reflect upon in years to come.

"Ben, what you're doing is wrong and you know it."

"Shooting an innocent man, ain't that wrong?"

"You got to let God handle that, Ben. You ain't God."

"I ain't God, but something gotta change or we all gon die, and God won't have shit to do wit it."

I found out later that morning that the innocent man Pop was talking about was Dr. Martin Luther King Jr., who was shot and killed six days before my fifth birthday. His funeral was taking place the day before my birthday and seemed like a much bigger deal. There was a lot of talk about God again, as there had been the previous year when Aunt Sister died. My curiosity about God and heaven resurfaced and undoubtedly was the most profound question of my first ten years in the world.

Who was God? Why couldn't I see him? Why did everyone seem to know something about God except me? Where did they meet him? Ma and Pop argued about God a lot. But it was usually Ma who brought God into the conversation. This told me she knew the most about God. Ma was always talking about God, and every Sunday she went to church where God seemed to spend much of his time. She even went to church on regular days like Tuesdays or Thursdays. But Pop never went to church. Like school, Pop dropped out of church long ago. According to him, God wasn't putting money in his pocket, and he wasn't putting any time into God.

Moving into the projects was a game changer for us. Pop was more uptight about the change. His side of the family lived on 119th Street and had been in Harlem since the '40s. He didn't like leaving them, not to mention the stoop action around 117th Street. There wasn't much stoop action in the projects. In the tenements, the stoop was where a lot of socialization and recreation took place. It was where I watched Pop hanging with his friends, huddled up with money in his hands and a brown bag wrapped around a bottle as he shot dice.

The stoop was hallowed ground in some neighborhoods. It was where you learned about your block. Street peddlers sold everything from sugar cane to Italian ice to watermelon slices from the sidewalk. When it was hot, someone got a big work wrench and opened the fire hydrant to let the water gush out into the street. Another person would grab an empty soda can and cut the top and bottom off, then smooth the jagged edges on the sidewalk. Once it was a perfect funnel, it was used to direct the high-pressure water to spray people and cars in the street. People would watch from the stoop or their apartment windows.

Life was a little different in public housing. Once we moved to 144th, Ma had trouble keeping Pop at our new place. He kept running back downtown to 117th Street.

"Ben, you need to stay home tonight."

"I ain't makin' no promises. I might be home. I might not."

"What you think gon happen if you get arrested? What if you lose your job? What are me and the kids gon do then?"

"I ain't getting arrested, and if I do, it won't be for nothin' I do tonight."

Ma and Pop's arguments consumed our first days in the projects, but I wasn't clear on what they were about. I knew it had something to do with stealing. One day Ma got under Pop's skin in a bad way and I heard him yell, "They been stealing from us for years!"

I figured I knew exactly who he was talking about: Miss Emma and Mr. Kitchen from Nanna's building. They were the only thieves I knew about. Nanna and I were down at Aunt Margaret's apartment one day, and she told everyone there that Miss Emma and Mr. Kitchen were some stealing niggas. She said she was at the corner store when she saw both Miss Emma and Mr. Kitchen stealing hot dogs and bologna. She also said Miss Emma stole one of her good seat pillows off the stoop. She said that stealing bitch had the nerve to take it on one of their bus trips to Atlantic City.

I was uneasy, and half scared of Miss Emma. I was less wary if other people were around, but didn't like being left alone with her, even if only for a couple of minutes. She liked to offer me candy, but she had a strange look and a way of looking at me, like she already knew every sneaky thing I had done or ever would do. I'd take one look at Miss Emma's big green eyes, and her white hair and lifeless, pale skin and trembling hands, and chills would fill my body. One day when I overheard Pop talking about Miss Emma, he called her an "albino nigga." He said she wasn't Black or White. I didn't know what an albino nigga was and didn't ask. I only knew Miss Emma didn't look like anyone else, so I took what Nanna said and put it with Pop's comments and figured being an albino must have something to do with stealing.

Today, as I dreamed about that red bicycle, I interrupted my parents' ongoing disagreement to ask a question about Martin Luther King's TV funeral.

"Ma, was Aunt Sister's funeral on TV too?"

"No, James, it wasn't."

"Why, Ma? Ain't she dead?"

"She's dead, James, but they don't put regular folk funerals on TV."

Ma's response only added to the mysteries of death, funerals, God, and stealing. Pop yelled all week about King getting shot, but I didn't remember any yelling about Aunt Sister's funeral. By the time King's funeral came on TV, Pop was saying a lot of things I was hearing for the first time, about "the crackers" that killed King. It was as if his experiences in the South were illuminated by King's death. When something serious or negative happened involving White people—like when the White cop Malhoney shot and killed Dewey, a twenty-one-year-old Black man from 120th Street, and no weapon was found, or when Mr. Casey, who was Irish, was selling bad meat that put people in the hospital from his store on 114th Street—Pop would start talking about his life and how he hated crackers, especially crackers down south.

It seemed like everything meaningful was run by crackers, and Pop had a lot to say about it. As I tried to get answers from Ma that morning about King, the funeral, and Miss Emma being an albino thief, Pop was in full rant mode.

"These crackers gon kill us all if we let 'em. They kill the one man talkin' bout peace, the one Black man tryin' to love these crackers. What you think gon happen to us if they killin' good niggas like King? If I'm gon die, I'm gon die shootin' back at somebody."

I'd hear similar words over and over, not only from my father but from those around him. Pop was born in the South but no longer talked like a Jim Crow Southerner. Pop was looking for something a lot of men came to Harlem for: respect.

King was shot and killed the day before Ma's birthday. My mother and I were irrevocably connected to King due to the timing of our birthdays, hers on the fifth and mine on the tenth. That day was also the beginning of my father's sporadic outburst about the evils of White people.

Martin Luther King's funeral was my clearest memory of watching TV with my father. There would be no movies, sporting events, or bonding moments for me and Pop. He would fade in and out of focus shortly after King's death, until it no longer mattered if he was around. By my eighth birthday, Pop was out of the house, and it didn't seem to matter.

As I listened to clips of Martin's speeches, in between Ma chastising my father for his rants, I heard words for the first time that would become part of my social indoctrination in life. This was the day I discovered where Pop was getting all the new stuff we were getting. The stealing conversation I overheard had nothing to do with Miss Emma or Mr. Kitchen. According to Pop, crackers had done *most* of the stealing. From my father's mouth to my ears, everything crackers had gotten came from stealing or taking it from somebody, so Pop was out in the streets, doing a little taking of his own. It's why we had a brand-new floor-model Motorola.

Pop and I never got a chance to talk about it. Soon after King's funeral, Ma was tired of fighting with him. She started second-guessing their marriage. When the Temptations came out with their hit "Papa Was a Rolling Stone" in 1971, Pop was one of the stones rolling out of our life. He moved back downtown to 119th Street and into Aunt Margaret's extra bedroom. He would live out his final ten short and complicated years of life within the mundane drudgery of 117th Street, never venturing much beyond its three-block radius. Like other absentee fathers of children living in the projects, he was out of our lives before I or my little sister knew why having a father mattered.

CHAPTER 5
DREW HAMILTON HOUSES: LIFE IN THE PROJECTS

OUR BUILDING WAS THE third of three apartment towers on Eighth Avenue between 141st and 144th Streets. There were two additional buildings on Seventh Avenue between 141st and 143rd for a total of five 21-story buildings. It was a different lifestyle than in the Barrio. For one, there were a lot more people living in closer proximity, especially more kids. My new building had eleven apartments on each floor. One Drew Hamilton building housed more people than ten tenement buildings in the Barrio.

The Drew Hamilton projects was home for Black and Puerto Rican families escaping the perils of bad plumbing, falling plaster, and dilapidated tenement housing rampant in East Harlem, Brooklyn, and the Bronx. There were more than 200 apartments in our building, and thousands of former tenement residents. The housing demographics in Drew was a mix of senior citizens, single mothers, and working two-parent families.

Public School 194 was in our backyard. In the mornings, children lined up as teachers with bullhorns organized them into groups. The groups were segregated by grade. I observed the spectacle from my kitchen window. The groupings of children navigated uniformly up the steps and into the six-story school building. Public School 194 was named after Countee Cullen, a famous Harlem Renaissance poet, but everyone just called it PS 194 or 194—similar to our lack of acknowledgment for the formal name of our public housing complex. Drew Hamilton Houses was named after significant historical figures Cornelius J. Drew, an outstanding community organizer and activist, and Alexander Hamilton, the nation's first secretary of state. Growing up, few people I knew acknowledged these men, let alone their historical contributions. For most, our neighborhood was simply known as Drew.

A fast learning curve for me was unavoidable. I was the oldest sibling, with an absentee father and a mother with little knowledge of Harlem life. I learned from day one that our neighborhood was about fighting and being willing to fight. I developed an elevated sense of awareness, learning who was who and who did what in my surroundings.

My first day at 194, I was wrestling with a boy during recess. I didn't know the boy. We were running side by side, and he grabbed me, so I grabbed him back, and we began jostling. Before I knew it, I had him on the ground and was on top of him. Then, two other boys jumped in and started kicking me in the side. All three whaled on me before the school guard pulled them off. I remembered one saying, "We gon fuck you up after school." It was the first of many threats.

Once the threat was issued, I could think of little else. The boys were older, bigger, and looked mean enough to kill me. I couldn't think about schoolwork, so I spent the rest of the day trying to figure out how I was going to get home without getting beat up. We had a spelling test, and I was good at spelling, but I didn't even bother with it. I just sat there thinking about what was going to happen to me after school. I turned in a blank piece of paper. When the three o'clock bell rang, I was nervous. As soon as I saw the door letting out into the street, I took off down 144th Street.

I repeated this process and other means of self-preservation for nearly two weeks. During recess, I avoided everyone and stuck to myself. I even skipped recess. It was my first lesson in understanding school was about more than the classroom. I started watching and observing people to stay ahead of the game.

And my lessons kept coming. I was at Mr. Henry's grocery store on 144th Street one morning to get some milk for the house. There was an older boy in the store I didn't know but had seen around. I learned later his name was Quentin, and he lived in the second building. He was standing behind me on the line waiting to pay for something. I gave Mr. Henry a dollar to pay for the quart of milk but was slow to grasp my change off the counter. The boy grabbed it and quickly walked out of the store. For some reason, I immediately looked at Mr. Henry, the reigning authority, but he looked back at me and said, "Boy, you better go and git yo money back. I ain't the police."

I never got the money back. Instead, I came home with a cut lip and nothing else. The milk carton fell and busted while I was fighting with Quentin. Ma's face had a look not of anger as much as disappointment. We were on food stamps and cash poor; that change was one day's bus fare to work, and the loss of milk meant no cereal for me or my little sister in the mornings. This wasn't the reason I began stealing, but that started soon after.

The lessons in Drew Hamilton were always there. Some were subtle lessons, others glaringly blunt. From day one I assumed these were lessons I had to learn on my own, and not necessarily ones I could share with my mother. She made this blatantly clear in little ways, undoubtedly without even realizing it.

I was five or six when Ma found a babysitter in building 2430 on Seventh Avenue. Miss Williams had a daughter my age, Tonya, who had been in my kindergarten class. I don't remember when me and Tonya started kissing, but I remember her asking me if I wanted to be her boyfriend. I said yes. One afternoon after school, Miss Williams caught Tonya and me kissing in the corner of Tonya's bedroom. I wasn't doing much kissing. I was allowing myself to be kissed. Since Tonya made me her boyfriend, I sat still and let her do what she thought a girlfriend was supposed to do.

After catching the two of us, Miss Williams told Ma she could not watch me anymore. I had never been kissed before and never thought about kissing before Tonya. I told Ma as best I could, "I didn't do nothin," but Ma wasn't convinced. It was my first butt-naked ass whipping, without a stich of clothing. I learned that day not to trust Ma to be on my side, even if I was right. The more things started happening around me outside our home, the more I kept them to myself, though there was another instance that cemented that lesson, when I made the mistake of asking Ma a question about faggots—a result of a conversation I overheard two older boys having in the elevator. I couldn't help myself.

I was on my way to Miss Johnson's place on the eleventh floor, and these two guys were talking about two poets I was learning about in school. These guys were saying Countee Cullen and Langston Hughes were faggots, and that a lot of great poets were "fags." I was already particularly interested in Langston Hughes by then, especially his poem "I eat in the kitchen when company comes." The older teenage boys talked like I wasn't in the elevator.

I felt like I knew what a faggot was by then. Whenever someone out in the park called someone else a faggot, there was usually a fight because if you didn't fight after that, it meant you really were a faggot, and everyone would be calling you a faggot afterwards. So, at the very least I thought a faggot was someone who wouldn't or couldn't fight. I got up the nerve to ask Ma about it.

"Ma, was Langston Hughes and Countee Cullen faggots?"

"Who taught you to say that word?"

"Nobody, I just wanted to know if they was faggots cuz—"

Ma grabbed me by the arm. "Listen, I don't want you using words like that again, you hear? Don't make me whip your butt."

"Yeah, Ma, but I was just askin' because someone said they was."

"I don't care what they said they was. You ain't gon be talkin' like that. Where do these two boys live anyway?"

It took me a few moments to realize she wasn't asking about the two guys in the elevator. She wanted to know who Countee and Langston were.

"No, Ma, they don't live nowhere. They jus some poets we learn about in school."

Once I started getting out into the neighborhood, it became natural to limit what I told Ma. Our lives were too different. I was growing up in the density of the ghetto, moving and mingling in the block. This had never been her scene and never could be. I learned early to filter everything when it came to the world and what I experienced outside our apartment.

What Ma did know was church, so this was where she tried to keep me. She made me join the usher board and young-adult choir. I grew to hate both. I escaped to the parks and playgrounds sometimes when I was supposed to be in church, even at the risk of an occasional beating. None of my male cousins were going to church, and few of my friends in school. They still had fathers around to advocate for their absence, but I didn't. How was church going to keep guys like Quentin from taking my money? Sometimes I wished Mount Nebo would burn down. I felt bad afterwards, and a little guilty for thinking that way about God's house, but these were genuine feelings when Sunday morning rolled around.

Our church was a prominent structure in the early '70s. Mount Nebo Baptist Church sat on the corner of 127th Street and Eighth Avenue, and you could see it from blocks away. Sometimes, if Ma had enough money, the three of us would grab a cab early Sunday morning down Eighth Avenue. On occasion she took a risk and gave me thirty-five cents for the bus and sent me to Sunday school ahead of her, unescorted. When the weather was nice, I always found my way to a candy store to spend that thirty-five cents and then to a park where there was a basketball court, church shoes and all.

I'm not sure what I hated most about church—the ridiculously long rituals of song and tradition, or the exaggerated sequencing of the sermon. Maybe it was those stained-glass images of pearly, white-skinned angels and our savior Jesus. I never felt the church thing. In later years I would question my own spirituality. I was so averse to the scene that I wondered if I was a bad person. I hated the perfumed and powder-scented smells cascading through the building when entering church. The best part of church for me was the end.

Away from church, I spent most of my time in the neighborhood park. We had one main basketball court, and everything else in the park seemed to revolve around it. The court was directly behind my building, so I had a complete view of the scene from my window. I knew who was playing when. I knew who came out early and who stayed out late. I knew when the firemen across the street came out to play or when the biggest games were going down. The park became the center of my world.

PART 2
1968–1975

CHAPTER 6
DREW HAMILTON
BASKETBALL

"FOUL!"

"What?"

"Foul, nigga!"

"Fuck you, bitch. That ain't no fuckin' foul!"

"My ball, mothafucka! You fouled me!"

Most days, a game between Bito and Big Steve was no big deal. Today it was about money, so it was different. Playing for money was about ego, personality, and machoism as much as anything else. Big Steve lived in my building, so we rode with him. Most cats hanging in the park aligned with guys they lived closest to. Big Steve lived on the tenth floor, and his younger sister Michelle was in my third-grade class. She was a quiet girl who rarely came outside. Steve was tall and well known for having the strongest arm in the block. People said he roofed a handball twenty-one stories on top of our building, but I missed it.

In the park, a challenge always loomed. This was the neighborhood. Bito wasn't a serious ballplayer. He liked to get high and ran around with Terry Reed and Butter Graham, local neighborhood hustlers. Bito wasn't too serious about street life either. Petty larceny, shoplifting, or being an occasional drug-traffic lookout was the extent of his crime life. Challenging Steve wasn't as much about basketball as it was about trying to hustle up a few dollars and saving face.

The game got traction because Bito was from building 200 on Seventh Avenue, our natural rivals. Our two buildings competed in the park when it came to almost everything. This wasn't about gangs, but every building had their own crews (the peer group you hung with).

Today, Willo and Terry Reed, both building 200 guys, spotted Bito $100 to play Big Steve. On our side was Big Nate, who lived on the twentieth floor of our building, putting up money backing Steve.

Both guys were giants to me, in stature and notoriety. People knew who they were. Bito wasn't graceful, but he was tall. Steve was even taller and very athletic. Neither were known as the best basketball players, but they were competitive enough for people not to consider them scrubs. There were a lot of guys, like Imp, Mike Daniels, and Wendell Ramsey, who were better basketball players than either of these guys, but since it was a money game, it got interesting.

Like many in our block, Bito and Steve used the basketball court, the hub of the neighborhood, as a venue for testing their manhood. I was supposed to be in church for choir rehearsal the day they squared off, but instead I was hugging the park fence to see what I could learn. It was the first time I watched a game that had almost nothing to do with athletics. This was more about what kind of person you were, and what you had inside.

Steve could dunk, something that greatly impressed me. I hoped I'd get to see that. He would drive down the lane, his big fro flailing, wearing goggles attached with a band around the back to keep them in place, and slam the ball through so hard the basket would shake the whole fence. It was always with the right hand, the same arm he used to throw his deadly fastball in a game of stickball.

Though one of the taller boys in the block, Bito couldn't dunk. He was slower and didn't block shots like Steve could. Skill for skill, Bito just didn't match up.

A small crowd gathered around the court, inside and outside the surrounding fences. I was on the corner outside the fence, a good spot near the water hydrant on 143rd Street. Steve started out good. He didn't have a great outside shot, so the game was slow. There were several minutes back and forth when neither guy could score. Steve was using his jump hook to his advantage. With Willo and Terry Reed urging him on, Bito tried unsuccessfully to block it, and ended up fouling Steve almost every time.

It got more interesting the longer the game went. Steve played more often and had at least one go-to move that was better than any offensive skills Bito brought to the game. But Bito wasn't without recourse. He had nothing to lose by fouling Steve as often or as hard as it took to gain an advantage. The question quickly became how much Steve was going to take. How was he going to respond? Was the game going to devolve into a physical confrontation, or a street fight between these two giants?

I think Willo and Terry Reed knew this was how it had to go down. Toward the middle of the game, fewer and fewer points were being scored and hardly any being attempted without a hard, flagrant hacking of the guy shooting the ball. Steve wasn't a punk, so Bito couldn't dominate with intimidation. Bito was the aggressor because he had to be. He scrapped and fought, making the game competitive and eventually forcing a stalemate, the best he could hope for under any circumstance. Had Steve faltered in will or heart, Bito would have won despite being less skilled.

This was how basketball was often played in the streets. It was a test of wills. We competed for everything in our neighborhood—notoriety, respect, or sport. Every aspect of your life was fair game and subject to scrutiny when you ventured outside for just about anything.

Playing basketball is how I learned to handle situations socially. It became a symbolic rite of passage that led to getting a rep on the streets. My neighborhood bred a thirst for competition and respect that often developed into pride, skill, and confidence. The block was where your heart was tested. It was where you developed creativity, style, and capability for handling pressure. How you dealt with pressure showed who the serious ballers were going to be and who might choose other paths in life. Some guys didn't want the burden of trying to be that good or didn't know what it took. A lot of guys found other things they were good at, and things that made them feel better about themselves.

I skipped church every chance I could to play ball. On warm Saturday and Sunday mornings, I was glued to the chain-link fence, to watch not only a game but also the drama surrounding it. Sometimes a money game was happening, but mostly these were hard, gritty games with guys playing for nothing more than pride and rep. You could see how guys reacted to physical and psychological threats. All of this gave me early insight on how to cope with situations like getting jumped my first day of school.

No neighborhood like mine is devoid of role models. We drew inspirations from personalities in a way that helped us make sense of our environment. It allowed us to cope and sometimes thrive despite extreme obstacles. Anyone who was good or had a rep for playing ball, I wanted to know about. On the other hand, anyone who had a rep as a tough guy, a fighter, or who demonstrated an ability for committing violence was also of interest for me. Bito's buddy Terry Reed was the first of many cats I discovered who could fight. Terry was a local hustler, short in stature. His girl Pumpsi lived on the fifth floor of our building, and so he became a familiar face.

Drew Hamilton was overrun with guys playing basketball. Some made the All-City team and had their names in the papers. Ted Campbell, Wendell Ramsey, Mike Daniels, and Daryl Barber were All-City players with solid reps in the block, and there were many others just as good, though some didn't play school ball. Because almost everyone played ball in our park, it meant even more if you could elevate yourself above the rest. Making All-City distinguished you as one of the best.

Once you were All-City, your rep followed you into the parks and everywhere you went. It became a part of your life. People identified you for not being like everyone else. Guys like Ted Campbell were treated differently because of what they did in basketball, even concerning issues that had nothing to do with basketball.

Ted Campbell played for Brandeis, a notable PSAL school. He was only five foot nine, but few in the block got as much respect as Ted. Terry Reed played ball also, even though he was already more gangster than athlete. Like Ted, Terry wasn't very big, but he was always doing push-ups and was a physical cat, a routine he probably picked up in jail. Despite his formidable rep as a fighter, Terry would compromise with Ted in ways that indicated he respected him.

A lot of rivalries in the park were centered around basketball. Someone was always someone else's nemesis in one way or another. Mike Rich and Paul Jinx were close to my age and had peer circles of their own. These two became natural rivals in the park. Mike Rich, whom I grew closer to as I got older, adopted the street name "Jelly," and "Jinx" got his name for being exceptionally elusive. He was like greased lightning; he wasn't that fast, but he used unique juke moves to shake—or "jinx"—anyone pursuing him.

Once I got tight with my own crew, these were the guys we came up playing under. Jinx and Jelly were point guards who liked to control the action on the court. Jelly was deadly from the outside and had a soft touch. He was the better offensive player but also a good defender who liked challenging people, using whatever he had at his disposal. On the other hand, Jinx played with instincts and flair and unwavering confidence. If you were playing with either of them, they always pushed you to perform at their intensity level; and if you didn't live up to the challenge, there were always consequences. When you stepped into the park, you were being evaluated and assessed by almost everyone out there. You were building your rep, one way or another, every time you walked outside your front door.

Jelly thought he was better than Jinx, but Jinx never conceded. Jelly played for a better basketball school, coming up behind Ted Campbell at Brandeis. He played more summer-league ball than Jinx and was coaching at a young age. When it came to basketball, Jelly was all in. On the other hand, Jinx was a more well-rounded athlete. He was as good in baseball as he was basketball and even played football on occasion. Jinx also seemed to have more people on his side than Jelly. He'd been in the neighborhood longer and had older siblings who helped to integrate him. Jelly arrived when he was in high school, from Teaneck, New Jersey. Me and my crew came up under these two dominant personalities, and the scrutiny was intense enough to develop tough skin.

If you failed to score when set up on a pass, your game was questioned. If someone scored on you at a critical moment, you couldn't play D. If you turned the ball over at the wrong time or consistently, you had no heart. In the park, you had to be ready at all times to excel and defend yourself psychologically and physically. That's just how it was.

Ted Campbell's main rival in the neighborhood was Wendell Ramsey, another high school player with All-City credentials. Wendell played for JFK High School. He lived on the seventh floor of our building, so, like Steve, he was one of our guys. Ted lived in the second building on Eighth Avenue across the street from our building and was part of a different crew. He and Wendell were the same age, playing for different schools, sharing the same park—more than enough to get a rivalry started. Both would get basketball scholarships out of high school.

What made their rivalry interesting was the contrast in styles of play. Ted wasn't a textbook, fundamental player in the way Wendell was, whether on or off the court. Wendell was a pretty good student; Ted seemed to go to school for recreation. Ted smoked a little weed, drank a little wine, and still managed to get a basketball scholarship to Coppin State. Wendell didn't smoke or drink. Ted socialized with more popular crews in the block. He had a steady rotation of honeys, while Wendell was more reserved in his personal relationships and wasn't as well liked as Ted. Different life choices and circumstances set the tone for how and why they went at each other so hard on the court.

Ted would break downcourt, stop at the top of the key, and release his shot and hit dead center. We didn't have nets, so sometimes the ball was so perfect you questioned whether the shot went in. Wendell was six foot two, a little taller and bigger than Ted, and would come back down, attack from an angle, pump a head, and shoulder-fake and then drop one in off the board. Wendell played like Walt Frazier. Ted was more unconventional, like Earl Monroe. He would dribble into a double team, spin away, and release another pretty jumper from long range. Wendell would come back at him, try to back Campbell down, and spin off him to get his shot. Ted, who didn't like being showed up, especially by Wendell, would body up and smack anything coming upward when Wendell tried to shoot.

Some days, Ted couldn't do anything with Wendell, who was bigger, had a decent handle, and was just as deadly as Ted on the perimeter. Other days, Ted overcame his physical disadvantages and outplayed his archrival in spectacular fashion. People gathered when they squared off because it was usually a heated confrontation, and you could always learn something watching a game driven by emotion and passion.

Their rivalry was natural. The contrast between them set the tone for nearly every situation I encountered playing ball in Harlem.

There was a sublime and sometimes blatant contrast between textbook school players and guys playing ball on the streets. These two worlds consistently fought and competed with one another for many years in Harlem basketball. Technically, Ted wasn't a street guy. He was a ballplayer, and his life centered around playing ball, but he socialized with guys who took more risks to get the things they wanted, so he was viewed as more "street" than Wendell.

The respect players received from their peers and onlookers had a profound effect on me, almost as much as their abilities. One day, I was shooting on the court alone when a few older boys, Quincy, Mike McKane, and his crew from the second building, told me to get off the court so they could play. This was known as "butching" the court, a common occurrence. Older boys would "butch" the court from younger, less established boys. Then one of them said, "No, leave him alone. Let shorty shoot. That's 'Little Ted.'" I don't know how or why, but one of the guys thought I was Ted Campbell's younger relative. It was the first time I experienced firsthand how much a person's rep meant in our world. I got consideration simply because someone *thought* I was "Little Ted."

CHAPTER 7

NBA, ABA, AND THE STREETS: THE BLACK BASKETBALL LEGENDS

"SERVE 'EM, JOE. THESE yo streets! Show dem suckas what it's like to play in Harlem."

It was a vintage 1970s summer game day—a Saturday, the best of all days in Harlem. The one day there was no church and no school. On Saturday you didn't have to learn anything you didn't want to learn.

Some of my best days on earth were Saturdays. Saturday was a movie day. The first time I saw *Enter the Dragon* was on a Saturday. I could stay out later. It was a Saturday when I finally cornered Angela in our building's laundromat, in the basement, and we kissed for the first time. Angela lived in the second building. She was Puerto Rican and wore her hair in one long ponytail. Sometimes when I thought about Saturdays, I thought about Angela.

This Saturday, people were draped over the sidelines, hanging on fences and on top of buildings, peering down at the 155th Street park. Some were yelling, others jumping up and down. Most people watching were loyal followers of the park's main attraction, Joe Hammond. We weren't old enough to vote, drink, or drive, but we were old enough to know a hero when we saw one: the newest personification of Harlem's street basketball folklore—a skinny, light-skinned, part-time hustler, full-time playground legend we called "The Destroyer."

I had a bad view. This was always the case when I went up to 155th to watch a game. It was punishment for failing to leave two hours early for a game only a ten-minute walk away. The high wired fences were packed with spectators. All the good tree spots were taken, and somehow people got into PS 46, a school sitting next to Rucker Park, and found their way up to the roof to peer down at the action.

Every square inch of the area was covered. When Joe Hammond was playing, it was like a holiday. If you were late, the best a young cat could do was to try and squeeze in or wait until someone moved so you could slide into their spot and hope no one older, bigger, and meaner than you wanted it.

People were selling food, clothes, and whatever they could to take advantage of the extra traffic. Hustlers were handling business, big-timers were profiling, and pretty girls were looking to impress someone worth impressing. Vendors set up frozen-watermelon stands, crab buckets, and shaved ice venues up and down Eighth Avenue in the vicinity of 155th. Harlem opened up and came alive when a big game was going on here.

A group of us from the block took the brief walk up to 155th to watch Joe Hammond play. We were only guaranteed glimpses of the action due to the massive crowd, but it was still enough to leave us dreaming. When it was over, stat keepers from the scorer's table spread the word. Joe dropped fifty-seven points despite showing up to the game almost ten minutes late. There were pro stars on the court with Joe. Some were in the ABA, and others, like Hawthorne Wingo, were playing in the Eastern League, but Joe was a king at 155th Street. He was routinely late and the main attraction. When he finally arrived, the crowd parted like the Red Sea, and the anticipation alone was enough to send chills down my spine.

Joe was Harlem. Every flamboyant, stylish, trendy, and colorful depiction you could think of was displayed through his game and how he lived his life. With the streets pumping sounds from Curtis Mayfield, Bobby Womack, and Marvin Gaye, he was our reigning basketball star, the one everyone was talking about. He was in his early twenties, and his legend was beginning to challenge the Goat's rep. Walking back to Drew Hamilton after the game, my friends and I were filled with fantasies and dreams of being as great as the Destroyer.

"Yo, Marky Rod, you think Joe can eat up Clyde like he did those niggas today?"

"Clyde can't fuck wit Joe! Joe can serve anybody, don't matter who it is. The White boy from the Knicks couldn't do nothin' wit Joe last week."

"What White boy from the Knicks?"

"The White boy Mike Riordan!"

"He playin' in the Rucker?"

"Hell yeah, and Joe ate his ass up, just like he did those niggas today."

"That don't mean he can fuck wit Clyde. Frazier ain't no joke, and he can play D. He locked up Jerry West."

"But Clyde ain't never seen nothing like Joe. That's a whole nutha game he playin' out there. I can't see nobody stealin' the ball from Joe like Clyde be doing those cats in the NBA."

This may have been true, but I would never find out. Older, experienced coaches and players talked about Joe and used words like crafty, skilled, deceptive, explosive, uncanny, and unpredictable. Before I even knew what some of these words meant or had any context for how people applied them to Joe, I knew it meant he was special. He was different. Whenever anyone smarter than me or more experienced had something to say about Joe Hammond, I had to listen.

Walt Frazier was probably the biggest pro basketball star in New York City in the early '70s. He had tried as a rookie to penetrate Joe's playground world in the latter '60s and didn't find it gratifying. Clyde was an NBA All-Star now but didn't demonstrate the same level of confidence or success in the Harlem summer league as an NBA rookie. One of the coaches in the Rucker, Peter Vesey, who eventually became an NBA columnist with the *New York Post*, coached Clyde that summer and later reported that Clyde didn't consider the games uptown to be "real basketball."

I didn't see Clyde play in the Rucker in '68 or '69, but the word was he was rattled by the pressure to perform before the manic, animated Harlem fans. It didn't matter how big a star you were coming into Rucker Park; you had to produce, or people let you hear it. Apparently, Clyde wasn't ready. When he didn't show immediate success, Vesey benched him.

Clyde's misfortunes in Harlem didn't stop him from becoming an NBA superstar who boys like me now idolized. I was ten years old when the Knicks won their second NBA championship by beating the Los Angeles Lakers, and that's right around the time people were saying Clyde was the answer to Jerry West. Clyde wasn't a playground legend, but he was New York's biggest basketball superstar and equally as flamboyant, stylish, and trendsetting within legal circles as Joe Hammond and Pee Wee Kirkland were in illegal ones. One of Clyde's teammates, Dean Meminger, was routinely outplayed in tournaments like the Rucker by guys like Joe Hammond, Pee Wee Kirkland, and Charlie Scott.

Unlike Clyde, another NBA superstar guard was dazzling crowds on the streets *and* in the NBA. In the 1972 to '73 NBA season, Nate Archibald, known as "Tiny" on the streets, became a phenomenon in the world of basketball by averaging thirty-four points and eleven assists per game. At six foot one, he was the first and only guy to ever lead the NBA in scoring and assists within the same season.

Smaller guards like Lenny Wilkins and Dave Bing, two guys on their way to the Hall of Fame, had often been compared to the great Bob Cousy, who was touted in the press as being the best of all small guards. Older Black guys in my neighborhood had a different opinion. They talked about Wilkins and Bing as being on par with Cousy, despite his seven or eight world championships with the Celtics. They pointed out who Cousy played with, which was basically the greatest team and coach of the modern era. When Tiny came along, even though he had yet to win one NBA championship, people around me were already saying he was better than Cousy ever was. Interestingly, Cousy, who himself admitted Tiny was doing things on the court he could never do, was the head coach of the Kansas City Kings where Tiny played.

Tiny was a South Bronx native—a tough neighborhood. Everyone said he was a different kind of dude. He carried himself with a quiet dignity that set him apart from other cats. He was a pro athlete who had the respect of the streets and many of the hustlers he grew up with, like Guy Fisher, a well-known hustler from the Bronx with connections to Nicky Barnes.

You might find Tiny hugging a park fence, watching a game that held no significance. It could be a game between eight- or nine-year-old kids, but he would be standing there watching intently, as if he was still learning something. When I discovered who Tiny was, I watched him as he watched other people play. I wondered what he was seeing. Why was a major pro like him watching a kids' game on 145th Street? But that's how he was.

Tiny was also acquainted with Pee Wee Kirkland, one of his most formidable rivals on the playgrounds. Pee Wee was even more well established in Harlem's crime scene than Guy Fisher was. Known in some circles as "the bank of Harlem," who even the most notorious gangsters and killers respected, Pee Wee was one of the best ballplayers in New York City in the late '60s and early '70s.

Despite not having disposable cash like Pee Wee or Guy, Tiny was respected by them for the life he chose and the more practical and safer future in the NBA.

My era of peers learned everything we could about life in the streets—some of it true, and some legend. We followed the new, playground-oriented basketball guys playing in the parks, so in a way we were a part of this rise of street culture by circumstance. We respected traditional basketball, but the pull of talent flowing into alternate leagues like the ABA and emerging from the playgrounds was too much to ignore.

All the best players had nicknames, or something distinguishing their style of play. The names cascading through the parks were as mysterious as the game itself. Names like the Hawk, the Doctor, Black Jesus, and the Helicopter made you want to see why they had these names, and how they earned them. The nicknames were indicative of changes taking place in basketball and on the streets, which became a significant part of basketball culture.

On-the-street players were evaluated through different lenses than in mainstream, traditional media. Our perspectives were predisposed to be nontraditional. In the "traditional" world, Bill Sharman was hailed as one of the smartest pure shooting players to ever play the game. But Sharman didn't get the same kind of credit in Harlem. In our world, his exploits, like many others, came with an asterisk because they emerged out of an inherently unfair system. As a result, few people around me were saying Bob Cousy was a better point guard than Nate Archibald or Pee Wee Kirkland, but when you read the newspapers or sport magazines, Cousy was the greatest point guard to ever come out of New York City.

When I watched clips of Cousy later in life, I thought he was slow. A lot of my peers agreed. We believed he was fortunate to be playing with Bill Russell and even luckier playing for a coach known for bending rules in his favor, Red Auerbach. These conversations still rang in my head years later when I watched Celtic highlights depicting the great Bob Cousy on TV specials. It looked like he was literally dribbling in circles and doing things he could never get away with against the players I grew up watching and idolizing.

Yet Bob Cousy was not only a Hall of Famer, he was a revered one. In coming years, the emergence of Lenny Wilkins, Dave Bing, Tiny Archibald, Isiah Thomas, and later John Stockton as prototypical "little" men would push Cousy further and further down the list of great point guards. Even point guards who were not as revered or popular, like Kevin Porter, who came along in the mid-'70s and would set several NBA records for assist, brought into question Bob Cousy's greatness. A lot of guys believed Porter was just as good; he just didn't play for the Celtics in the 1960s.

Not surprisingly, Cousy wasn't the only White athlete reevaluated where I lived. Nor was basketball the only sport reassessed. Most White sports legends got a different reaction in the ghetto than what was portrayed on TV, in magazines, or within the average White American household. Rocky Marciano, Babe Ruth, and Mickey Mantle were consistently counterbalanced with Muhammad Ali, Hank Aaron, and Willie Mays. Resentment simmered where I lived, passed down from years of discrimination against Black athletes. It was a resentment further antagonized by the glorification and reverence of White sports legends in everyday media.

John "Hondo" Havlicek, George Mikan, Bob Pettit, and Bill Bradley were great basketball players, but how good were they, really? Things were so unequal for so long that we questioned the accomplishments of any great White athlete emerging from an era rampant with discrimination. The inequity over the years seemed to validate those who believed that a large part of the success of White professional athletes—be it in baseball, football, boxing, or basketball—resided in their benefiting from a system that was never fair to anyone non-White. As my generation came of age, this historical fact not only inspired an alternative style of play in basketball; it was also fused with a post–civil rights, progressive mindset and alternative reasoning that made us feel whole, and worth more than our meager, substandard social and economic stature suggested.

We didn't revel in the legend of Babe Ruth. When a special came on TV about Ruth's life, old heads like my uncle Preston and my senior-citizen neighbor Mr. Tramble snickered. They were compelled to talk about other baseball players I had never heard of—players like Satchel Paige, or "Cool Papa Bell." They talked about how Hank Aarons and Josh Gibson were discouraged from playing in the '20s and '30s. They talked about Babe never facing the best pitchers or athletes of his day because many weren't allowed to play. The average fan might think it was time to "get over it," but old cats like Uncle Preston made sure we understood what the real deal was.

That Black basketball players were inherently marginalized in sports was further substantiated when someone from the basketball ruling class came up with the bright idea to ban dunking in college basketball in 1967. Right away, those hip to what was happening had another shining example of White men in control flipping the script for their own interest, to the detriment of others. A lot of Black guys saw the ban on dunking as an indictment on "Black basketball" and Black players. In our eyes it was an attempt to "fix" the game to get an outcome the people in charge could accept and control.

We loved dunking. It had become an art in Black neighborhoods and an area we obviously excelled at above all others. Some thought the no-dunk rule was introduced to curtail the dominance of Lew Alcindor, who became Kareem Abdul-Jabbar after his career at UCLA. Similarly, the rules in basketball had been changed when Wilt Chamberlain came into the pro league in 1960.

However, Kareem's college career was nearly over. More importantly, the dunk was not even his most formidable weapon on the court. Nobody from our basketball culture understood how banning dunking made the game better. We knew that jumping higher, and playing quicker and with a unique style or rhythm, was *our* game, the Black man's game. Taking the dunk out of high school and college basketball was in many people's eyes an attempt to minimize our unique athletic talents in favor of those areas White athletes could compete more favorably in, like shooting.

Maybe they didn't want to see a six-foot-four David Thompson powerfully dunking over six-foot-ten Bill Walton. The imagery was all wrong. Symbolically the dunk represented the beginning of Blacks taking over in basketball. Many of these blue- and green-eyed men thought taking dunking out of basketball maintained the purity of the sport; they didn't want the game to change.

I learned to respect traditional basketball and pros like Walt Frazier, Oscar Robertson, and Jerry West. But I found myself gravitating to younger, creative players like "Pistol Pete" Maravich, Charlie Scott, and George Gervin. Pistol Pete's career captivated me. I read everything about Pete—how he lived in West Virginia before moving to Louisiana, how his father drilled him every day until he became the best offensive machine college basketball had ever seen. I started pushing myself, incorporating Pete's ball-handling routines, shooting drills, and exercises into my own practice routines. I kept two basketballs and learned to dribble both at the same time. I'd get out extra early to find a remote park where I could be alone to practice.

Pete averaged forty-four points a game his final year at LSU and scored fifty or more points more than thirty times in his college career. They didn't win a championship, but he was remarkably prolific. He was one of the few guys I knew could match Joe Hammond point for point if they ever faced each other. Pete was taller than Joe and just as skilled on the perimeter. Joe was an unbelievable shooter, even in the parks, where the wind didn't always agree with a person's shot. But Pete was excelling against the best in the world on a day-to-day basis, and no one could stop him. The talent of these two men, one in the pros, the other on the streets, impressed me almost to a point of obsession.

In 1977, Pistol demonstrated his most proficient offensive ability when he went against Earl Monroe, Dean Meminger, and Clyde Frazier, and exploded for sixty-eight points (without the three-point rule) in a televised game against the Knicks. Everyone got a shot at trying to stop Pete that night and could do nothing with him. Monroe and Frazier, two future Hall of Famers, combined for less than twenty points that night. Ironically, Joe Hammond had equally impressive numbers facing off in the summers against pros like Monroe, Meminger, Charlie Scott, and Archie Clark. Hammond had back-to-back fifty-point performances in the same day against these same NBA players.

Toward the end of the decade, there would be another high-scoring, frail-looking talented super scorer who got my attention. In 1978, George Gervin, who they called the Iceman, emerged as a six-foot-seven scoring machine in the NBA. I felt Ice was an even better offensive weapon than Pete or Joe. I remember watching Ice and Pistol playing games of H-O-R-S-E on ABC television as though I were watching a real game. I was fascinated by their offensive skills. Put these two guys in a summer-league game, and I would expect the same fifty, sixty, or seventy-point scoring binges Joe Hammond was famous for.

Holcombe Rucker, the founder and organizer of the original Rucker Tournament, died of cancer in 1965. Had it not been for guys like Bob McCullough, a Rucker protégé who played for Benedict College in the '60s, a lot of young cats wouldn't know anything about Mr. Rucker.

The Holcombe Rucker Tournament started around 1950 and became a place for streetball players to compete against pro stars. The tradition of the Rucker was strong due to the involvement of pro guys like Ed Warner, Roger Brown, Wilt Chamberlain, Connie Hawkins, and Kareem, but the vibrant and competitive nature of the league was always harnessed through the street guys. These guys always had something to prove to the pros. They wanted them to know that being pros didn't mean they were always the best ballplayers in the world.

A lot of times, this was a fact. Earl Manigault, AKA "The Goat," Connie Hawkins, AKA "The Hawk," Jackie Jackson, Pee Wee Kirkland, and Herman Knowings, AKA "Helicopter," and now Joe Hammond, gave basketball a new attitude that helped increase the legitimacy of new, upstart professional leagues like the ABA. The street game added color to the action, and that trend exploded in the '70s.

Like anything on the streets, there was always a negative side. A lot of guys good enough to shine in the local park would never play in any of the Rucker divisions. And some guys good enough to shine in the Rucker Tournament would never become pros. Once you excelled in tournament ball, particularly in the Rucker, it separated you from the average guy out in the park. Some guys were not as good under the whistle or playing against better players, and the Rucker league prepared you to sink or swim.

In the park, you could carry the ball, palm it, take an extra step, and debate whether you did it. You also could foul deliberately as many times as you wanted without penalty. Some cats who never played tournament ball developed bad habits and flaws in their game because they were never legitimately challenged within an organized venue. There were a lot of park players who had talent and who could play but never made the transition to tournament or organized ball. This was true even at the pro level of the Rucker Tournament where guys could perform out there but couldn't make the transition to big-time NBA ball for one reason or another.

For example, Crazy Nate was one of my best friends in the sixth and seventh grades. He was from a loose home and lived on Bradhurst Avenue on 144th Street where some of the worst-maintained tenements were. Nate had an uncanny leaping ability and reflexes that, combined with his strikingly dark skin, made you think of a panther. He got to balls you didn't think he could get to and made shots because he could propel himself to the basket with force. Nate had a full-grown goatee and could dunk the ball in the seventh grade. Some people said he was an island boy from the West Indies or Jamaica, but Nate didn't have a Caribbean accent. We called him Crazy Nate because he was always ready to scrap and looking for trouble.

Nate was top dog among his age group playing in a park near Colonel Pool on 146th Street. He was always over there, and no one could do much with him. Someone would ask Nate, "Hey, man, why don't you come down to Milbank or over to Minisink to try out?" Nate would always say he was going to go and never show up. We found out after a while that he was stealing cars with his cousin JoJo and selling them to chop shops in the Bronx. Before I made it to the ninth grade, Nate was busted for grand theft auto and sent to Spofford Juvenile Detention in the South Bronx. By the time I finished high school, he was at Rykers.

I learned from Nate's experience why pro guys, mainly guys in the NBA, looked at street guys as if they could never make it in "legitimate" organized basketball. This was true for a lot of guys playing on the streets, but no one could say that about Joe Hammond.

Hammond would never make All-City or become an all-American because he did not stay in school long enough. Despite never playing a day in college, the ABA, or NBA, Joe Hammond embarrassed and outplayed enough pro players in NYC to get a rep for it. His two 50-point games on the same day became a well-circulated legend. The first fifty-point explosion came against a team featuring two future NBA players, Tiny Nate and Dean Meminger, both in college. Tiny was at Texas El Paso, and Dean was playing in the Ivy League for Columbia. After dropping fifty-plus on their squad, Joe hung around and followed it up with another fifty-point performance against NBA All-Stars Earl Monroe and Archie Clark. Joe was only nineteen.

Joe's name was so prominent on the New York basketball scene that it began to ring out in far-off places. He was offered tryouts and contracts to play with the Nets in the ABA and Los Angeles Lakers in the NBA. Unlike other players breaking their necks to get a pro tryout, pro scouts came looking for Joe. Players like the Goat and Pee Wee Kirkland, who were legendary in their own right, had at least played high school and college basketball. Joe wasn't playing for any school and somehow mastered and developed a polished, professional game.

His reasoning for passing on pro-contract offers from the NBA and ABA was equally surprising for someone not living in Harlem: "I make more money on the street right now than they gon pay me in the NBA. Why should I go play for sixty grand a year and risk sitting behind some sorry-ass White boy when I can make a hundred grand in a couple of months on the streets and play whenever I want? Shit, I got over a hundred grand in my closet. I can't make that kind of money in the NBA."

Hammond, just coming into his twenties, was selling drugs and hustling dice games. His free-flowing hustle encompassed more risk, but it also netted him a bigger cash return than most people playing in the NBA. Walt "Clyde" Frazier entered the NBA in 1968 on a salary of less than $30,000 a year. It took Clyde four years to crack $100,000, even as an NBA All-Star. Joe's lifestyle was as addictive as the narcotics he was selling. He was spending more money than the biggest stars in the NBA, driving Rolls Royces and Cadillacs and boasting about not even having a driver's license. Scaling down his lifestyle to playing eighty-two games for a minimum contract was something he wasn't interested in. Joe also may have felt he was as big of a star and as legitimate a player as any of the top

NBA players, even though he hadn't proven it in the NBA.

Joe wasn't big or physically imposing. He was lanky, and his gift was finesse. He was a devastating scorer, the kind that made defenders second-guess their own ability. He only needed an inch to get his shot off and was an expert at changing speeds and using feints to get you off balance. He shot the ball when you didn't expect it or couldn't do anything about it. I never saw Joe get his shot blocked. Most people, when they realized what they were up against and the depth of his skills, just wanted to get out of the park without getting embarrassed.

By 1973 there were few players on the street in Harlem more celebrated than Joe Hammond. His cat-like reflexes and uncanny timing made some sequences look animated. The only replay available was the one in our heads, so sometimes it was as if your mind was playing tricks on you. Hammond wasn't scoring sixty or seventy points by shooting the ball all the time; you couldn't get a rep for just putting up a bunch of shots. Joe's style and scoring efficiency and consistency is why people tuned in. For someone who wasn't a high school or college star, he had remarkably polished skills.

He would spin and weave with such a fluid groove it was like he was dancing in slow motion, then suddenly change speeds and do something explosive and totally contradictory to the first groove he was in. His wizardry around the basket was also unique. He used the backboard at almost any angle with mind-boggling precision that left everyone admiring his ability and touch on the ball. I thought only Gervin used the backboard like Hammond. It also wasn't uncommon for him to flip behind-the-back passes after making a dazzling move and hit his teammates in the face with the ball, like Pistol Pete was rumored to do.

However, the most important lesson I learned watching Joe came from watching how he handled everything going on around him while performing. He didn't get nervous, wouldn't rush his shot no matter the situation, and he didn't panic or lose focus. The only thing Joe did was play, expressionless, like he was removed from it all. He might make a move that defied gravity and reality, but it didn't seem to mean shit to Joe. It was as if he expected to do every amazing, fantastic move he pulled off, and this stuck with me. Through him I realized how important it was to keep your cool and perspective on the court to perform at a high level.

Joe Hammond had no parallels on the court; however, his childhood friend, Pee Wee Kirkland, was the bigger personality in Harlem. Kirkland was on a first-name basis with the biggest narcotics dealers on the East

Coast, including guys like Nicky Barnes, Frank Lucas, and Frank Matthews, who operated in Brooklyn. Owner of a Rolls Royce by his twenty-first birthday, he was as big as it got when it came to money and organized crime in Harlem. He was also meeting and hanging out with celebrities like Muhammad Ali, Stevie Wonder, and Marvin Gaye. Pee Wee was hardwired to the hustle going down in Harlem. It was in his blood. No one fucked with Pee Wee, and no one fucked with Joe because he was tight with Pee Wee.

Pee Wee happened to also be a great basketball player. He attended Norfolk State in the mid-'60s where he played alongside Bobby Dandridge, who would go on to play for the Bucks and Bullets. Kirkland was also offered pro contracts to play for the Bulls and a few ABA teams.

But just as intoxicating as playing ball was the "shot callin'" lifestyle and free-flowing ebb that life on the streets provided. Kirkland and Hammond practiced when they wanted, stayed out as long as they wanted, and lived free of demands other than the ones they dictated. The life of a hustler made it difficult to stick to a more disciplined path for becoming a professional athlete. For guys like them, the NBA life waned in comparison to the life they were living, and for guys like me coming up behind them, we took notice.

Kirkland stopped traffic at any intersection, especially when driving his Rolls. He could be rolling with a chick, diamonds on his fingers, big fro, customized suits, and you automatically knew he was somebody important. He was as much of a showman when it came to basketball. Kirkland would score twenty or twenty-five points in one half and decide to skip the rest of the game to go play somewhere else if the competition wasn't up to the challenge. Like many coming up after him, he took half the crowd with him when he left the park.

It was part of a hustler's style to keep it interesting, always leading into something bigger and better. If someone came out with a new Cadillac with Corinthian leather or lambskin interior, then another cat had to come out with something to top that. If a cat told a joke about someone's mother, then you had to come back with a better one about his. Competition on the street was intense no matter what you were into—violence, drugs, sports, it all ran together, and everyone was trying to make their mark.

Pee Wee wasn't the first big-time hustler to get busted, but word traveled all over Harlem when he did. In 1971, shortly after Red Holzman invited him to try out for the New York Knicks, he was arrested on a narcotics conspiracy, ensuring he'd spend the rest of his twenties and almost all of his thirties behind bars. After being sentenced to Lewisburg Federal Penitentiary, he pulled together a team that was allowed to play in a semi-pro league. A few years after his arrest, I saw a clip from a newspaper where he scored 116 points or something crazy like that against a team from Lithuania.

Kirkland and Hammond learned to play the way most of us did—in the parks and community centers. Despite our being heavily influenced by the reputations and style Kirkland and Hammond exhibited, many other guys were equally credible in basketball without illegal activities.

There were players like Charlie Scott and Julius Erving. Charlie wasn't as celebrated on the streets as Joe or Pee Wee or even Tiny, but Julius was. When it came to reverence and celebration, nobody was outdoing Dr. J on the basketball court. I remember people asking why guys like Charlie and Doc were playing in the ABA with teams like the Virginia Squires and New York Nets, and not for the Celtics or Knicks. The answer wasn't easy to figure out as a kid, but it was fun to listen.

The fact was the history of the NBA wasn't much different than that of other professional sports leagues, which for years marginalized and discriminated against Black players when it came to compensation, contracts, opportunities, and business. Even Bill Russell, the center of professional basketball's most successful team, the Boston Celtics, was on record talking about unfair practices against Blacks and quotas perpetrated in the NBA to try and maintain mostly White NBA teams.

The Knicks of the early '70s introduced a more harmonious and diverse NBA. They exhibited a sense of teamwork across racial boundaries, winning two NBA championships, enough to inspire Pete Axthelm to write *The City Game*, which highlighted greater diversity in the game. The book also focused on the reality of the ghetto and the disparity many felt existed between White and Black players. This historical discrimination may have inspired collegiate all-American Charlie Scott to go to the obscure Virginia Squires after being drafted by the Boston Celtics in 1970.

There was always someone talking about disparities in pro sports, driving me to search a lot of books for an answer. After reading *FOUL*, about the life of Connie Hawkins, I realized that at the end of the day, Black athletes were just Black people, and Black people got fucked over in sports just like anywhere else. At least, that's what people in my neighborhood like Hal Ramsey were saying.

"Man, if you look at a guy like Mike Riordan compared to Joe Hammond or Pee Wee Kirkland, it really ain't no comparison. They gon always find a spot on a team for somebody like Mike Riordan. The NBA make superstars out of guys like Gail Goodrich and Bill Sharman.

"Don't get me wrong, I know they're some bad-ass White boys out there, like Rick Barry, Pistol Pete, and little Ernie D., but most of the White guys in the NBA can't touch half the niggas out in these streets. The ABA is only gonna get bigger and better, and that's why people come from all over the country to play in the summer Rucker Tournament on 155th Street. Shit, they know where to come to git a real game!"

Hal was one of the few cats in the block respected for being book smart and equally as street tough. The Ramsey boys were high achievers in school and had a father who didn't mind venturing out back into the park to see what was going on. Everyone knew Mr. Ramsey, but when it came to political commentary, his oldest son, Hal, was the one spitting perspectives and getting deep on us.

One of the reasons the ABA was becoming more popular on the streets than it was in the '60s had to do with many of its best stars playing in summer leagues like the Rucker Tournament or Sonny Hill league in Philly. Philly also had the Baker League, and in DC the Urban Coalition attracted street and pro players. It wasn't uncommon for professional stars like Marvin Barnes, Larry Kenon, and Spencer Haywood to be seen in a street game or in a public park. A lot of NBA guys were bringing their friends to play, the way Wilt Chamberlain had often done in the early '60s.

The ABA didn't have the marketing budget and television connections of the NBA, so their games were hard to catch on TV. But what the ABA had was our young imaginations and a growing respect from the streets. We were drawn to the run-and-gun freestyle professional league because that's what we saw on the playgrounds. At the time, many of us didn't know about the war taking place between basketball purists in the NBA and the rebellious upstart renegades of the ABA.

The ABA went to war with the NBA by signing guys like Moses Malone out of high school and free agents like Spencer Haywood and Rick Barry to larger monetary contracts. Barry even managed to get a piece of a team he played for. Nobody in the NBA was doing things like that in the '70s. NBA owners weren't signing guys out of high school and for years had marginalized Black players not deemed "superstars" but who were still better than many White players in the league. The NBA was run by wealthy White men and managed by shrewd attorneys like David Stern, a hired legal gun. Stern eventually became the NBA's commissioner, but before then was instrumental in litigating to have Connie Hawkins banned from the NBA for his rumored association with gamblers.

George Mikan was considered one of the NBA's greatest players in the '50s. When he became commissioner of the ABA, it gave the league a marginal level of credibility. In a sense, this respected Hall of Fame player and trailblazer defected to go against the ruling-class brass of the NBA by helping to organize an alternative league.

By the early 1970s, when it became obvious that basketball talent emerging from Black culture could no longer be marginalized, the NBA brass realized they were losing talented players who could help their teams win. They envisioned more profits but not necessarily an even playing field. Some players, like Connie Hawkins, were blackballed and slandered in an attempt to crush the credibility of the ABA.

Charlie Scott, a Dean Smith disciple at UNC and one of the first Black players to play in the Atlantic Coast Conference, was one of many great athletes to turn down the NBA and join the ABA. With better and better Black players more likely to "defect" to the ABA, the NBA was confronted with the reality of not securing the best players in the world, posing a serious threat to their bottom line in the future.

By the time I learned to do crossovers and dynamic spin moves to the basket, the issue between the ABA and NBA was no longer seen as a lesser league trying to keep up with the bigger, better NBA. The best ABA guys were on par with the best NBA guys. Some were actually *better* than the NBA guys. By attracting players like Charlie Scott, Moses Malone, Artis Gilmore, Julius Erving, George Gervin, and David Thompson, all future Hall of Famers, the ABA could boast that they had the best players in the world too, and there was nothing the NBA could do other than try to stem the tide.

The appeal of the ABA for young players coming out of college or high school was about freedom and money. They watched unproven rookies like Gail Goodrich and Pete Maravich come into the NBA and get million-dollar contracts, while proven Black veterans like Lou Hudson, Lenny Wilkins, and Dave Bing were getting much less. In Atlanta, Hudson was vocal about the talented Maravich signing with the Hawks for millions fresh out of LSU. Lou was already an NBA All-Star when Pete came in. Not only was Maravich's contract more money than the entire Atlanta Hawks roster, but also the Hawks traded Lenny Wilkins, a future Hall of Famer who they refused to pay a fraction of what they paid Pistol. Guys wanted to know: where were the million-dollar contracts for unproven Black players?

By far the most vivid example of a Black player being treated poorly by the basketball establishment was the Connie Hawkins story. Connie's rep had simmered only slightly since the 1960s, but people still talked about his ordeal with the NBA, which barred him from the league for merely being associated with someone embroiled in a point-shaving scandal. His court case was settled in 1970, allowing him to enter the pro league after years of playing for the Pittsburgh Pipers, a semi-pro team in an obscure league known as the ABL, the precursor to the ABA. Unfortunately, the ABL in the 1960s didn't have many great players to help raise the level of exposure or elevate Connie's game. Connie dominated the league, but few people knew or cared. He was still great in 1970, but a lot of people believed his best days were behind him. They said the uncanny, high-leaping and artistic athlete of the early and mid-'60s was gone forever. Without the challenge of going up against the best NBA players, his development as a pro most likely suffered.

Despite his exile, Connie's name was still royalty on the playgrounds of New York City. His basketball life symbolized the ongoing struggle. The war between the ABA and the NBA mirrored the conflict raging between street players like Connie and basketball fundamentalists and purists. It was the same war waged between the establishment and those in the civil rights movement, the same war Ali, Fred Hampton, and Malcolm X fought in. This conflict was about the established order of the collective (the rule) and the uncompromising freedom of individuals (the exception). The ruling-class majority and the underclass minority confronted one another in sports as they did in all facets of society.

The NBA of the 1970s was shaped and driven by strong, unwavering, mainstream traditions. Connie had to be kept out. He had to be suppressed and discouraged—not because he was a bad guy, or even guilty of anything, but because of what he represented, the streets. The streets consisted of alternate rules. Connie was Black, poor, semiliterate, from the ghetto, and like many of us was viewed and handled with a level of caution and skepticism within the White world around us. It didn't matter that Connie had never harmed anyone or that he was a nice human being. The NBA lawyers still attempted to crush the only life he had, a life of basketball.

The old guard of the NBA included basketball icons like Red Auerbach, who characterized the ABA as a renegade league of undisciplined, immature hotshots. Red believed players in the ABA weren't capable of excelling in the NBA. They played with a red-white-and-blue-striped ball, used a lot of gimmicks to help market the league, and had a fundamentally lax style of play. Many establishment guys like Red felt justified in their opinions, especially with guys like Marvin "Bad News" Barnes and Fly Williams playing in the ABA. These were guys who didn't necessarily leave the streets behind just because they were pro ballplayers. Fingers were quick to point: "See? I told you these guys are hoodlums."

However, nothing could stop the inevitable. The two leagues merged in 1976, and the best players from the ABA became some of the most exciting and dominant players in the NBA. In the '77 to '78 NBA season, David "Skywalker" Thompson scored the most points of any guard in NBA history when he dropped seventy-three in a showdown for the scoring title with the twenty-five-year-old George Gervin. Ice ended up winning the scoring title by knocking down sixty-three on the same night, thirty-three of which came in the second quarter. The two greatest scoring guards up until that time, Jerry West and Oscar Robertson, had never accomplished anything close to what Thompson and Gervin did.

Gervin would lead the league in scoring for three consecutive seasons, while Julius Erving and Moses Malone, also ABA alumni, became two of the best players the NBA had ever seen. Billy Knight, Bobby Jones, Larry Kenon, Artis Gilmore, Charlie Scott, George McGinnis, Mo Lucas, and "Super" John Williamson were just a handful of ABA guys moving into the NBA who did quite well despite Red Auerbach's perceptions.

As a young boy learning the game, I was presented with a choice of ideologies between the ABA and NBA leagues. I was a ghetto kid living an underdog ghetto life, so I gravitated toward unconventional approaches to life, and consequently to basketball. The ABA guys had more style, and they weren't kissing ass. Despite the bad press, I respected players with fancy titles and unconventional skills, and so I admired the ABA guys. The ABA for many of us was a professional extension of the playgrounds, with a direct link to one major landmark: the Holcombe Rucker Tournament on 155th Street.

But I still had respect for the history of the NBA, having watched young, incoming superstars like Pete Maravich, Kareem, and Tiny Nate. I loved the great Laker and Celtic teams and the rising Bucks, Knicks, 76ers, and Bullets.

I wasn't sure if David Thompson or George Gervin were going to be better than Oscar Robertson, Jerry West, or Walt Frazier. I only knew they were fun to watch. I didn't know if Connie Hawkins and Julius Erving were better players than Dave DeBusschere or Hondo Havlicek, but I always tuned in to see what amazing feat Dr. J was going to pull off. The newer players brought the element of the unknown to the table. When I watched Hondo Havlicek playing with the Celtics, I felt like I knew what he was going to do. I learned to anticipate his ball fakes and movements on the court and how he moved without the ball to get open. When Hondo got loose, it was not always about his individual ability. His success was more about what the defense *didn't* do to stop him. If you played these guys the right way, they could be contained.

Watching someone like Erving or David Thompson was different. With these guys, you could do everything right on defense, and they could still outplay you. I was part of a world of basketball that believed if you were "that guy," no one person or system could stop you.

I was a product of new cultural trends taking place in the 1970s. Historically, Black culture was known for improvisations that were formed and shaped with meager resources and under oppressive circumstances. The new things I witnessed on the asphalt playgrounds could be likened to the innovations Sugar Ray Robinson brought into boxing or what Myles Davis and Charlie Parker brought into the world of jazz. By the time I was in high school, another innovation was gaining momentum and heavily influencing what happened in Harlem's playgrounds. We called it hip-hop.

The ABA, like basketball in the playgrounds, was overrun with raw, unrefined talent. It was an underdog league that paralleled our underdog existence. We rooted for ABA guys and the nontraditional path because it was the genesis of our creativity. Our existence was filled with love and hate—a love of life that was counterbalanced with a hate of hard life. Talent manifested itself frequently uptown, but, often beautiful and tragic in the ghetto, it was inspiring and misleading at the same time.

"How many points you gon git today, Supa John?"

"Oh, I don know, young fella. How many you wont me to git?"

"Can you drop thirty?"

"That's all you *wont*, young fella? *Thirtay*? That ain't much. What's yo name?"

"James."

"Okay, James. I see what I can do for ya, young blood."

Maybe scoring thirty points in a summer league game was a little on the low side for someone like John "Super John" Williamson. He could be an unstoppable offensive force. A few years later, in 1977, he dropped fifty on his former team, the Indiana Pacers, while playing for the New Jersey Nets, and had forty-three and forty-eight in two separate games that same season.

When Super John Williamson shook my hand outside the park fence on Eighth Avenue and 155th Street, I had not come to watch him play but was still on top of the world. His big round face and bright smile nullified the fact that his shorts looked too small. He was as physically imposing as anyone I'd seen up close, and most importantly, he was a pro! Supe was only six foot two and wasn't much of a dunker, but he was a strong, solid player and an offensive force who didn't need to jump high or move fast to be productive.

Like my Southern migrant uncles, Super John wasn't a fancy guy, at least not on the court. And even though Williamson didn't grow up in the South, his deliberate, slow pace reminded you that he was ready for a long day's work. You weren't going to see spectacular dunks or dizzying shake moves from Williamson. But he was still big-time, and when you were big-time, even the simple things looked special.

CHAPTER 8
THE MINISINK CENTER, 142ND STREET

ONE OF THE MOST important moments in my life occurred on a cold December day in 1976. Around this time, I started living out my basketball dreams and fantasies. I and twenty-two other twelve- and thirteen-year-old Harlem boys sat with bended knees on a hard gym floor, waiting for our names or numbers to be called. Twenty-two was a low number for a Harlem tryout, but Minisink was still new on the basketball scene. Minisink was located on 142nd Street and Lenox Avenue, just a few blocks away from Colonel Young Park, a popular Rucker-site venue. A local social service and recreation facility, the building was rarely heated sufficiently, especially when the temperature dropped below forty. The floor was cold as an iceberg. Black, brown, and a few yellow boys were wearing canvas Pro-Keds, Converse, and Pumas, vehicles that would carry us to our dreams. Most of us were hungry and willing to do whatever to make the team. One look into our eyes told you everything you needed to know about Harlem basketball.

Basketball began to completely take over my life. I had played in the parks for almost five years but became more serious about it. I was part of a crew that played ball almost every day. These were mostly boys from my building, and every now and then one or two boys from other buildings would join us. We fought other crews for court time. We fought each other in our spare time. Fighting and sporadic violence was a part of the social grind in Harlem. Playing basketball couldn't protect you from an occasional beef until you demonstrated a reason it should.

You played one of two ways in Harlem. You were either a park player who built your rep from neighborhood to neighborhood, or you could venture into the organized leagues, where rules, standards, and organized competition pushed your skills. I got my first taste of organized competition at the Minisink Center. I had played in a few tournaments at school and in the neighborhood. A lot of guys preferred the parks, and some showed a lot of promise early in life, only to lose interest as they got older.

Many park players developed habits and styles that never got challenged in a regulation game or organized environment. People wondered why a guy wasn't in school or on a team after having so much success in the park. They didn't think about basketball as a team game. Maybe a guy was a great leaper and could score but was a poor shooter or ball handler. Maybe he never learned how to pass or how to make the right pass. Some guys couldn't handle the pressure of spectators and expectations and consequently folded in big moments. Others were less effective in organized basketball but still exciting enough to draw a crowd on the playground. A lot of these guys could never be pros but were still credible in the summer leagues.

In my first tryout, we ran three-man weaves, layups, and two-on-one drills. We all lined up in segments, nervous and anxious to show what we could do. Four other players from my crew were also trying out: Mike Poole, Quarter-field, J-Mac, and Greg Poole. Mike and J-Mac were two of the best players in my crew. Mike was the better athlete, but Mack had all the innate intangibles, though smaller in size.

Greg wasn't really a part of our crew. He was Mike's older brother and only occasionally in our circles. I knew all five of the Poole brothers very well since moving into the building in 1967. Mike, John, Quarter, and I were lifers, meaning we tried to play ball every day we could. Greg was big but only played every now and then. He liked to mix it up and didn't lack for confidence, even though his skills were somewhat suspect.

I sized up the competition at the tryout to work through my fear of failure. I took note of who missed layups. Who was throwing the ball away? Who was fucking up the cohesion of the three-man weave? If you were paying attention, it was easy to see guys on their way to being cut. This was a one-day tryout, so whoever made it through was on the team. I also noticed the boys who seemed to be light-years ahead of everyone else.

Torrie Cotton was the only boy in the tryout from the South Bronx. He could have been a special invite. This distinguished him from every other cat in the gym. Guys struggling through drills eliminated themselves, but the truth usually bore out in scrimmages. It was obvious Torrie Cotton was real. Torrie knew how to split defenders, when to stop and pull up in the lane or switch gears to blow by someone. He was average sized, but, like most accomplished players, his air of confidence was unavoidable. In my crew, Mac was good at splitting defenders, and so was I, but neither of us were as confident as Torrie was at the tryout. Cotton dismantled anyone guarding him in the scrimmage. The only guy even close to his confidence level was Howie Thompson from 142nd Street.

When it was over, we all made the midget squad for Minisink. Minisink wasn't as established as some other Harlem rec centers. Milbank had been at the top of the basketball food chain in Harlem since the '60s. You couldn't go over to Milbank and expect to make the squad if you didn't have a big game and an even bigger rep. A lot of young boys in Harlem played basketball like grown men, full of confidence and uncanny ability. Milbank wasn't a place for a rookie like me, just getting my feet wet in organized ball. There could be fifty boys trying out for Milbank, and at least a third of them were good enough to play in divisions one or two years above their age limits. Other rec centers in Harlem were also producing coveted players, but Milbank was like the Mecca for young players in Harlem.

The PAL center on 124th Street sponsored a team called the Sundevils, another mainstay of young talent. With Milbank not far away on 117th Street, a rivalry between these two camps developed quickly. The Sundevils were grooming players like Steve Burtt, Troy Roscoe, Troy Truesdale, and Kevin Williams, all future All-City players and superstars in Harlem. Little Mike "Boogie" Thornton was also a Sundevil. Boogie was eleven years old when I started playing at Minisink and already a prodigy whose name rang out in tournaments and parks across Harlem.

The Boys of Yesteryear on 135th Street was another talent magnate in Harlem. They featured two of the better young guards in Harlem, Ike Garrow and Alvin Lott. Both were my age and would eventually make All-City in the Catholic high school division. Boys of Yesteryear was also where Wendell Ramsey, a future All-City player, and his older brother Greg played in their younger years. Other organizations like Abyssinia Church on 137th and Stone Gym located in lower Harlem had credible community teams also. At every tryout there was a big turnout, and in each situation there was always a coach, a supporter, or someone trying to get the best guys on their teams.

The Minisink Center was newer to the scene, trying to put together winning teams to challenge these organizations and keep us off the streets.

Teams outside of Harlem also competed for the talent pool uptown. Organizations like the Gauchos and Riverside only became more popular and dominant as years progressed. These AAU programs were well funded and enjoyed a certain level of prestige and credibility among the best players in the city. They sponsored international trips to Europe and Israel, something none of the local community centers had funds for. The farthest we traveled for a game was a quick trip across the GW Bridge to Jersey.

With leagues like the Rucker, Each One, Teach One, Citywide, LaGuardia House, and Kennedy Center, AAU organizations began feeding the enormous demand for ballplayers in New York City. With the right frame of mind, it was easy to find a place to play basketball every day of the year.

• • •

"Washington, keep your damn eyes on the ball, boy. What's wrong wit you?"

"Mike, I was just—"

"Shut up and git your scrub ass downcourt, shit! And don't call me Mike. Call me Coach, scrub!"

Mike Williams was one of the youngest coaches at Minisink. He started working at the center when he was only seventeen. He was at least twenty-one or twenty-two by the time I got there. Mike was brash and talkative and usually in someone's face. He liked to keep the crowd popping, always saying something colorful or comical. He made a point to know all the best ballplayers uptown. After making the cut, it didn't take long for me to dislike Mike, mainly because he was good at putting you in the spotlight, and I was nowhere near ready to be there.

Since I didn't talk much and Mike Williams was loud and abrasive, he rubbed me the wrong way. Later, as my confidence, rep, and talent grew, he became one of my biggest supporters. But I was a few years away from that maturation. During my initial practices and games, I looked at Mike as a guy willing to make a fool of me, leveraging insults he thought would motivate me. Any area of weakness, or innocent misstep, was fair game for ridicule. An untied shoe, and you were a bum who didn't care how you looked. Walk in with uncombed hair, and you were sloppy and tacky—if you weren't considered a *star*. If you were Torrie Cotton with uncombed hair, or untied laces, then you were a crazy don't-give-a-fuck type of nigga declaring his unique defiance to the world. When you could ball, unconventional behavior signaled promise—that you were willing to carve your own path on your own terms. That meant a lot in Harlem.

I was one of the taller guys on the team, so almost immediately more was expected. But I wasn't someone Mike saw immediate potential in. Having played little organized basketball, I didn't attempt a lot of the things I was routinely doing in the park. The freedom of confidence just wasn't there. I developed a nice jump shot from the baseline, and my long arms allowed me to get rebounds and make shots around the basket that were out of reach for other guys, but I wasn't a consistent starter because I was still uncertain about my ability. Fortunately for me, Mike Williams wasn't the only coach at Minisink.

Ray Jay was the head coach of our team. He was thirty, more experienced, and had a different approach from the younger, more brash Mike. Ray Jay, with his full-grown, bushy mustache and fro combed to the back with an eagle point, was more like a teacher. He came in from Queens to coach and work at the center. Mike was our motivator, more like a hype man in a hip-hop group, in their good cop, bad cop coaching relationship. Between the two, every personality on our team was covered. Ray Jay related to laid-back beginners like me, and Mike motivated the more confident and accomplished players, like Torrie and Howie Thompson.

Everyone in the ghetto wasn't destined to be a great athlete. Anyone could see Donald Johnson was never going to be one of the most gifted basketball players. Donald was a year younger than me but was already hanging with an older crowd, staying out late and skipping school. By these standards, he was older than I was. His pants were usually too big, and he was one of those kids that seemed to belong more to Harlem than to any parent or guardian. On the street, Donald was called LA. He lived somewhere on 144th Street, but I never saw his mother or father, and he didn't talk about having either. LA stayed at a lot of different places. Sometimes he was over on Lenox at another relative's place. Since the day we met at PS 194 in the fourth grade, I knew LA was living a quicker, faster, and more unrestricted life than anyone else I knew. His premature exposure to the streets showed me something I never saw before or since.

One day LA came to school with two black eyes. It caused a big stir in the schoolyard. LA was olive-skinned yellow, so the startling visual of two dark-black rings under his puffy eyes was hard to forget. LA liked to talk, and walked with an exaggerated bop, but his willingness to come to school in his condition told everyone what type of cat he was even in the third or fourth grade. I wouldn't want to leave my house if I looked like he did, but he just didn't seem to give a fuck. I suspected Wee Wee's crew from 143rd Street, but that was before my friend Cherry from Seventh Avenue told me what really happened to LA.

LA's beatdown was the result of a lesson administered by one of his guardian angels on the street, Georgie Sweet. Georgie had an older cat kick LA's ass after learning he was hustling dime bags of weed. LA was already trying to hustle when he was nine or ten. According to Cherry, LA put up a fight, but the older cat was too good and experienced.

Georgie Sweet had a rep further downtown, first as a ballplayer, then as a hustler. He was associated with Freddie Meyers and his crew, a Harlem-based heroin ring operating around 116th Street. It was speculated Freddie Meyer's organization earned as much from the heroin trade as any crew in Harlem. Georgie must have thought LA needed a "scared straight" lesson. Unfortunately, a life of hustling was already becoming a reality for LA. His two black eyes were like a confirmation. For now, basketball kept LA off the corners, but not entirely. Like many other Harlem hustlers before him, he loved ball but also loved hanging in the block.

LA wasn't a better player than anyone in my crew, but he had unparalleled confidence. Full of street bravado, he talked a better game than any of us played. On the court, he was slower than almost everyone. LA wasn't big enough to play forward or quick enough to play in the backcourt. When we ran sprints, he was always last or nearly last downcourt, but he made the team almost entirely on confidence.

From day one, even without the blessing of athletic or physical talent, LA commanded a spotlight through the sheer flamboyance of his personality. He compensated by using exaggerated hesitation moves and perfecting ball fakes. Mike Williams let it slip one day that LA had a heart condition and he suffered from chronic colds and asthma. He took medication when he remembered, but rumors circulated that he was born addicted to heroin. Whether true or not, it was believable because his life was laced with the streets. For someone so young, LA was always somewhere he wasn't supposed to be.

• • •

I was playing at Minisink when I was ten, but it took three years for me to try out for the team. And even then, being tight with my crew gave me the extra confidence I needed to do so. I was determined to make my mark and started practicing obsessively. I went from hoping and dreaming to knowing and believing in less than a year. On warm days, I was up at 5:30 and hit the courts at 6 before anyone was out there. I played with my crew in the block, but it became habit to play in solitude, when no one else was out there.

Early on, I'd go to pick up J-Mac, but it didn't last very long. Mac was a Sagittarian, and often a late riser. I'd have to wait for him to get ready, so I started picking up another boy, Walter Welch from the fourteenth floor. Walt wasn't as good as Mac, and I only picked him up on weekends. During the week I'd go to school early to play with D-Mac and Al Lott at the Dime.

A lot of guys talked shit on the court. Mental and psychological warfare came with living in a maximum-density ghetto. This routinely spilled into basketball. Older guys pushed younger guys around, especially when pride was at stake. Sometimes less talented players, like Bito when he went up against Big Steve, dominated a game because they had a different perspective and approach to life. A guy might threaten to punch you in the mouth to gain an advantage or elbow you in the stomach when you went up for a rebound. If you didn't respond, your talent didn't mean shit.

Guys reacted differently. Some passed up shots or shied away from getting the ball if they thought they were going to get hurt or get the wrong cat angry. I watched lesser players dominate a game because they were looking for a fight no one wanted to give them. Playing ball on the street, you found out quickly who you were and what risks you were willing to take.

Once I started ramping up my game, some things came quickly and more naturally to me. People marveled a few years later at how quickly I rose to noteworthy status, first in my neighborhood and then all over Harlem. The next eight years of my life became one, long, never-ending season of basketball.

I studied players who interested me, taking note of mannerisms, reactions, and habits: the way a guy cut, or the advantages of a low dribble, and how to protect the ball and keep guys off you, like Brooklyn's Sam Worthen effectively did. I practiced shooting on balance and off balance. I watched, learned, and took everything back to the park. I took in basketball knowledge whenever, wherever, and from whomever it presented itself. Some of my earliest constructive criticism came from dope fiends like Hunter Bean and El. These guys came through our park sometimes at dawn to buy heroin. One of the greatest Harlem legends to ever play basketball, Earl Manigault, had been a heroin addict, so it wasn't far-fetched to think other guys who got hooked on dope in the '60s could have been pretty good ballplayers at one time. Some old-head dope fiends really knew the game.

I got to see a lot of Harlem on those early mornings. People came through my block I never saw during normal park hours. They came at sunrise to get heroin. Some drove cars with out-of-state license plates from North Carolina, Virginia, Maryland, New Jersey, Massachusetts, and Connecticut. These travelers would stand in line in a vacant schoolyard at sunrise on a Saturday or Sunday morning just to buy dope. They came for the white lady, horse, smack, duji, and a few other heroin titles littering the Harlem landscape. Heroin was an industry in Harlem and its biggest economy in the '60s and '70s.

Despite dope fiends coming through our park, early mornings were my personal sanctuary. I went to bed thinking about the next morning and playing basketball. I couldn't stay out late like some of my boys, but Ma didn't care how early I left the house. It was often dark when I left, but it was the only time of the day Harlem was still. Being out there alone, working on my game, and dreaming of playing in Harlem's biggest tournaments provided a tranquility I gravitated to like a fish to water. This serenity was where I fashioned my dreams for becoming a great player.

PART 3
1975–1978

CHAPTER 9
THE DIME

I STARTED AT THE Dime in 1975. Ronnie Snoop had gone there. So had Skip, Claddis and Terry Reed, gangsters from my block I knew well enough to know they were tougher than me. Lonnie Green scored eighty-eight points in a class-tournament game at the Dime. Lonnie's name rang out uptown enough to make some people glad to go to the same school he attended.

"The Dime" was really Intermediate School 10, known as IS 10. It was named after Frederick Douglass and attended by prominent historical figures like James Baldwin and Charlie Rangel. In 1975, it was just a school with the same old problem as most public schools in Harlem: too many kids and too few resources.

I was headed to a new neighborhood, which meant new friends and new enemies. Changing my routine made me anxious. At times, my anxiety led to violent encounters, like the time I punched Freddie Sweeny in the face because I thought he wanted to fight me. It turned out Freddie never said he wanted to fight me; an older boy Thatius made it up to see us fight. Or like the time Reiny said she was going to get some boys to beat me up, and I played hooky the next day. Whenever trouble was waiting for me, I tried to deal with it as soon as possible so I didn't have to think about it.

I was comfortable at PS 194. It was in my block, so I didn't have many problems on the schoolyard once I learned to navigate it. But the Dime was five blocks away on 149th Street. Five blocks felt like five miles for a house boy who didn't spend a lot of time in the streets. Each block in Harlem took on a different demeanor, character, and circumstance from one street to the next. When you traveled outside your block, even if you were only a few minutes away, it could feel like foreign territory unless you knew a lot of people.

The only boys I knew who were almost always out on the streets were LA and Cherry. Cherry lived on Seventh Avenue with his mother and four brothers, and LA seemed to live wherever he wanted. I got a lot of information about uptown from these two guys.

The Dime was located next to the last stop for the number 3 subway line on 149th Street. The school was a basketball factory, but there was a lot to focus on even if you didn't play ball. From here a lot of cats were headed straight to Spofford, while others were headed to some of the best academic high schools in the country, like Choate.

The basketball competition was tough in the Dime. I would become a much better player each year, despite developing a few other interests.

CHAPTER 10
COMICS, ART, AND GRAFFITI

I RAN WITH A crew that was into comic books. We liked Marvel mostly, so it was all about Spiderman, the Hulk, and my favorite, Thor. We copped all the books we could get our hands on and hustled them to one another.

I was copping issues every month. In less than two years, I had more than 300 comics, half of which I'd bought—the others I hustled somehow. Some issues were older than I was. I started boosting, trading, and selling comics outside of school and downtown to keep a little money in my pockets. The more seasoned and comfortable I became at the Dime, the more risks I took.

I was taking a risk the day I was busted shoplifting a few comics at the Cards n Stuff on 148th Street and Seventh Avenue. I was a fairly good petty thief by then. The only other time I was caught stealing was when I snatched a bag of potato chips at the Woolworth's on 145th and Broadway. On my way out the door, the assistant manager chased me down and detained me all afternoon.

Everyone in my comic book crew was busted stealing at one time or another. My two closest friends from my comic crew were Anthony and Kenny. Anthony lived on Saint Nicholas on 147th Street. He had over 500 comics. Ant was small and wasn't into sports, so comics and baseball cards were his world. Kenny lived in the Polo Grounds and had nearly a thousand books. My whole comic crew was thieving, but I think I was better at picking my spots and taking chances. I didn't like all comic books, so I stole books other guys might like. With the money I made, I bought the books I liked.

I also got into drawing and became really good at forging fake bus passes and tagging up subway cars with graffiti. We would draw comic strips in class and make up our own characters to pass the time. For the first time, school was more of a social thing for me than it was academic. I became concerned with self-image and self-preservation.

Attending the Dime was my first real interaction with harsher aspects of life. A lot of other poor kids were doing stuff I had no idea about, but my eyes were opened at the Dime. Shoplifting, graffiti, and train hopping were routine. Whoever I rolled with that day often determined the severity of crimes I committed. I'm not sure when my willingness to steal became strong enough not to fear the consequences, but it intensified at the Dime. Maybe it was one of those hungry days when I decided to snatch something to eat. Some days I knew the only things waiting at home were empty cabinets and condiments in the fridge. I didn't pass up an opportunity to grab a bag of chips or one of Mr. Henry's spiced-ham-and-cheese hero sandwiches.

Showing no inclination to take risks opened some boys up for being victims of someone who was. I was never the roughest or toughest boy in the Dime, but I stayed on top of things and kept from being a target. I didn't have an older brother, cousin, or father looking out for me like some of my friends. I was going it alone. Some days I ran with a good crowd that didn't steal or get into fights, but on other days I ran with boys who were a little more reckless. It was easy to walk with the wrong crowd at the Dime.

I expressed creativity in a variety of ways, most of it positive. I still made posters for Ma's church whenever there was an event. I think she liked telling people I made them. Drawing signs for Ma was my way of showing I was actually a good boy and not the sneaky boy always ducking out of church every chance I got.

I liked drawing, and people said I was really good at it. The Dime was over a train yard, and I started running with a few boys who liked to sneak down to the tracks to airbrush and spray-paint the subway cars. Todd Woods from 144th Street was the first to introduce me to tagging up the subway. We hooked up with some other boys from 142nd Street, "Scheme," "Pras," and another boy who went by the tag "Toro" from the Polo Grounds. All of us tried to outdo the others, riding up to Jerome Avenue to see if our tags were viewable from the street. Jerome Avenue had an elevated subway station that ran outside, so you could see trains from the street as they came and went. I wasn't good at large tags yet, but Scheme, whose real name was Bobby actually got to see his name in lights on the number 4 train. For me, avoiding train conductors and mechanics was part of the challenge of tagging.

The other was staying away from the mutated rats in the subway tunnels. If anything was going to discourage me from tagging up the subway, it was the rats. Rats in subway tunnels were not afraid of people. We were bigger, but NYC rats didn't scatter just because they were smaller, especially when there was a pack of them. Stray cats stayed away from the subway tunnels because they didn't stand a chance against sewer rats. They were some ugly and aggressive creatures.

My three-year experience in the Dime was a roller-coaster ride I half enjoyed and tolerated because it was the life I was dealt. By the time I reached my eighth-grade graduation, I was looking forward to newer challenges and hoping for another change. I was optimistic and unsure about my future in school and life—and became even more so the day I ran into Johnny Pimp.

CHAPTER 11
JOHNNY PIMP

I DIDN'T KNOW HOW Johnny Pimp got his name, but he had a mild reputation for cruelty. He'd stomped a few guys in school, and I saw for myself the day he spat in Tommy Ortiz's face for mistakenly stepping on his new Playboys. Tommy wasn't much of a fighter, so nothing happened, but it could have. Tommy was Puerto Rican, and the PRs from our block were tight and stuck together. All Tommy had to do was tell the right person to get some payback.

I walked by Pimp's block most days on my way home and clocked him on the corner of 146th Street, shaking guys down for their pocket change as they passed him. My walk-home crew frequently changed. The day I ran into Pimp, I was with a middle-of-the-road crowd, fair game to juvenile street predators. They weren't timid guys, but like me, they were non-engaging, not outwardly aggressive, and they didn't have street reputations. If I wasn't getting together with my graffiti cats, or some of my basketball friends, I walked home with these guys.

Pimp and I had crossed eyes before and were content with staring at one another. Eye contact was one way of indicating I wasn't one of the suckers he routinely shook down. Looking away invited trouble.

Pimp approached me out of the crowd on that fateful day and asked if I had a dime. A five-year-old in Harlem knew this really wasn't about the ten cents he asked for. I had three dimes in my pocket and planned to use every one of them at Mr. Levy's candy store for some Boston Baked Beans, Skittles, and a pack of green apple Now and Laters. Pimp asking for a dime was a common shakedown line. He was feeling me out and checking for weakness. I knew then he was going to try to take whatever money, pride, or dignity I had.

A few guys told me Pimp was Baby Dow's cousin. If this was true, it was something to worry about. I knew Baby Dow's rep very well. My first year at the Dime, in the sixth grade, I was jumped by Dow and his crew behind Harlem River Houses, and it was the worst beating I'd ever taken. I was with a group of four friends, and the only one spared that day was William Allen, a boy who lived on the thirteenth floor of my building. William escaped the beatdown because Dow knew his older sister Kay and he liked her. He thought she had a nice ass, and so Kay's nice ass saved William's that day. The rest of us weren't so lucky.

I didn't have a rep for violence or for being a tough guy. I also didn't have an older cat looking out for me. I had to think hard about tangling with Pimp.

He was skinnier and shorter than I was and didn't have an athletic bone in his body. I was wrestling and boxing with cats a lot bigger, heavier, and tougher. Without his street connects, I wasn't worried about a fight. Unfortunately, things might play out in his favor if it came down to who knew who.

Some guys would deliberately lose a fight to avoid the backlash from friends or relatives of the boy they were fighting. They didn't want to get jumped. I'd done it myself on occasion. I'd mess around with some guys, testing their fight skills, and figured I could probably beat them, but in the back of my mind I also knew they had older brothers or cousins I couldn't beat, so I kept our fight on the "friendly" side.

This was a potential situation with Pimp if we wound up disagreeing. I didn't know the guy, had never seen him fight, but he was so frail that he looked sick. He reminded me of my cousin Lester in Brooklyn. Lester and I were the same age, but Lester had been diagnosed with a brain tumor at nine years old and was dying. He spent a lot of time in the hospital. Growing up, he suffered just trying to do basic stuff, and gradually lost strength every year. He wouldn't make it past fifteen.

Pimp's skin sagged off his bones, his eyes were droopy, and he was often smoking a cigarette. The cat should have been in high school, but he was still hanging around the Dime, shaking down dudes for their money. I didn't want any trouble but didn't want to back down either. When I came near the corner of 146th Street that day on my way home, I would never forget the words I'd heard many times before then.

"Yo, you gotta dime?"

Picking me out of the crowd was the first insult. Why didn't he pick some other nigga to fuck with? This meant that out of the school of fish, he saw me as the most vulnerable. Maybe he just didn't give a fuck.

"Na, I ain't got no dime," I said, making sure to put on the appropriate scowl as I stared at him.

His response was "All I find all I keep?"

"All I find all I keep" was textbook extortion. If you let a dude pat your pockets to see if you had money, it was worse than losing a fight. At least in a fight there was a struggle, but to allow a cat to take your shit or act like he was going to take your shit, as others watched and you did nothing to stop it, was the ultimate dis. That kind of talk got around. Then you had to fend off three or four aspiring gangsters, some of whom were only masquerading as tough guys, trying to get extra change in their pockets. I learned this much early in life.

"I ain't got no dime," I said as Pimp moved into my walking path.

I stopped walking instead of trying to get around him. The crowd I was with kept moving. A few of them lived in my building. I wasn't close with any of them. These guys were into baseball cards, and I traded with them from time to time. Fat Raymond Ramos lived on my floor, so we were neighbors but weren't close. I didn't expect anyone to do anything more than continue to walk away and be thankful Pimp hadn't decided to fuck with them. If he had picked one of them out of the crowd, I would have let them handle it on their own too.

If anything was going to jump off, it wasn't going to be on the corner of 146th Street. This was his block, and I didn't want to take a chance of getting jumped again. If there was going to be a fight, and I'd decided there was if I wanted to buy those Skittles, it couldn't be on 146th Street, so I ran. Sensing fear like a hyena, he chased me. Had I kept running, he would have never caught me, as slow as he was. But once you start running, you have to keep running every time you walked out on the street. So I slowed down midway down 145th Street between Seventh and Eighth Avenues, feeling I was far enough away from where he lived and close enough to my own neighborhood.

This street was neutral and a main throughway uptown. People on their way to the Bronx or further west to Riverside Drive came back and forth through 145th. When I stopped running, it should have put him on the defensive, but it didn't. He got agitated and more aggressive.

"Why the fuck you runnin', nigga!?"

"I ain't runnin' now." I frowned.

"Gimmie yo fuckin' money."

I was more angry than afraid, so I yelled, "What the fuck you want?!!"

He responded, "You heard me, mothafucka!"

As Pimp reached for my pocket, I swung and caught him on the side of his jawbone with a right hand and felt an exhilarating chill in my soul when he screamed. I got it in my head at that moment he was some kind of bitch. He was one of those masqueraders running around fucking with everyone just because he could.

If Pimp was Baby Dow's cousin, I was going to get jumped or killed anyway, so I fought and kicked his ass for all the times I'd gotten my ass kicked. He was slow, uncoordinated, and couldn't handle anything I threw at him. Fighting with Johnny Mack, Mike Poole, and my neighbor Tony "Nose," I had good reflexes and long arms. The preceding weekend I fought June Bug three times in one day and won two of the three fights. June Bug was from Brownsville Brooklyn, the grandson of my neighbors, the Trambles in 21K. He came to visit on the weekends. We usually went to the breezeway to get it on. Not only was June Bug a good fighter, it was really all he knew or wanted to do. He wasn't into playing ball or anything else; he just liked to fight. Going toe to toe with boys like June Bug gave me a lot of confidence.

Pimp was swinging wildly and missing. I landed punches to his droopy face on three separate occasions. I dropped his ass after throwing him in a headlock, and, feeling particularly mean after throwing him to the ground, while he was dazed and off balance, I kicked the side of his head into the sidewalk. His screeching yell gave me another chilling rush. An older cat watching the struggle from across the street ran over and grabbed me.

I didn't stomp Pimp into the sidewalk, but my adrenaline was running so high I could have done anything. Stomping in the '70s was almost the violence equivalent of drive-by shootings in the '90s. It was a statement to any witness as to how cruel you could be and how crazy you were. It was a sign not to fuck with you because you didn't care about life. I'd won the fight. He couldn't beat me, and I could see it, but kicking Pimp, taking it to that level, gave him an understanding, perhaps a fear he would carry with him for the rest of his life. I wasn't sure what it had given me.

Dazed and bloody after his head was kicked into the street, the fight in him was gone and so was I. I ran to my block almost as soon as the older guy released my arm. The adrenaline was pumping so fast I left my book bag on 145th Street and had to run right back to get it. I was paranoid, fearing Pimp went back to his block and organized a search crew to find me. But I was alive now, and I felt particularly good about what I'd done.

The fight with Pimp occurred on a Wednesday, and I shot hooky the next two days of school. The weather was nice, so I hung out on Riverside Drive near the park. I missed a few tests and had to make them up. I became paranoid about the fight with Pimp. I avoided the gym entirely. I snuck out early to avoid crowds. I walked down Lenox Avenue instead of Seventh, staying as far away from 146th Street as I could. I didn't know who was looking for me. I'd heard about guys getting stabbed, cut with bottles, jumped, stomped, and beaten up for less than what I'd done. There were always a few guys around who liked hurting people. It didn't have to be their beef. Some guys wanted to be in on the beatdown because that's what they liked doing.

Fortunately, it was near the end of the school year, and Pimp never approached me again. I saw him several weeks later, in the hallway the last week of school, and he avoided eye contact. Maybe he was biding his time. Once he avoided eye contact, for some reason I felt really, really good about it. Maybe I would do what I'd done to Pimp to some other perp.

In the end, despite all the different interests and new friends I made, there were some things, particularly when it came to violence, I didn't like about the Dime. I was sick of guys like Pimp and Baby Dow having a free reign and knew it would be more of the same in high school.

CHAPTER 12
SCHOOL DAZE AT THE DIME

COMING INTO THE DIME, I was an A student, and so were most of my classmates in the sixth grade. These same students were kept together in the seventh and eighth grades unless, like me, they slipped academically and got replaced by someone who was higher achieving or performing better.

Once I became a C student, my academic standing never quite recovered. I kept my face in a book, but my academic discipline declined each year. There were enough lower-achieving classes and teachers in my eighth-grade year that I passed without really studying or pushing myself. In some classes, student behavior was so bad that a guy like me could get by with minimal work because the teacher had no control of the classroom. This happened at least half the time in the Dime.

I didn't know much about the high school of Music & Art, but I knew it was one of only two high schools in Harlem. I'd heard Kurtis Blow had gone there, and Kurt was rocking hip-hop parties uptown and in the Bronx. I found out more about M&A around the time I was busted tagging up one of the school bathrooms at the Dime by Mr. Willis.

Mr. Willis was a janitor. He was a short, stocky, mean-looking man, with scars on his brow and a rigid demeanor that implied his life was never easy. He had graying hair, and I never saw him smile, not even for teachers. Willis may have been pushing a broom at the Dime, but he got as much respect as anyone in school, including the principal. We knew not to fuck with him.

Willis lived two blocks away from school on 147th Street. I saw him a few times while riding my bike down Seventh Avenue. I never tried speaking to him. He would be walking his German shepherd or hanging out with a few of his buddies on the corner, never smiling or laughing like the other men I saw out there. Short, dark, and direct, Mr. Willis didn't play around, especially with smart-mouth kids.

"Boy, what the hell you doin' messin' up my bathroom?"

"I'm sorry, Mr. W."

"Sorry? No, little nigga, you gon be sorry. I spend all my time cleaning these got-dam bathrooms, and you kids come and fuck it up."

I was scared of this guy. He had a grave voice that sent chills through me, like *The Exorcist* movie. He looked like death, or death on the way. He didn't hesitate to grab a kid by the collar to make a point. I guess firing Mr. Willis would be hard to do, especially since he helped keep things under control after the first airing of *Roots* in 1977. When *Roots* came on TV, it changed how a lot of us looked at White people. *Roots* illustrated a tragic evil perpetuated against our ancestors. It also reawakened an intense resentment. A lot of White teachers in the Dime had it rougher after *Roots*, but Mr. W helped settle things down.

He would cuss, sometimes under his breath, and no one thought it was odd. A lot of teachers and staff were routinely disrespected by students, but Mr. W squashed beefs when they got out of hand. Scared and searching for words to atone, I couldn't look him in the face.

"Stand up straight, boy. You gon clean that shit yoself, hear me?"

"Yes sir." I never called anyone sir, but it seemed the appropriate thing to do to save my life.

"And then, you gon clean all the rest of these bathrooms around here, the girls' bathrooms too, understand?"

"Yes sir."

"I'm not going to the principal or the dean with this shit. You gon stay after school and help me every day. Tell anyone who ask that you're volunteering, understand? Or do you need me to contact yo mama?"

"No sir, I can clean it."

Ma didn't know much about my day-to-day in Harlem, and I rarely told her. I doubt I would have known how. She was working or in church and didn't know how many times I got shook down for money or how many times I'd stolen something to eat when my pockets were empty, or how many fights I'd been in. She certainly didn't know I was tagging up subways and bathrooms with graffiti. For me, basketball, graffiti, and comic books were a part of my lifestyle. They were how I coped in my environment.

Fidgeting as Willis spoke to me, I tried to pick my graffiti book off the floor, and it fell open. It was a hardcover, neatly bound, black art book I'd stolen from Gimbels down on Thirty-Fourth Street just a month before. Willis picked it up. He peered with his tiny eyes at the "tags" and other designs I'd been doing and said in a gruff voice, "This all yo shit?"

"Yeah," I answered.

"And you wasting yo time running around painting in bathrooms? Do you draw in school?"

"Yeah, we have art class, but not this kinda stuff."

"Do you go down on those subway tracks with this shit?"

"Na, I—"

"Don't lie to me, boy. You know what vandalism is?"

"No."

"Vandalism is a crime, and fucking up public property is vandalism. I can have yo little ass arrested if I really want to!"

I had stopped going to the subway tunnels because it was hard to get supplies and I was tired of stealing them and running the risk of being caught. I knew there was an end date to my criminal activities and the hourglass was running.

"Look, little nigga, I know you be going down under them subways doin' this shit. As a matter of fact, I seen this shit somewhere before."

I couldn't believe it! *Willis saw one of my tags?* I tried to contain my delight that he recognized something I had done.

"I'm lookin' at this book, and you can draw, but you wastin' it out here, spray-paintin' subways and bathroom walls. You can git paid for doin' this kind of thing, understand?"

"How?"

One look at his face, my first look up since he busted me, let me know Mr. Willis didn't have an immediate answer.

"Listen, you gon have to work for anything you git, and right now, I need you to work on these floors. Here's the mop."

I cleaned bathrooms after school for two weeks before Mr. Willis gave me my graffiti book back. It was perfect since I was still trying to avoid running into Pimp after our fight. I realized the third day in that Mr. W was hustling me, but I didn't care. I could have skipped out on him, but he managed to teach me a lesson and eliminate some of his work at the same time. Even people on the straight learned to hustle in Harlem.

As far as I can remember, I was always into art. I'd been drawing signs and cartoons since starting school and decided to try my hand at graffiti. My art and ball-playing groups never crossed.

I had never received any formal art education. Like basketball, there weren't many outlets to learn the fundamentals. My art skills were technically limited, raw, unrefined, and undisciplined, like my basketball skills. As a result, when I decided to apply to Music & Art and Art and Design high schools, I had a limited portfolio filled with ghetto depictions, cartoons, and street-laced memes. Some of the art teachers at the Dime tried to prepare me, but landscapes and oil paintings just weren't my thing.

Tagging up subway cars was a far cry from knowing what a linear perspective or three-dimensional concept was. In the subways, we went with the vibe, and what we were feeling, not by anything practical or technical. Graffiti for us was an emotional, creative cultural experience. When I attended the orientation and entrance examination at Music & Art, I knew right away the kind of stuff I did wasn't represented anywhere.

Despite a cultural artistic divide, M&A was still only a ten-minute walk from my block. If I cut through St. Nicholas Park, I could get to school in no time. Located next to City College, Music & Art was obscure as a result of being in a comparatively serene area of Harlem. Though surrounded by potential chaos in every direction, M&A was in a very quiet, peaceful setting. Convent Avenue was known as Sugar Hill back in the day, and possessed some of the most expensive, affluent real estate Harlem had to offer. Alexander Hamilton's home, known as Hamilton's Grange, sat on the corner of 139th Street and Convent. Convent Avenue was where you could still see expensive red-brick brownstones worth millions. We were at the height of Harlem's economic decline, but Convent was where you still saw White faces walking down the streets.

At the entrance examination, I was immediately challenged in ways that made me uncomfortable and unsure of my artistic ability. I was asked to use mediums I'd never been exposed to, like charcoal. I had to use paintbrushes and watercolors for the first time. I wasn't much of a painter. Before the exam, the only thing I'd used for my personal projects were magic markers, pencils, and spray-paint cans.

I also didn't see many Black faces at the entrance exam, adding to my trepidation. Other students were coming in with big, elaborate portfolios, some with attractive oil paintings, others with acrylic and watercolors. It didn't take long to feel I was in the wrong place. The interviewer glanced at my graffiti pieces and flipped the pages so abruptly he couldn't possibly have looked at them with any interest. His eyes angled down toward the eyeglasses on his pointy nose. I saw a smirk. Maybe it was just his dismissive attitude, but I'd seen the same smirk before on the faces of store clerks downtown when I walked in with my crew to look at the comic books on their newsstand. Sometimes that look alone was enough to feel some kind of way about yourself and the situation.

It was the same smirk a White landlord gave a Black applicant he didn't want to rent to. I didn't know as a child that I'd see that smirk again in later years on job interviews or when I applied for loans. After a while, that smirk became virtually transparent and expected. Maybe I even saw the smirk when it wasn't there.

When I got word back from M&A saying I wasn't accepted, it didn't surprise me. I didn't let myself get too excited even though I dreamed of getting in. I adjusted mentally to going to Brandeis. Brandeis had a JV basketball squad, and I wanted to make the team. Playing JV basketball for a city school felt more natural than going to Music & Art, even though M&A was a much better school.

Public schools had an interesting correlation in the 1970s that was common in most big cities. Areas with the highest concentration of Blacks usually had the best athletes but the worst educational environment and school infrastructure. The environment I encountered at the Dime—of lower grade expectations, wilder students, and poorly trained, overwhelmed teachers—was duplicated in many city public schools. Fights, confrontations, disorganization, disorder, and poor educational standards was the norm. The experience could be different if you were in magnate classes, but I no longer was. I wasn't flunking out of school, but I skipped class more often, sometimes just to be away from unwanted drama taking place around me.

The upside was that I would face the best basketball players the city had to offer. Brandeis was in the PSAL (Public School Athletic League), which didn't lack for talent. The only thing I had going my way socially moving forward was basketball, so I focused on that. If I went to Brandeis and did what I was supposed to, I could make a name for myself.

CHAPTER 13
ALVIN LOTT: A PRODIGY

MANY OF MY SIXTH, seventh, and eighth-grade mornings were spent playing one-on-one with Alvin Lott on the courts behind the Dime. When we met, Alvin was already a great player and would eventually become one of the better point guards in New York City. When the weather was warm, which for us was anything above fifty degrees, we would get to the Dime around 6:30 in the morning to play until school started. D-Mac, from 146th, and a few other players from 149th Street were early-morning regulars also.

D-Mac and I became good friends and eventually playground teammates later in life. The first school bell rang at 8:40 AM, so we got a good two hours of playing in the mornings before school. We usually played again in gym class, then again at lunch and sometimes more after school. Alvin was good enough to stay on the court with whoever was out there. Even as a sixth-grader, he was out there with eighth-graders like Lonnie Green.

I was forced to sit out when some of the better seventh and eighth-graders got on the court. But by the end of the eighth grade, I was over six feet tall, and the skill gap between me and a lot of cats had closed considerably. I still wasn't pushing to get out there when the bigger games rolled around like Al was, but I knew I was more skilled than some of the more well-known guys. D-Mac and I had this in common.

Mac's real name was Daryl MacDonald, and like me, he was skinny, quiet, and a notorious park rat who was a lot better than people knew he was. We were all learning from each other, but I think I learned more from Alvin than anyone else. Alvin was intense on defense. He hated losing. He ripped you if you had any weakness or lack of confidence in your handle. My ball-handling skills improved playing against Lott because he challenged my ability to protect the ball. In the coming years, as my rep on the playgrounds grew, so did D-Mac's and Alvin Lott's.

Once I started getting recognition as a player, I felt a lot better about myself. I started to believe I had more control over my life. The pat on the back I got from an established player or the words of encouragement kept me going and dreaming, and this kept my anxiety in check. When guys of stature took notice, it meant I was becoming *somebody* in a place where distinction meant almost everything. Every one of us wanted respect in Harlem, and any boy without a father in his life, or an older brother, or someone who could relate to the life we lived, wanted it that much more.

Our eighth-grade graduation was held at Riverside Church on 122nd Street and Riverside Avenue in 1977. People said Riverside was the richest church in the city. I wore a navy-blue suit with a red bow tie, our school-assembly colors. Ma took time off work and, along with Nanna, Aunt Margaret, and Uncle Preston, watched me graduate. Pop didn't make it, and I was relieved he didn't show. I wouldn't know what to say or how to act. At the same time, I was angry he wasn't there. This was one of many contradictions shadowing my young life.

Leaving the Dime meant no more one-on-one games with Alvin. He was on his way to Cardinal Hayes, one of the better Catholic high schools in the city. Playing for Hayes, he would get a lot of exposure and become one of the best players in the Catholic High School Athletic Association (CHSAA).

Alvin was a little more destitute than I was when it came to his living circumstances and resources. Sometimes his sneakers had holes in the bottoms, his pants too, and the only thing that kept guys from snapping on him all the time was the fact that he was such a good basketball player.

His game fit his body type. He was short and compact and developed a deadly outside shot. He used compact spin moves to shake people loose. On offense he beat you with head fakes and dynamite ball-handling skills that made him hard to stop. Al also played fearless. He played like an older, mature player and didn't get nervous in pressure situations. His unusual poise on the court helped him take charge and fuck with less confident people's heads.

The week before graduation, Al and I were in the back of the Dime after school, playing a game with a few guys from 149th Street. Jeff Carter was there, and so was Coco Mo, two of the better players in the Dime. A few other guys I knew through reputation were on the sidelines, watching. Baby Dow was with Larry Sprye and Vonn Zipp, watching Stymie Singleton, who was playing against Mega, another talented young player from the Dime.

Dow didn't seem to remember me from the beatdown he gave me and my crew a couple of years earlier. Of course, I hadn't forgotten him. Stymie, Mega, and Alvin were three of the better small guards in school. Coco Mo, Jeff Carter, and Stan, Big Lou's younger brother, were also pretty good, and all of them were up there that afternoon. Mega was a little better than Stymie, but neither had anything on Alvin. What set most guys apart at this stage was their handle, and all these guys were wickedly good off the dribble.

In New York, ball-handling skills were a significant tool of the trade when it came to playground basketball. The flashier you were, the better. Between the legs or around the back, when a guy handled the ball well, it could be a thing of beauty until it no longer was.

Stymie was a cult figure uptown. He knew everyone and was cool with guys like Baby Dow, Ronnie "Snoop," and Pepsi Dow, guys already hustling at a young age. Whenever I saw Stymie, he was knee-deep in a mixed crowd of females or rowdy guys. His muscular older brother Craig Singleton had beaten enough people up for everyone to know not to fuck with the smaller, more popular Stymie. Stymie and Craig were the younger brothers of Small Paul, one of the more notable gangsters operating uptown. As a result, few people fucked around with the Singletons unless they were looking for trouble.

Today Mega was eating Stymie up in a game of three on three. He was shaking him up so bad Stymie got mad and started 'bowing (elbowing) Mega and trying to start a fight. All of Stymie's clique was on the sidelines, so Mega curbed his game just enough for Stymie to get back into it and outshine him. Sensing Mega was intimidated, Stymie, who was normally easygoing and nonconfrontational, uncharacteristically hit Mega in the jaw with another deliberate elbow. Mega was a baller, not a fighter, so he quit and retreated to the sidelines, holding his face.

"Yo, we need another man," Stymie yelled, probably happy to get rid of Mega. That's when Alvin stepped up from the sidelines without hesitation. He nearly ran to the court. Alvin didn't have anybody up there other than me and a few other guys we played ball with. There was nothing we could do for him if Stymie's crew decided to get crazy. I wasn't in good with any of those guys and didn't know anyone as ruthless as the cats watching from the sidelines. Nevertheless, when Alvin got in the game, he took it over. Stymie had a rough time with Mega before, but it was pure hell trying to stop Alvin Lott.

Al started spinning with his back turned to his defender, shielding the ball and shaking Stymie loose and getting to the basket. He made his first three baskets coming straight in from the sidelines. On defense, he locked Stymie up so bad he didn't score another basket the rest of the game. People on the sidelines started barking, talking shit, yelling for Stymie to retaliate, but Alvin kept doing his thing like they weren't even there. His team won, and Al embarrassed Stymie in a game a less confident player would have stepped into cautiously because of the hostile scenario. As it turned out, quite a few people lost a few dollars on that game, and Stymie was in on a cut of the bet. Alvin cost him some money. But I guess even Stymie had to respect a special talent like Lott. He settled his crew down and even shot a wink to Al as he left. We stuck around after everyone cleared out and played a few games of twenty-one.

In later years, this game behind the Dime reminded me of a story I heard of another Harlem superstar of another sport, the great Sugar Ray Robinson. Apparently, a few organized crime figures approached Robinson to fix a fight with Jake LaMotta, who they had a controlling interest in. They asked Ray to lose purposely as the favorite so they could capitalize on the odds. He refused to play ball, and uncharacteristically, they never came after him, even though they had gone after others who refused. Some said they didn't mess with Sugar because he was such an exceptional athlete; they admired his talent too much to threaten it. Others said it had something to do with Bumpy Johnson, the Italian mob's operative in Harlem, who also happened to be a friend of Sugar's. Either way, what happened that day in the back of the Dime with Al Lott showed me how much respect someone got when people thought they were special. This is one of many reasons basketball became a social platform for me, as much as an athletic one. I wanted to be special.

When I learned Al was on his way to Cardinal Hayes, I didn't ask how he could afford the tuition. I knew his dire economic situation. It was no different than Isiah Thomas getting help to attend Saint Joseph's coming out of Chicago's West Side. Cardinal Hayes would open different opportunities for him, the same way Saint Joseph's had for Isiah.

Snatching ghetto ballplayers and enticing them to attend mostly White, prestigious institutions was becoming somewhat of a routine for my generation, in a complete reversal from how the previous generations of gifted athletes were handled. Now, more White scouts were coming to the ghettos, dangling scholarship carrots before our eyes. In the '50s and '60s, Black players were going to Howard, Winston-Salem, and Hampton. My generation was saying fuck that—we wanted to play on television. A lot of guys were still going to Black colleges like Clark, Norfolk State, and Virginia Union, but it was usually because they were either underexposed, had academic issues, or just weren't good enough for D-I. If you were the best, you wanted to be on TV, and the formula for that was to go to big White colleges, the same schools that a decade earlier only ignored us.

A few people my age asked why it was like this. Why had so many great players before us willingly operated under a system of marginalization and underexposure? Players like Earl Monroe and Pee Wee Kirkland had relatively few options other than Norfolk State and Winston-Salem. What would change if athletes from the ghetto, universally considered as the best athletes in the world, continued to go to schools like Norfolk State in place of Marquette, Georgetown, or UNC? Would television contracts and the millions of dollars funneled through the NCAA find their way into Black colleges instead? And if they did, would the economic paradigm shift? Would our schools, housing, and quality of life elevate to a higher plane? And more importantly, would these athletes return to where they grew up instead of being economically inspired and driven to escape their own upbringings?

The one person who seemed qualified to answer some of these questions was my neighbor, Mr. Washington from apartment 21G. Mr. Washington was like a street sage. He was a working senior citizen who still occasionally smoked weed or tobacco in a pipe. Mr. W was tall and loved jazz. He wasn't a mentor, but he was one of the few older Black men around with a deep opinion. I was intrigued by him because his opinions were usually on an island apart from everyone else's. I ran errands for Mr. Washington from time to time. He would catch me coming out of the door and ask if I could pick him up a pack of cigarettes. Only in the worst ghettos could an eight- or nine-year-old boy walk into a store and buy a pack of cigarettes, but I could. Some store owners, like Mr. Henry or Mr. Willie, wouldn't sell cigs to kids, but I learned which store owners didn't care who bought their cigarettes.

A lover of Miles Davis and Charlie Parker, Mr. Washington was once an aspiring trumpet player who must have missed his opportunity window. He was in his late sixties now, working for the city parks and recreation maintenance department beyond retirement age; he planned to work until he couldn't. Mr. Washington was always talking to Ma and the other neighbors about White people, what they had done and why life was so hard for Blacks. They rarely agreed with him, so it always made for good listening.

"A lot of what goes on out here on these streets is by design, like somebody wrote a book on it. And when you start pokin' around you'll find some White guy or a group of White guys behind it. Drugs, crime, even the schools is designed to keep us right where we at, in the ghetto, working and scrappin' to survive. We ain't nothin' but modern slaves."

This kind of talk always enticed someone to challenge Mr. Washington.

"What you mean slaves? So, we ain't free?" one of the neighbors would ask.

"Yeah, sho you free. You free to do exactly what you been taught how to do, pray, sing, dance, and play ball."

Mr. W was so comedic in his delivery the neighbors would break out into hysterical laughter, each one taking turns in rebutting his commentary. But he continued talking, stroking his two-day-old shave, pausing and sucking his teeth in between his banter.

"I work in these school parks every day, and you a fool thinkin' these kids in Harlem, the Bronx, and Brooklyn is being taught to compete wit the ones up in Scarsdale or those over on Jones Beach. That ain't gon happen. Most of these kids is prepared for a life in and out of jail or working for dem kids up in Scarsdale or in Jones Beach. Either that, or they gon be doing what I'm doin', pushing a mop and a broom. Some of 'em might git out, if they can bounce that ball or git in the Army, but mos of 'em ain't gon git outta here cause they ain't being taught how."

If I was around when Washington was talking, I acted as if I wasn't listening, like it was no big deal and nothing he said was important, but I always listened with intent. I hung on to his words, even if I was in the next room. I wanted to know if he was right. I thought he was old and a little crazy, but when he started talking about White people and why things were so fucked up in Harlem, he had my attention. Mr. Washington made me think maybe Pop wasn't so crazy with all his rants about the White man.

Everyone on our floor said Mr. Washington was crazy, even though he was the only Harlem native among all the neighbors. He'd lived in Harlem since the 1920s. Ma and the other adult neighbors were either migrants from the South or Puerto Rico. They hadn't grown up in the city. While they were learning how to live and cope in New York, Washington was homegrown and looked at things differently.

People coming up from Alabama, the Carolinas, Virginia, and Mississippi had their eyes wide open for any opportunity. Some got good jobs, usually working for the city or in government, but not everyone was finding good jobs. When they didn't, they discovered they needed one job to go with another one. Many working families making good money left Harlem as soon as they could. The exodus of middle-class Blacks left behind the working poor, people on public assistance, and the unemployed. Most of us were living lives revolving around a palette of public housing, public school, and public assistance. Almost everyone I knew struggled through these circumstances.

Mr. Washington hadn't convinced me I wanted to leave Harlem yet, but like he said, "bouncing a ball" looked like my best shot at it. I planned to bounce it until something shook loose. One day he and I were waiting for the elevator, and he asked me if I loved my basketball more than he loved his trumpet. I told him I didn't know, but people would rather watch me play basketball than listen to him playing his horn. He laughed loudly and seemed to respect me as a thinker after that. He started saying things like "That boy smart." I was quiet, often ignored, and generally inconspicuous, but every now and then I randomly blurted out an observation or information an adult didn't know I was able to discern.

One person on his way to "getting out" of poverty was Alvin Lott. I wished I could get into a great school like Power, Rice, or Tolentine. But I could only prepare myself for another dose of public school at Brandeis and all the wonderful lessons waiting for me there.

PART 4
1977–1980

CHAPTER 14
BLACK AND WHITE BASKETBALL: PHILADELPHIA 76ERS VS. PORTLAND TRAILBLAZERS

DESPITE FINISHING SECOND IN the Pacific West Division of the NBA, the Portland Trailblazers weren't good enough to win the NBA championship in 1977. Or so we thought. LA, New York, Philly, and Boston were the NBA teams me and my crew kept our eyes on, but none of us were checking for the Blazers. My man Mo was a die-hard Doc fan, and he was heated.

"Man, I hate Portland. How the fuck did they make it to the finals anyway?"

"Yeah, I hate doze fuckas too. Mothafuck Big Red," I agreed.

Talk against the big redhead Bill Walton was a little harsh in Harlem going into the summer of 1977. Walton had a rep as a hippie rebel, the kind of White cat that would probably get respect even in Harlem, but he still wasn't a dude most boys in the ghetto saw as the best.

Harsh talk about Walton was irrelevant. Despite the consensus of most of my basketball-loving peers, Portland beat Kareem and the Lakers in the 1977 Western Conference finals to make it to the NBA championship. Not only had they beaten the Lakers, the number one seed in the West, but they swept them four to zero, and Walton played his best against the great Kareem. Some were even saying he outplayed Kareem, but that was bullshit. The truth was Kareem dominated his individual matchup with Walton, and still lost. The miracle didn't end there for Portland.

The NBA championship was as pressing as any issue in my life in 1977. The year before, I watched the greatest basketball game of my life on CBS. I would never forget the triple-overtime game between the Celtics and the Phoenix Suns. This one game opened me up and had an incredible impact, despite the fact that my childhood hero, Charlie Scott, only managed six points before fouling out. The Celtics went on to win the 1976 championship, and I wanted nothing more than to be a professional basketball player.

A year later, I was fully engaged with the NBA, trying to figure out how Bill Walton and the Portland Trailblazers beat Dr. J and the Philadelphia 76ers four to two in the championship. It was the first year after the ABA/NBA merger, and three of my favorite players—Doc, David Thompson, and the Iceman, George Gervin—had become NBA All-Stars.

Fans full of playground vigor, long on athleticism and short on understanding, were left wondering how the Blazers upset the 76ers, despite seeing it with our own eyes. Philly had Daryl Dawkins and Lloyd Free, two young players with the best raw talent in the league. They had the most exciting player in the game, Dr. J, and another ABA superstar, George McGinnis, as well as Doug Collins, an NBA All-Star. How did a team with so much talent and innovative creativity lose to a bunch of no-name wannabes from Portland? I hadn't paid much attention to Maurice Lucas, Johnny Davis, or Lionel Hollins. I also didn't know much about Bobby Gross. How did they win?

The 76ers' defeat sent shock waves through the streets. The 76ers embodied the freestyle of street basketball. People read Bill Walton's comments in the papers, about how Philadelphia was a team straight from the playgrounds, a team full of selfish ball hogs not worthy of a championship. We felt like Walton wasn't just talking about the 76ers; he was talking about players from our neighborhoods. We identified with the 76ers because of their colorful playground personas. We were amazed by Lloyd Free's spin moves and leaping ability, Daryl Dawkins's raw talent for dunking, and Dr. J's style. It captivated the imaginations of athletically gifted players. The Knicks were dead to us. They didn't seem to have any style or success anymore, especially once Clyde was traded. The Knicks nose-dived toward the bottom of the Eastern Conference, and we looked forward to watching the 76ers so we could try and cop some of their moves.

When the 76ers went up two to zero early in the series, we were excited and ready to see Dr. J make Walton eat his words. We expected the super-talented 76ers to blow the Blazers away in four straight games, but it didn't happen.

Maybe the 76ers had one too many one-on-one players, but on paper it looked like Philly could win at least three championships without half trying. They were what people call a super team today. In comparison, Portland was just Portland. They were bland and offered no color. We didn't know much about these guys, and most of us believed Bill Walton, who once idolized his UCLA predecessor Kareem, was overhyped due to his UCLA pedigree and pale skin.

The Blazers were victims of two of the most awesome, dramatic slam dunks ever captured on live television. When Doc threw it down on Bob Gross and Bill Walton on two separate spectacular moves, people talked about it for days afterwards. I replayed these dunks in my head every night, lying in bed, imagining myself getting an awesome dunk like that in a big game. However, despite the great dunks, the style, and creativity, the Blazers came back to win four straight games and walk away as the 1977 NBA champions. The Portland Trailblazers were limited on creativity, but they were a team and long on heart.

After the ABA merger, controversy still lingered over which league had the best players, especially concerning the most-publicized ex-ABA player, Julius Erving. The 1977 NBA finals featured at least five other players from the ABA, all of whom were starters. The Blazers' Mo Lucas and Dave Twardzik had their beginnings in the ABA, and so had George McGinnis and Caldwell Jones of the Sixers. Doc was lighting the NBA up as he had the ABA, leading Philadelphia to the NBA championship one year after playing in the ABA. As a result, the basketball purists were out in full force, talking about the wild, freestyle renegade play of the 76ers. For a lot of basketball enthusiasts, Portland represented *real* basketball, and how the game was supposed to be played. Doc's new team reminded too many people who didn't like the ABA of what the ABA was about.

However, Doc, with his colorful style, helped legitimize the people coming into the NBA from the ABA, while exposing the NBA to more flair than it had ever experienced before. In his first year playing with what White old heads still called "the real professional basketball league," Dr. J was almost as unstoppable in the NBA as he had been in the ABA. His scoring average dipped from twenty-nine points per game to twenty-one, but he was sharing the offensive load with George McGinnis, who also averaged twenty-one. Unlike Connie Hawkins, who lost most of his prime years playing against lesser competition, Doc was still in his prime coming into the NBA and could still take over a game.

On the streets, the '77 Trailblazers were perceived as a precursor to system-oriented teams like the Utah Jazz in the John Stockton and Karl Malone era of the '90s. Most players from the inner city didn't like the Blazers—not because they won but because of how the media depicted them in winning. Portland was given credit for having smarter players than Philadelphia, not for being better coached. As a result, when they won, this message hit home loud and clear. People could talk all day about the fantastic dunks Doc got over Walton, but it was Walton who walked away a champion in 1977.

Controversy regarding style, intellect, and athleticism in basketball always bubbled beneath the surface of how people looked at the game. Guys like me, who learned to play innately, were unpredictably talented, innovative, and breathtakingly creative. We were also undisciplined risk-takers who frequently disregarded the tenets of fundamental basketball. Skill and athletic prowess made us formidable, but when a team or a player came along who was limited athletically and still able to challenge and compete, this provoked a natural conflict of ideas and concepts about the game.

I saw daily examples of this in Harlem. Dancing Dujii lived in my building on the eighth floor. His real name was Gerald Thomas. Dujii wasn't what you considered a fundamental player. He was fluid and played with deceptively effective offensive skills comprising off-speed and hesitation feints and moves. He wasn't fast, or overtly strong or athletic, but he was skilled and had an innate ability for playing defenders out of position through sheer trickery. At his best, Dujii played guys guarding him like puppets, thrilling crowds in the process. In comparison, Wendell Ramsey was a more fundamental player. He knew how to use his body and employed head fakes and textbook ball-handling skills on his way to becoming an All-City basketball player at Kennedy High School. I became acutely aware of the distinctions between players like Wendell and Dujii and what they meant in the game of basketball.

Should I jump over a guy or stay on balance and play by position? Should I stay on my feet or risk flying to the hoop? Should I flick the bounce pass, or do I launch it up top for the exciting alley-oop? Should I throw a two-handed chest pass or a one-handed look away? As my game developed, the style vs. substance contrasts stood at the forefront of basketball, and the NBA championship series in 1977 began to put it into perspective for me.

New attitudes and flavor resonating from the streets were a result of the very playgrounds Walton criticized the 76ers for being too much like. The 1976 NBA/ABA merger was just beginning to generate dollars from these new styles and trends. Names like "The Doctor," "Skywalker," and "World" Free, gave the game a new sense of theater that was marketable. Fans came to see the "Iceman," not George Gervin. We wanted to see "Pistol Pete," not Pete Maravich.

Nothing demonstrated this compelling drama of style vs. substance more than the reemergence of the dynastic Boston Celtics in the early 1980s. The Celtics had slower players, guys who didn't jump or run as fast as many other teams in the league, and yet they became championship contenders. Led by Larry Bird, Kevin McHale, Dennis Johnson, and Cedric Maxwell, these guys were great players, and not necessarily great athletes.

Individuals in the media capitalized on the contrast between the Celtics and the high-flying, athletically dominant Lakers featuring Magic Johnson, James Worthy, Kareem, and Michael Cooper. Like Bird, Magic, though the catalyst for the Lakers, wasn't an outstanding leaper and didn't have blinding speed. However, he was a physical freak of nature as a six-foot-nine point guard. The contrast of styles between the Celtics and Lakers fueled renewed interest and dollars within the NBA. Part of that theme played along racial lines and emphasized the smart vs. flamboyant player contrast, which sold tickets.

The renewal of the Celtics/Lakers rivalry in the early '80s was talked about in sweaty gyms, parks, and street corners all across America. Fans of the Celtics talked about how smart the Celtics were, and how wittily, hard, and cleverly they played. On the other hand, they could only think about how athletic and physically talented the Lakers were. The buy-in to this theme was intensified because it was the Celtics, the NBA's most revered team and the last of the great White era, beating the charismatic, mostly Black Lakers. The Trailblazer/76er matchup in 1977 was only a precursor to the 1980s Celtic and Lakers rivalry.

The average fan focused less on Bird and Magic revitalizing the game of basketball. Some didn't even consider how much the two had in common. The average guy on the street was generally talking about one thing: Who was better? Who was more valuable?

Both put in long, hard hours of preparation. Both were winners with heart and determination, and neither happened to be very athletic. They were more alike than any two players in the league. However, much of what the non-basketball public tapped into was that Bird was White, playing for a great White team, and Magic was Black, playing for a mostly Black team. Bird was in Boston, Magic in LA, Bird was a workaholic, Magic an entertainer, Bird was smart, Magic was talented, and that's how the script rolled out across the American basketball landscape.

The public are not basketball purists. Many aren't even basketball fans. The real market interest generated from the matchup between Bird and Magic fed into the non-basketball public's perception. Race, politics, and culture naturally became part of the spin because it was part of everyday life. Consequently, a lot of people were cheering for Bird and the Celtics not because they were basketball or Celtics fans but because they could relate to them culturally. The same was true of people pulling for Magic and the Lakers.

It was no different for us in 1977 rooting for Philly over Portland. We related to their style of play. We remembered Doc from his Rucker days and felt he was a better player than Walton or Bobby Gross. We couldn't root against him.

On the street, particularly in New York City, we often went out of our way to be flamboyant, challenging the boundaries and concepts we thought invalidated our worth. We did things the way we did on the court because it made us feel special. In some cases, this meant attacking the game with a vengeance, as though the game itself owed us something. A lot of guys became men on the basketball court; it was an environment where, with the right skills, you dictated your own terms.

The guys I fucked with on a day-to-day basis lived the game. It was Harlem. When *Sports Illustrated* published articles about how hard players like Walton worked, or when Tommy Heinsohn raved on TV about how smart Bobby Gross and Hondo Havlicek were, but in comparison only talked about how high Dr. J could jump or how athletic David Thompson was, a lot of Black guys resented it. Guys like me didn't.

I chose to revel in the distinction. I wanted to jump higher, run faster, and be smarter all at the same time. Players who preferred a more exciting, faster style of play tended to minimize players like Bill Walton. They overlooked his passing ability, and his defensive skills in the post or his movement without the ball, all of which were exceptional. Guys from my walk of life were products of a built-in, generational resentment that contributed to a backlash against teams labeled in the media as being smart, like the Trailblazers, especially if their main guys happened to be White. But what if the Blazers really had played smarter, like most of the press indicated? Why were people equating smart play with being White? Being a smart player often meant learning to play within your limitations, specifically when you knew what they were.

No one was better at pointing this out than Bubblegum, one of our neighborhood's wisest basketball scribes. When Portland put a beatdown on the Philadelphia 76ers, Bubs had a lot to say about it and a perspective I would never forget.

Bubblegum was in his mid-twenties and already part of the folklore in our projects. The middle brother of three in the Ramsey clan, he had excelled athletically and academically in high school. People from my building believed Bubs was on his way to becoming a scholar when he left for college on an academic scholarship in the early 1970s. Even though Bubs didn't drink and never got high in high school, he returned from college years later hooked on PCP, and that's how the legend picked up steam.

No one in my crew knew the whole story. We only knew he was a straight A student when he left for school up north at his Ivy League college and was never the same after returning.

Despite living in an environment rampant with drugs and addicts, most people in the projects never bothered getting high. On the flip side, we always heard stories about how many middle-class and affluent White kids tried every drug they could find in high school and college. The rumor was a White kid got close to Bubs and either knowingly spiked him or convinced him to try LSD. The White New Englander was supposedly motivated by envy and like many White kids already an experienced drug user. Once it got to a point Bubs couldn't handle his new drug life, the White kid quickly distanced himself, and Bubs's college life fell apart in short order. He was no longer a threat to anyone as the smart nigger from Harlem.

Bubs was back home for good now and spent most of his time fading in and out of reality, making a whole lot of sense when his mind was straight and talking like a crazy nigga when his habit had the upper hand on him. Everyone loved Bubs, even when he was fucked up. Fortunately for me, there were always enough sober moments in between his binges to learn something from him. He had a lot to say after Portland beat the 76ers.

"When you can't run as fast, or jump high, it becomes natural to play in a way to compensate for what you can't do. You try to anticipate better because you know on instinct you just ain't that fast. You move lateral, not vertical. You use your hands or body and try to strip the ball low and pick up little things to compete with other guys out there. That's how I used to play.

"See, you guys who run and jump real good, y'all problem is y'all don't know what you can't do. When you got hops, speed, and all that, it makes you think you can do some shit you might not be able to pull off all the time, know what I mean? Maybe you can't out-jump a guy for a rebound; maybe you can't outrun a guy. What the fuck you gon do then? Guys who can't jump, who don't run that fast, who ain't that coordinated, shit, they already know what they can't do. They got less choices. It's easier for them to stay on track and be focused. And it's easier to coach guys like that, too. Talented guys are harder to coach cuz they can do so many things."

"Yeah, Bubs, but that don't make them smarter" was my retort.

"That's up to how you play. What I'm sayin' to y'all is don't get too caught up in the stunts you see out here in the street. You still gotta learn to play the game to be good."

Bubblegum was six foot two and weighed over 300 pounds. His real name was Greg Ramsey. When he was lucid, I just wanted to hear him talk; it didn't even have to be about basketball. He was an early riser, so at times he'd be sitting out on a park bench at six in the morning by himself. I'd be out there shooting alone, and he never bothered me. He wouldn't even come over to ask for a shot, as so many did from time to time. He'd just sit there and watch. It was as if he had respect for what I was trying to do, like he knew the only reason I was out that early was so I could practice alone, undisturbed.

Sometimes Bubs became determined to lose weight. He'd run sprints in the schoolyard, and it seemed like it took him five seconds to go just a couple of feet. Sometimes he'd run in a wool knit sweater in the hot sun. He said the more sweat, the better. But his workout routine would only last weeks, sometimes a few months. He'd try counseling and rehab, but then he'd relapse and be strung out again. I never asked him what happened at the New England college or about how he got hooked on drugs. I just took him as he was.

In the aftermath of the Trailblazers beating the 76ers, Bubblegum's analysis made sense. It helped me decide I didn't want to be one of those "incomplete" guys who could only run fast and jump high. Watching Dr. J was more enticing than watching anyone on Walton's team, but the fact was that the Blazers won the NBA championship, not Doc and his crew. Bubs warned us not to get too caught up on what we saw in the playgrounds, but it was easier said than done. Trends were being established in parks all over the city, and innovations and improvisations would continue. Doc's team may have lost, but where I lived, sometimes memories of the spectacular superseded practicality.

CHAPTER 15
THE LEGEND OF
ARTIE GREEN

ONE DAY BACK IN 1975, I found myself in the back of Harlem River Houses on 150th Street one day when I wasn't supposed to be. Ma sent me to the corner store to get groceries. We were leaving for South Carolina the next day, and she wanted to make sandwiches. I wound up several blocks away from the corner store because the store was crowded, and I had a pocket full of food stamps I didn't want anyone to see me using.

Ma would have been tipped off I wasn't coming back anytime soon if she'd seen me take my five-speed, black Drag Stripper with the handlebar gearshift. It had the banana-boat seat and a rearview mirror on the sides. I was riding down Seventh Avenue on the sidewalk in front of Harlem River Houses when I heard a loud roar coming from the back, near Harlem River Drive. I turned into the Harlem River complex to see what was going on.

When I reached the back, people were crowded all around the fences. A game was going on. There were no referees, but I quickly noticed people focusing on one particular player. They became animated with every move this guy made. Like everyone else, I homed in on the nappy-haired, dark figure in high tube socks, dungaree shorts, and a T-shirt.

There were a few giants out there that day—guys so big they looked like lumbering dinosaurs who shook the ground as they ran. They could trample me and my five-speed like it was nothing. One of these giants went up to grab the defensive rebound as the ball came off the rim. He clearly had the ball in his hands. But then the smaller guy, the one with the dungaree shorts, grabbed the ball out of the giant's hands while they were both in flight. Before the bigger guy could hit the ground, the smaller guy, while moving upward, snatched the ball out of the giant's hands, cocked the ball behind his head and tomahawk-slammed it through the rim.

The eruption afterwards was so deafening, I jumped as chill bumps raced across my body. People screamed and yelled at the guy in dungaree shorts, saying, "Artie the Grasshopper." It was my first Artie Green encounter, the first time I'd laid eyes on the legend.

•••

Our park was a world of concrete, iron, and stone. It was reinforced with cold steel and hardened hearts, highlighted by brief patches of grass, trees, and wooden picket fences surrounding the exterior of mammoth-sized buildings. Tenement buildings hemmed in the taller project houses. In the park, we clung to our world as tightly as the tall chain-link fences surrounding it. On the hottest days, vapor rose from the asphalt, as hot as the boiling blood and competitive spirits of the residents living in the five 21-story, public housing buildings known as the Drew Hamilton public housing projects.

It was six o'clock on a Sunday morning. The sun was just rising over the South Bronx cityscape, and I was out practicing new moves I saw Artie Green make the night before in a game at Whitney Young Park on 139th Street. Three years had passed since my first glimpse of the legend behind Harlem River Houses in 1975, and his star had only risen higher since then.

By this time, Ma had given up trying to keep me in church. I guess she figured it was a lost cause. Maybe I was going to hell like Pop. She prayed for me, but the court was my sanctuary now, and she and I prayed to different gods. Over the years I pulled every trick in the book to get out of church, and now it was paying off. I used to get up early to leave for Sunday school, knowing it was shorter than morning service. Then I'd skip out before morning service started. If that didn't work, I snuck out during services to roam the parks, to return later with scuffed shoes.

I'd do almost anything to avoid Reverend Gardner's long sermons and that dreadful organ music. I hated the oversaturated smells from all the different perfumes, powders, and colognes people drowned themselves in. Some people only went to church once a year, Easter Sunday, and I hated this day most of all because it was always extra and overdone. The church would be overwhelmed with non-regulars and backsliders. And they would all be dressed to a T, new shoes, new dresses, haircuts, and hairstyles, and I hated all that shit. My stomach would be in knots until I got out of there. I didn't even hang around for the food.

I preferred the solitude of an empty park and a bouncing ball. Across the street, firemen stood in front of the fire station, watching as I dribbled up and down the court, imagining myself in a big game, shooting one shot after another at net-less iron rims. I invented new ways to challenge myself. How many could I hit in off the board? Which side of the court was my weak side? If I missed more on the right than on the left, then I worked on the left. No angle escaped my daily regimen. I shot bank shots from left to right, corner shots, shots off the left-hand dribble, then off the right, then off left and right foot and from the top of the key. I knew the court better than I knew myself. The firemen could set their alarms by the bounce of my ball any morning of the week.

Some of those morning sessions were spent thinking about Artie Green. Artie made his mark in basketball early in life. He was known for his athletic flair, and especially for dunking on people, particularly bigger, taller guys. Even before he could dunk, people were saying he was special. He had the confidence and dynamic ability that excited people. More than a dunking machine, Artie played with a style that led to comparisons to Earl Manigault. At six feet tall, he wasn't the Goat, but some said he had "Goat-like" tendencies. The shrewder old-timers didn't go for it. They said Artie didn't measure up to Manigault, but that didn't mean much to me.

Commanding the respect of frenzied crowds, his rep was built on serving older and more established players. Artie was blessed with the ability to fly in a way no one his size was doing in Harlem in 1977. A lot of cats could jump and get up high, guys like Steve Burtt, Abjack, Troy Truesdale, and Tony "Red" Bruin from Queens, but no one finished like Artie.

When contested on a shot, he went over you. Against smaller guys, he went up and over, and the taller, bigger guys, he went around, over, or in between. People watched Artie to see that one phenomenal move they would flash back to in their minds and retell a thousand different ways afterwards. This is how legends are created—variations of the same event retold from a thousand different perceptions. It was the lifeblood of playground basketball.

Such an event took place some years later over the summer of 1981 in a pro game at Columbia College. Columbia and City College (CCNY) were summer-league venues for the Pro-Am league where a lot of pros played. That summer, Ray Williams, the younger brother of NBA All-Star Gus Williams, was playing for the Knicks and going up against Artie. The Williams boys grew up in Mount Vernon, NY. Pros like Jeff Houston, Sugar Ray Richardson, Hollis Copeland, Bob McAdoo, and several other pros were playing that summer. I hadn't planned to go to the game that day, but most of my crew was going, so we scrambled together a few dollars and jumped into a cab down to Columbia. I knew my way around Columbia pretty good by then because I'd spent a lot of my high school days sneaking into their gym for pickup games.

Artie was playing with his former Marquette teammate, Sam Worthen, the skillful six-foot-four playmaker from Brooklyn. Sam was the playground personification of Magic Johnson and knew how to get the best out of Artie. The other team featured Hollis Copeland, an NBA vet, and Ray Williams, who was on his way to making the NBA All-Star team himself. Ray would score fifty-two points against the Pistons.

On one play, Artie caught the ball on the outside wing on a break and attacked the basket with Ray Williams as the first one back to challenge him. Artie gained momentum as he advanced the ball downcourt, his huge, overdeveloped calf muscles tearing up the court as he took off for flight just outside the hash-mark area inside the foul line. Artie wasn't a glider; he was an explosion off the floor. He exploded straight up and over people, usually off two feet. What made him so dramatic was watching him continue rising as others reached their ceiling.

But Ray wasn't a land lover. He could get up in the air too. As Artie rose, so did Ray, and it looked like he would block Artie's shot. But Artie kept rising and moved the ball to his left hip to avoid Ray's hands, and then down to his bending knees while in flight. Time stood still for a split second . . . waiting for the inevitable outcome . . . and then . . . *BOOM!* He dunked the ball so forcefully Ray had to duck his head under the rim. In later years I'd see a similar dunk by Dominique Wilkins on the Celtics. Since Artie was at least seven inches shorter than "The Human Highlight Reel," it was one of the most astonishing things I'd ever witnessed.

The entire gym erupted. People on the first rows jumped up and ran on the court as the referees blew their whistles uselessly. There was no foul, only pandemonium. Artie's dunk stopped the game before someone called a time-out. I watched Ray closely after the play and saw him shaking his head. That dunk by Artie was the talk of the summer, and even today when people of my generation talk about dunks, they ask if you saw the dunk Artie got on Ray Williams up at Columbia's gym.

Artie didn't live in our neighborhood, so when I watched him play for the first time in our park, I stared at him like he was from another world. One afternoon, Mo Blind shook the radiator pipe running through both our apartments to let me know Artie was playing in our park. We jetted down the back staircase to get a spot near the fence. Artie was recognized everywhere, and the crowd around the fences of our court swelled like a block party was going on. Artie sported a Slick Watts hairstyle this time, his dark-chocolate skin glimmering in the sun, making him look like a gladiator. I marveled at his spin moves to the basket. He also had a dynamic handle, which, along with his quick explosiveness to the rim, was probably his greatest asset.

He was the first cat I saw put the ball between his legs and behind his back while in the air before dunking it. Artie could also do a 360 while rotating the ball around his body. I was in awe of his physical ability. If there was a key to stopping Artie, it was to not let him near the basket. When he was airborne, anything could happen and often did.

Artie played for Taft High School where he would become a high school all-American. On the streets, I started following his career when he was playing with the LA All-Stars. He was one of the premier players at Whitney Young Park on 139th Street. The Whitney Young league was an attractive tournament for guys in college, or in that age group not yet playing in the pros. Guys like Dave Crosby, Sam Worthen, Wendell Ramsey, Steve Burtt, Imp, Dave Britton, and Gary Springer all played up there, thrilling and entertaining standing-room-only crowds on the corner of 139th Street.

When he was recruited by Al McGuire to Marquette, I hoped Artie would do as well in college as he did in high school and on the streets. McGuire was a New Yorker himself and recruited a lot of guys from the city, particularly from neighborhoods like Harlem. I wanted to see Artie on TV like some of the other big college stars, including Daryl Griffith and his cousin Butch Lee.

However, as I got older and more astute about the game, the shrewder and more cynical I became about playground legends, including Artie. He had flamboyant moves with the ball, but his outside shooting needed work and he didn't always see the court well.

I was already aware that a lot of guys I now idolized in the playgrounds would never make it to the NBA. As much as I liked watching Artie play, I knew he liked to get high and drank wine every now and then. A lot of guys smoked weed, and drank a little wine, and then before you knew it, they lost a step and were trying something harder, like coke or dust or some other crazy shit.

CHAPTER 16

THE EMERGENCE OF JAMES ICE

GAMES IN OUR BLOCK were hard edged. People brought egos, personal problems, and frustrations to the court every day. Drew Hamilton Houses was a hot sight for good pickup games and attracted players from neighboring areas, like Artie Green. It wasn't unusual for an All-City or all-American player like Gary Springer to get a game in our neighborhood. I hugged the sidelines for years, watching guys with big reps from other neighborhoods battling guys from our block like Imp, Daryl Barber, Wendell, Ted Campbell, and Mike Daniels, another All-City player in the Catholic division.

Gary Springer was dominating the PSAL (Public School Athletic League) in the late 1970s. He played for Ben Franklin, where they had a powerhouse team. His playing alongside the tall, lanky Richie Adams, another high school all-American, made Franklin one of the top schools in the nation. Listed as six foot seven in the papers, Gary was probably closer to six foot six, something I would only discover once I grew tall enough to look him eye to eye. When I saw big Gary in the park, wearing his Junior Olympics sweat suit, sky blue with the red-white-and-blue stripes down the side and the letters *USA* on his back, I thought he was the biggest star in the city. He was.

Like Artie, Springer was an exceptional athlete. He was physical, ran the floor well, and flew over people, dunking on everything in his way. As a "big" man, Gary was also known for sticking people's shit to the boards and snatching offensive rebounds out of the air to slam them back through the rim with force. Big Richie was probably more talented, but Gary was getting bigger press in the *Daily News* and *Post*. His girlfriend, Sharon Johnson, lived on the eleventh floor of our building, so this kept him around the block.

Seeing great players come through the park gave me bigger dreams of being great. When someone like Steve Burtt showed up, people immediately treated him differently. When he walked into a local McDonald's, he often got his food free. If Gary needed a favor from someone, even if they hardly knew him, he could get it.

Drew Hamilton Houses was condensed and concentrated like everywhere else in Harlem. We lived in an intense, combustible demographic that attracted all kinds of guys. Almost everyone who came through thought they could play basketball. The ones who fouled all the time were called "butchers." Guys with weak games were "scrubs." Guys were doing other things, like boxing, playing baseball, stickball, and other sports; however, basketball was the game that got adrenaline going and formed crowds around the fences. Playing in Drew also involved a certain level of risk. You learned which risks to take and which ones to avoid.

From the first day I went out back to play basketball in our park, I was tested. There were five 21-story buildings sharing one full basketball court, making the competition tough. Every building had a crew, and each crew sought dominion over the court. Younger guys had the court at the most unfavorable times. Older guys didn't play when it was too hot, at night, or early in the mornings. We didn't have lights out back near the courts, and it was hard to see at night. The older cats also didn't do rain, snow, or cold, so that's when young guys got out there to develop our skills.

We played games against rival crews, like Larry Dog and his boys from 144th Street or Johnnie Tucker and his crew from building 200, and in each case, bravado, risk-taking, and competitive intimidation was as frequent and consistent as crossover dribbles, finger rolls, and dunks.

I wasn't much of a talker but dealt with talkers routinely. It didn't always matter how good a guy was, or whether he could shoot, pass, or dribble. The game was also about attitude and confidence. There was always someone out there whose talent was superseded by their will to be relevant. Quarter-field was our biggest talker. He was Cowboy's younger brother, who was well known, so Quarter often got considerations some of us didn't. Mo Blind was the best debater in our crew, but it was Quarter who always had something to say. His mouth kept shit going.

But everything wasn't always funny when it came to playing ball in our neighborhood. There were always a few out to punk and intimidate you if they could get away with it. If you were outplaying someone, making them look bad, and it was obvious, a guy might elbow you or try to intimidate you physically to slow you down.

By the time I was fourteen, I was better skilled than not only the guys in my crew but also most of the guys my age in the neighborhood. Some of the older guys would select me from the sidelines to play in their games where the stakes were slightly higher. Guys like Marc Johnson, Mike Rich, Steve Hicks, and Paul Jinx were all starters for their respective high school teams. They were the next peer-group level up for me, and they began selecting me in pickup games. These guys were on the court with the very best players in the block, so I had to prove I could play with them.

Older players were stronger, and more confident and mature; if they didn't match you in natural skill, then strength and size could get them over. If you couldn't deal with it, then you weren't ready. If a guy was a lot stronger than you, you had to be quicker and faster; if he was bigger, you had to be smarter—figure out where he was weak and try to exploit it. In most cases, there wasn't time for prolonged thinking. You had to observe, adapt, and know what to do in certain situations, or it was going to be a long day. It was probably the best environment for honing natural basketball instincts.

My long arms gave me a physical advantage, and I was quick on my feet. When I started playing in bigger games, it was obvious my moves were different than what was already out there. I developed certain spins and change-of-direction moves that threw people off and shook them up. I'd do quick half spins back and forth to freeze the defense to get my shot off or get into the lane. I changed direction on a dime and was as good a shooter from the outside as anyone in the neighborhood. I would stop, reverse directions with either hand, and elude defenders to get off my shot with an ounce of daylight. Someone would reach for the ball, and I'd flip the ball behind my back, change direction, and take off. Or I'd throw it between my legs, spin, and stop short for a pull up. There were few guys my height playing like that. Guys started calling me James Ice or "Ice" after NBA All-Star George Gervin. It was the official beginning of my Iceman experience.

I was becoming a headache to defend, and I secretly wanted a nickname of my own, something no one else had. George Gervin *was* the only Ice that mattered. And Brooklyn's Jerry "Ice" Reynolds was already the most well-known Ice in NYC. At the same time, I thought it was lame to give myself a nickname, so I didn't do that either. I answered to Ice.

Around this time, guys began trying to slow me down by playing physical. Bigger, less talented players scored on me because I couldn't jockey with them for position. I hated that shit. If the physical stuff didn't work, intimidation wasn't far behind. Guys fouled as hard as they could or tripped me before I made my move. If it was a big game, a game with spectators on the sidelines, I never got the call. If I started to beef too much, someone might want to take me out. The unspoken rule was to call your own fouls, but as a rookie, a young boy with no rep, you weren't getting a call. I couldn't go out there calling a lot of fouls and risk being called soft, so I usually didn't say anything playing with older guys. You had to play through it, and sometimes it could cost you the game.

Fortunately, I wasn't exactly a lame duck. A guy could get embarrassed playing me without any thought to strategy. This was often true when a guy guarded me for the first time. Depending on the circumstances, I got players off balance and out of position with moves that made people on the sidelines take notice. Guys didn't like being embarrassed, especially if a younger player was the one shaking them up and scoring buckets.

The trials and tribulations of becoming good and respected in street basketball started in your neighborhood. This was where your rites of passage began. Each small accomplishment prepared me for summer competition and year-round challenges. When I was fouled hard, I came back harder. Even without the body weight of most guys, I blocked a lot of shots in the park and got unconventional steals by reaching around and slapping the ball free, something I was getting away with for now. On the street, when a person got ripped, there was no referee to bail them out. When he got his shit blocked clean, it wasn't up to someone else's perception.

A blocked shot done right got the crowd going almost as much as a great offensive move, especially if you pinned the ball to the backboard. Getting "stuck" was a custom trademark on the streets, and I was already good at sticking people. Sometimes after a guy got stuck, his perspective changed, and he became skeptical on offense. That's when you knew you had the edge on someone, something you could use. I didn't have any big-name rivals yet, but I was already looking for one.

One summer afternoon, I was playing one of my best games ever and noticed Suki draped around a fence pole, his eyes searing the court, fiery and intense in the same way he played the game. Suki was one of those guys who didn't care how hard he fouled you. He liked it; holding, tripping, pushing—it all made sense to him. Basketball was meant to be played hard. He must have thought his job was to make us tougher and meaner.

This afternoon, sirens cascaded in a background of cars, buses, and park chatter. A throng around the court's park fences hemmed us in. I caught another set of eyes near the fence: Hunter Bean's, his gold tooth visible as he brandished a brown paper bag wrapped around a bottle of Wild Irish Rose.

I was supposed to be at my job at Woolworth's department store on 145th and Broadway. I was the dishwasher. But I missed a lot of playing action because my shift was from three to seven every afternoon, the same time the best games took place in the park. Today, I skipped Woolworth's in favor of playing ball, and it was something I was never sorry about.

People squatted along the sideline park curb, legs bent, rows of Converse, Pro-Keds, and Adidas lined up for action. Eyes peered through the wired fences, hands hanging from the metal links, fingers pulling back and forth as it swayed. The park was alive, a combustion of games, conversations, debates, people passing through, bikes, big wheels, lodie tops, tennis balls, broom handles used as baseball bats, Now and Laters, Squirrel Nuts, Mary Janes and Skittles, sodas, chips, hero sandwiches of spiced ham and cheese; it was the neighborhood I knew and loved.

"Yo, Ice, keep yo head up on the break, baby, r-ight?"

"Yeah, r-ight, Steve."

Steve Hicks lived on the third floor of my building and was down with an older crew of sports fanatics. He played high school ball for a powerhouse Division B school. Steve wasn't an overtly athletic guy, but he had good size and was a smart and tough guard. As a respected leader in his crew, Steve was an all-around athlete and well liked in our block. He and I were on the same team in a full-court game, and it was prime time. Prime time meant people were waiting on the sidelines, evaluating you for when they stepped up to challenge you. Prime-time games featured the most spectators and were the most intense games because no one wanted to sit down and wait to get back on the court.

I'd never played in a prime-time situation before, but all the conditions were set for it to happen today. The weather was nice. The sun was going down, and the looming shade from the tall buildings washed away the rays. This was the time slot that pulled the regulars, the serious players who didn't come out to the court until the sun was low in the sky.

"Good shot, baby, good shot!"

Steve was pushing me. He sensed I was in an unfamiliar place. Today I was feeling the game as much as playing it. I also felt all those eyes around the fences.

Full-court games went to forty points by two. The first team to reach twenty prompted switching baskets to indicate the second half. Craig was on me, an older boy from the second building who also answered to the nickname "Ice." He was aggressive and no slouch to contend with. Craig had strength and experience. He was explosive when attacking the basket. But he was already aware I had a few things that would give him trouble too.

His title wasn't as widespread as Jerry's in Brooklyn, but a lot of people knew him as Ice. It was just another reason I didn't want this title. Craig was a high riser starting for Rice High School. He was into the weights. Maybe he resented my becoming known for the nickname he'd adopted, but I wasn't sure. The Ice thing had chosen me.

So many young guys were copping Ice as a moniker that players had to distinguish their titles. All over the city, there was a Greg Ice or Jerry Ice or a something Ice. I didn't think Craig looked or played anything like the original Iceman. He was smooth, had nice moves, and was an excellent defender, but it was obvious people felt my likeness was closer to the real thing. George Gervin was noted for his ability to score and his extraordinary finesse. He was an extremely skinny guy with a nice touch from the outside. Craig was two years older than me, but his game didn't resemble Gervin's, and I didn't think he could handle me. I wanted to prove it this afternoon.

"Yeah, Ice, take him to the hole. It's all you."

A shot fake got Craig off balance. I drove around him toward the baseline for a reverse layup, flipping the ball backwards off my fingertips at the rim. As I let the shot go, my back was to the basket, and I focused on the faces around the sidelines, never bothering to eye the rim. The ball bounced off the board and flipped in for two points. Murmurs escaped from the crowd as I ran up court.

"Gimme the ball, gimme the ball," Craig demanded.

Catching the ball, Craig crashed into me with his shoulder, his head down to make his move, then faded backwards to get his shot off, a shot I'd seen him get off a dozen times in the park.

"Good block, Ice! Tell him to git that weak shit outta here!"

Steve was hyped to exploit the situation, like any good playground player would, so he fed me the ball again. A jab step without the ball got Craig's attention as I feinted baseline, stopped short, and darted back toward the top of the key where Steve hit me with a pass. Catching the ball and turning toward the basket without hesitation, in one fluid motion I let the shot go for another two points, my second basket in a row.

Still steaming from the blocked shot from the previous play, Craig became more determined. It looked like the youngest player on the court was taking him to school.

Fat Larry, who lived in the building on 141st Street, was on the sidelines yelling, "Git that young boy off you, Craig!" Looking up at Larry, I noticed new faces huddled around the fences, and people from my crew, with a few older, more established players. I didn't look at anyone directly, but I drew energy from them. It was intoxicating. I've heard drug addicts strung out on smack for years say the first high was the one they would chase for the rest of their lives. This afternoon, I was experiencing my first high, and I would chase this feeling whenever I stepped on the court.

The crowd was the game in Harlem. When I was a skinny kid looking for a spot on a fence, I knew Harlem crowds were as much a part of the game as the players. Players didn't play for themselves and in some cases didn't even play to win; we played for the love and intoxication of the crowd.

If you kept the attention of the crowd, your self-esteem, stature, and rep was elevated. The eyes watching you, looking on with admiration, respect, and envy, was what made playground basketball. After long hours of practicing, shooting thousands of shots, practicing new moves I witnessed in the parks, and testing them on my friends, I was ready to make my mark, and ready to play for the crowd. Today, I had the attention of people I respected most. I'd prepared for this kind of game.

From the corner of my eye I noticed Ted Campbell watching, one of the best deep shooters in Drew Hamilton, with Dujii standing next to him. Both were respected prime-time players, and I wanted to impress them.

"Watch yo back, Ice. Watch yo back!" Big Artie from the nineteenth floor yelled to warn me shortly after inbounding the ball. I anticipated Butter Graham coming up behind me while eyeing Craig trying to cut me off ahead. Splitting defenders wasn't a fundamental move, but it was common practice on Harlem's playgrounds for those able to pull it off. It was becoming one of my trademarks.

With Butter approaching to force a trap, I kept my dribble low as Craig moved to cut me off. An aggressive move to my right forced Craig to shift with me. There was no time to turn and see Butter, so I had to feel him coming behind me. With my body leaning and the ball in my right hand, I stutter-stepped before stopping on a dime and reversing my direction with a spin. During the spin, I threw the ball between my legs, leaving Craig and Butter disoriented and me a clear path toward the basket. The two of them nearly collided trying to trap me, and the sidelines erupted into a frenzy of frantic screams and howling.

Chills ran through my body as I continued to attack the basket. It was time to finish things off, but BG jumped into my path as I ascended. I left my feet and adjusted in midair by turning my back slightly while airborne to shield the ball. BG was at least six foot three and a good shot blocker. He cut me off from the basket, but from my peripheral I noticed Steve breaking to the lane, so I wrapped my right arm across my body, flipping the ball behind my back for a wraparound pass and the score.

It was improvisation at its pinnacle. Again, the crowd erupted, giving me another adrenaline rush, bigger than the first. "Go 'head, young boy! Go 'head!" Even Big Larry, one of my most outspoken critics, was slapping high-fives. I had done better moves before, made defenders look worse, but never to players as good and as experienced as Butter, Craig, and BG. I began to feed off everyone else's expectations.

But then, I ran into a problem. A lesson about the streets was about to be reinforced: basketball in Harlem was about a lot more than fancy moves and dunks.

Butter Graham was a gangster. More importantly, he liked being a gangster. Butter also had a rep for not being too smart, and this combination made him dangerous. I didn't fuck with Butter. He was good enough to play for Benjamin Franklin's basketball team but dropped out and was now a full-time thug who occasionally played basketball. He hung out with Terry Reed and Willie Green, guys who talked about deliberately getting themselves busted to guarantee having warm places to sleep over the winter. Willie Green was a notorious extortionist who didn't live in the block. He wasn't a fighter and didn't look physically imposing, but a lot of people didn't fuck with Willie, especially with Butter as his muscle.

Earlier in the summer, Dujii was lighting Butter up in an afternoon game. Butter couldn't guard Dujii but switched off on him anyway because Dujii was eating up Fly Tye from the second building. Dujii went deep into his trick bag, and Butter couldn't do anything with his hesitation feint moves and was overshadowed by Dujii's off-speed, unorthodox offensive skills. Rather than deal with the embarrassment, Butter popped Dujii with an elbow in the neck. He acted contrite, like he didn't mean to do it, but everyone could see it was deliberate. Dujii was a low-key dude. He sucked it up and kept playing, but all that spectacular shit ended. He didn't score another basket the rest of the game.

Butter got his name because of his caramel-colored skin. Possessing good hesitation moves and a soft midrange jump shot, he was one of the best players in our block and won hundreds of dollars in one-on-one and two-on-two games for money. He didn't practice or play for any team and only played when he felt like it. I was having a breakout game this day, probably the most significant in my neighborhood up until that time, and had gotten Butter's attention.

"Let that little skinny mothafucka come this way wit that weak shit. Craig! Git on that mothafucka!" he shouted.

I acted as if I didn't hear Butter's words, but he wasn't the type you could ignore. And no one on our team had enough juice to curb his attitude if things got out of hand and he wanted to bully the game. Butter was the type of guy who wasn't going to respect your talent on the court if you didn't have his respect off it. For a guy like him, you had to be willing to challenge him physically, in any situation. He didn't respond any other way.

Craig seemed to take himself out of the game mentally after getting his shot blocked twice, and Butter took over on offense. His physical talent was outclassing Big Artie. He would spin back and forth, double pump, and hesitate while airborne, making basket after basket. Then, after working Big Artie over on the inside, he stepped out and hit the medium-range jumper. Usually, when a player like Butter got on track, Big Artie would have been on his own. Team defense wasn't a mainstay in street basketball. Sometimes a player was left to die at the hands of a superior offensive player. If you didn't have like-minded guys playing team defense, one guy could be the reason a team lost. Today, I saw Butter beating us by himself, and something inside me screamed to win.

The game was tied thirty-eight to thirty-eight, known as "point up" in the block. A normal game was forty, but since it was tied at thirty-eight, you had to win by two baskets, so the game point became forty-two. If the score made it to forty to forty, then the game point was forty-four and so on. You had to win by at least two baskets, for a total of four points. This was our version of overtime. I watched some games get into the sixties between two teams that wouldn't give up.

With the game tied, Butter was backing in on Big Artie with a hard-high dribble. I anticipated him setting up for his move, using the off-arm elbow to keep the big guy off balance the way Adrian Dantley was doing in the NBA. Butter was about six foot one and over 200 pounds; he was a smaller Dantley who played bigger than his size. Big Artie's six-foot-four 230 waned against his assault. With Craig not really trying to get the ball, I waited until Butter made his move and capitalized on one of Butter's weaknesses: court vision.

Coming in from the weak side, I swooped in and knocked the ball away from him and began making my way up court. I took two dribbles before Butter reached out and grabbed me by my shirt and threw me out of bounds like I was a toy. I tripped and fell, scraping my knee. The crowd howled as Butter glared down at me, daring me to act like I wanted to get up too quickly.

"Fuck you, skinny bitch."

If it were someone else, maybe someone like Johnny Tucker or GE, normal peers and rivals, I could swing and look forward to the fight. But swinging on Butter was suicide. I decided I wanted to live a little longer. There wasn't anyone with a big enough rep looking out for me, or who had my back, and since I couldn't kick his ass, I had to suck it up. It was our ball, but I was hurting. Then someone on the side threw me a lifeline.

"That's r-ight, Ice. He mad cause you servin' they ass," someone shouted. It was Blue, one of Big Larry's six brothers.

Unlike Big Larry, Blue was in my corner. He pushed me to play hard and to be tough. Blue was in his mid-twenties, but I played a few one-on-one games with him and he always hacked and muscled me throughout the game. I liked Blue, but I hated playing against him because he was always using his weight and strength to disrupt my offense.

There were people on the sideline who could have stepped to Butter. Someone like Big Larry, who even Butter didn't fuck with. But I was still the equivalent of a rookie. I hadn't proved to any of them I had heart. Older cats were watching to see if I would quit and how I would react. The street was always watching.

I stayed out of the way the next few plays as the game went back and forth, point up, point, and finally point game our way, and our ball. One basket could win it, and the game was a lot more physical and serious. No one wanted to lose and sit down. Spectators were waiting, and whoever lost wouldn't get to play the rest of the day. In the half-court, it was easier to grab someone, foul, and make them take the ball out of bounds rather than give them a chance to score. It was harder in the half-court to surprise the defense and get a better shot.

"Here, Ice. It's yo show, baby; take that mothafucka."

Steve passed me the ball in the backcourt, but I didn't want it. I wasn't sure I was ready to take the last shot in a game like this. It was our point, our ball, and our game to win. If I scored, I was the hero. If I missed, I was a young boy who wasn't ready. I had gotten into Craig's head a little bit, but now I had to deal with my own. What if I missed? What if Butter came over and crushed me? Worse yet, what if Craig stripped me before I even got a shot up? He was known for that kind of thing.

I felt like everyone was watching. A lot of my crew was there. And when I looked to the outside corner of the sidelines, I noticed someone else's eyes focused on the court. Artie Green, the legend, was leaning on a fence, in civilian clothes, taking a look at the action.

His presence alone made the game more important. When a guy like Artie was watching, everyone played harder and tried to impress even more. If I took myself out of the action, no one could blame me. I was younger and had already impressed the crowd with a few moves. I also went head-to-head with Craig, a more established player with nice skills. Maybe it was time for the older, hardened veterans like Phil Walker or Big Artie to take it home.

But Butter was virtually wrestling with Big Artie until he didn't want to be on the court, much less near the ball. Steve was having a hard way with Puerto Rican Pedro hawking him, another college-bound player incapable of backing down. And Phil was having an off game even though he usually got the best of BG.

Getting the pass from Steve in the backcourt, I moved cautiously across half-court. Craig wasn't pressuring me like before. He was playing back, biding his time. It was smart, but it could also mean he didn't think he could rattle or take the ball from me. I was alert, but I didn't even look at the basket. I didn't want anyone thinking I had any intention of trying to score.

I decided to make my move on the left wing. Even if I didn't take the shot, I had to get Craig off balance to make something happen. I drove to the right aggressively, stopped short before reaching the baseline, and pivoted back to the left. He was shook, but only slightly, and Pedro slumped off to help, so I couldn't get my shot off. I immediately hit Steve with a pass. As I made the pass, Craig recovered and tried to get back in position. I darted in the opposite direction, back toward the baseline.

A lot of bodies were clogged in the lane: Big Artie, Butter, BG, D Allen. I used them all as picks to lose Craig as I ran to the opposite side of the court across the baseline. Steve was reading me, reversed his dribble, and hit me with a pass on the opposite side of the court. Craig wasn't close enough. As I caught the ball, I eyed the basket. I was on an angle, about twenty feet out, about to take a shot I took almost every morning. The catch and release, as before, were virtually simultaneous, and it had to be as Butter lunged toward me, knocking me down as I released my shot.

The ball hit the backboard once and went straight through the basket, a sweet bank shot. It was game! "Yeah, slim!" someone yelled. I stayed on the ground awhile, listening to the murmurs of the crowd. "Yo, that kid gon be nice."

I looked up to see a smiling face offering me a hand up.

"Good game, slim," the owner of the hand said.

It was Artie Green, the Black basketball god. The same god who didn't know I existed before today. Before today, I was just like all the other little niggas trying to be like Artie. But now Artie knew me, he saw me, and that was worth getting up that morning. It was worth skipping work at Woolworth's and the bloody knee and swelling ankle I got from Butter. It was worth everything.

From that moment on, my perspective changed. I knew I could play with the big boys. I stood up to Craig and Butter, and enough people saw it to know I was to be reckoned with. My rep was going to grow. My status among my peers was elevated higher than it ever had been.

I got picked more often to play with the older guys—not all the time, but enough. Players like Ted Campbell, Marc Johnson, Wendell Ramsey, Imp, and Phil Walker, all high school starters and college players, were offering advice and took an interest in my personal development. Soon I was on the radar of the main hustlers in the block, guys like Wayne Davis, Nut, and Big Nate Hall. When I played, people expected something exciting, like I was carrying their expectations into my games around Harlem.

Being accepted, respected, and admired for what I could do on the court gave me an identity at a time I was searching for one. I wasn't a man yet, but you couldn't convince me of that when I was on the court. From that day on, James Ice from Harlem was only going to get bigger and better.

CHAPTER 17
THE HIGH SCHOOL OF MUSIC & ART

I HEARD THE PHONE ringing in our apartment before I got through the door. Fidgeting to unlock an assortment of three locks, I hoped the call was from Danielle Spencer, a short, curly-haired cutie I met the previous weekend outside the Polo Grounds. Her reddish-auburn hair was pulled back into a ponytail, with curls dangling down the sides of her face. She had butter-pecan skin, glistening in baby oil. In our brief exchange, I could see she was quick tongued, like Danielle Spencer from the TV show *What's Happening.* I stopped Dee coming out of the 155th Street subway and wound up walking her back to building 6 in the Polo Grounds projects. Not knowing what else to say before she left me standing there, I asked for her phone number. She took mine. Rushing through the door, I dropped my book bag, dashed toward the ringing yellow phone hanging on the kitchen wall, and picked it up.

"Hello."

"Hi, may I speak with James Washington?"

"This is James Washington."

"Hi, James, this is Miss Arnold. I'm the admissions counselor at the high school of Music & Art."

My heart nearly jumped out of my chest. I forgot all about Danielle.

"James, it seems there was an error made when calculating your standardized test scores from your previous school. There is a minimum academic requirement for our school, and your scores along with the other entrance examination requirements met the minimum standards for admittance. Are you still interested in attending the High School of Music & Art?"

I wasn't one for impulse, so I paused to make sure I was sane. Maybe she was making another big mistake. I knew my art portfolio wasn't like any I'd seen the day of my examination. Both of my graffiti and comic book partners from the Dime were rejected by M&A same as I was. I'd also had a great summer of basketball in 1977, and all summer I had prepared myself for a tryout with the Brandeis junior varsity team.

Before receiving that call from Miss Arnold at M&A, my first day of high school at Brandeis Annex went pretty much as anticipated. It was mild mayhem. Students strolled into class, some with notebooks, others with nothing but attitude. The raunchiest and loudest students immediately attracted attention, some already falling into character as the cool, crazy niggas they thought they were. These were the kids already tapped into the word-of-mouth networking groups that would become the social cogs around school. Loners like Walter Welch, and other stragglers no one paid much attention to, were either smart or unlucky in school life. I preferred the company of loners. They weren't as phony. But I had to avoid being around loners exclusively. Loners were always on someone's target list, so I was going to play the middle the way I had in junior high.

The array of students coupled with frightened, intimidated teachers highlighted how badly Brandeis Annex was overwhelmed by sheer numbers. Despite only carrying the ninth and tenth grades, it was still overcrowded. There were forty students in my homeroom, and a third of our gym class wouldn't have lockers. At the Dice, the moniker for the school, it seemed like more people were interested in sporting new gear and dominating the social scene than anything else. The fly cats were fading British Walkers and Playboys; some were flossing suede Pumas and shell-toe Adidas. Image seemed to trump nearly everything else.

I washed dishes at Woolworth's all summer to save up a few dollars for new school clothes. I rocked a new pair of white-on-white shell-toe Adidas and a blue Adidas sweat suit with white stripes down the side my first day at Brandeis. Sporting a fresh cut from Jerry's Den Barbershop on Lenox Avenue, I was ready to mix in with the rest of my image-driven classmates. After Miss Arnold's phone call, that all changed.

"Yeah, I'm still interested in Music & Art," I answered her.

"Good, James. We're sorry for the misunderstanding, but you should report to our office tomorrow morning and not Brandeis. We will request your records be sent to us."

"Okay."

"Do you know where we're located?"

It was a dumb question, but I didn't care. All that mattered now was that I was leaving Brandeis Annex and going to another school. It didn't even register that I was leaving a superior basketball school. I was still happy. A lot of famous people had gone to Music & Art, like Billy Dee Williams and Diahann Carroll, and I wouldn't have to take the train to school.

"Yes, I know where it is. Same place we took the test, right?"

"Oh yes, you're so right. That was a dumb question, wasn't it? Well, we expect to see you tomorrow, okay?"

"Okay."

I didn't see this coming. I liked the idea of attending Music & Art, but I had to think about what that meant for playing basketball.

Eugene Robinson lived in the neighborhood in the first building on Seventh Avenue and 141st Street—the only project building without a notable or dominant crew represented in the park. We hung out when we happened to run across each other. I met Eugene in church, somewhere neither of us wanted to be. Eugene and I had a few things in common other than hating church. We liked fighting each other. Boxing, wrestling, it didn't matter; we were always mixing it up.

He was the younger brother of Freddie Jackson, who was just becoming a notable singer in New York. Through Eugene I found out Freddie had gone to M&A. Freddie was a featured singer in our church, Mount Neboh Baptist. Freddie could sing, and he was a big guy, but people on the street said he was a homo, and he was feminine enough for Eugene to socially distance himself in public. Homo or not, people came to church just to hear Freddie blow.

Most cats from our block attended mainstream public schools. If you were an outstanding student, or had developed an athletic skill or taken up a trade, there were other alternatives. A few guys from my crew managed to avoid standard public schools. Mike Poole was accepted into Printing, a trade school in Midtown Manhattan; Sputnik and Wil Allen got academic scholarships to high-achieving prep schools out of state; and Mo and Dee White's parents made enough to send them to Rice, a private Catholic school. Johnny Mack was at JFK in the Bronx, one of the better performing public high schools, and D-Ferg, from the second building, was accepted into Art & Design, another specialized school for the arts. All of these schools, with the exception of JFK, had acceptance criteria and academically outperformed high schools most Harlem kids were being funneled into, like Franklin, King, GW, and Hughes.

My new school sat prominently on the corner of Saint Nicholas Terrance and Convent Avenue at 135th Street. You could see the building as far away as Fifth Avenue. It looked like a castle, complete with gothic towers and decorative gargoyles. There was nothing modern about the building, but it seemed to fit the surrounding area.

Convent Avenue, once known as Sugar Hill, surpassed Striver's Row when it came to affluence during Harlem's Renaissance of the 1920s and '30s. Despite Harlem's drastic decline in quality of life, a lot of the property up on the hill was still coveted and, according to some, very valuable. Unfortunately, it seemed like the rest of Harlem, especially the East Side, was falling apart.

Our neighbor Mr. Washington was legendary for his conversations about Whites wanting Harlem back. I always wanted to know when they had it to begin with. He talked about how convenient and profitable it would be for major businesses if Harlem were a more suitable place to live. A place with less drug activity, violence, and poverty.

Washington, in his slow slang, would say, "Niggas don't own nothin' in Harlem no more." He said Jews and the city owned most of the property and let housing standards decline almost as soon as they started letting more Blacks into the area. Despite being the primary residents, native Blacks, islanders, and Latinos owned and controlled very little real estate in Harlem. Whites getting Harlem back wasn't going to be hard whenever the time came.

I was very familiar with the serenity of Convent Avenue and how different it was up there. I spent many Saturday mornings riding my bike up the long hill on 141st to Saint Nicholas Terrace overlooking Saint Nicholas Park. I liked riding up there because it was always quiet and hardly anyone was up there. Occasionally I would stop by a few of the courts in Saint Nick Park for a quick game. A few students from City College might be hanging around, but there were rarely any sirens or police cars driving up and down Convent Avenue like they were on Eighth, Seventh, and Lenox Avenues.

Music & Art was part of the scene on Convent Avenue. Despite being hemmed in on the east and west by ghetto neighborhoods, Music & Art maintained its distinctly artsy liberal arts environment and demeanor. Having produced talented performers like Eartha Kitt and artists like Reginald Pollack, the area was a relative haven. I wanted to embrace both worlds: the serenity and tranquility of M&A, but also the ghetto where I was becoming a notable basketball player.

After I hung up with Miss Arnold, I had to call someone to let them know my life had just changed forever, so I called the one person who might give a damn.

"Ma, guess what?"

"What, James?"

"Guess!"

"James, I'm at work and don't have time to play games."

"Ma, I made it into Music & Art!" I blurted out.

"Really? Oh, that's so good, James. I'm so proud of you."

"Yeah, they told me to come over there tomorrow."

"What did they say?"

"They said it was a mistake on one of my test scores."

"See, the lord works in mysterious ways, don't he?"

"Yeah, Ma, I know he does," I lied.

"So what do you need to do?"

"I just have to go there tomorrow. I need art supplies, just don't know what I need."

"James, I won't have any money this week, but don't worry about that now. Just be happy you're in. Have you thought about asking your father for money to get supplies?"

The thought of Pop snapped me back from my euphoria. She knew I wasn't thinking about asking Pop. It had been a very long time since I asked Pop for anything. Between her two jobs, Ma managed to get money from Pop when she could, but I was older now, a lot more stubborn, and learning to cope without the benefit of experience or guidance of an older man. I'd rather steal my art supplies than ask Pop for money to buy them.

"Okay, Ma, I'll see you when you get home."

It felt like I'd really caught a break. Getting into a specialized art school was one miracle, but staying close to home made it even sweeter. There would be no subway rides to school for me. I started putting together all the advantages of going to M&A, and before I knew it, I wasn't even thinking about playing for Brandeis.

Ironically, getting accepted into Music & Art came at a time when my artistic interests were declining just as basketball was rapidly expanding my life. I hadn't picked up my art book the entire summer and was no longer doing tags in the subways. It was all about basketball now.

At Music & Art, I was going to get a taste of what life was like on the other side of 110th Street, the downtown side where options weren't as bleak and the dialogue not as harsh.

At the bottom of the hill at 135th and Saint Nicholas Avenue was the Eighth Avenue subway line. Most of the M&A students and teachers emerged from this station every morning. Others came in on the Broadway line at 137th Street. Directly in front of the Eighth Avenue subway at 135th was PS 136, my former rival junior high school when I was at the Dime. Every year featured rumors of a big fight going down between 136 and IS 10. Usually someone issued a threat, or they beat up one of our guys or vice versa, and then everyone would be talking about the big fight between the schools, usually scheduled for a Friday.

That life evaporated. My first day at Music & Art, I watched as a White stream of students poured out of the 135th Street subway station, walking up the steps through Saint Nick Park and toward the Terrace. Some came from as far away as Rockville Long Island, Ozone Park Queens, Flatbush Brooklyn, and Chinatown. Others were a little closer, traveling from Midtown Manhattan or the Village, but no matter where they came from, they appeared carefree and somewhat less animated than my classmates at the Dime. One policeman stood at the entrance of the subway station.

CHAPTER 18
WILLIE BOSKET: BABY-FACED KILLER FROM HARLEM

AS I SETTLED INTO the idea of my new fairytale high school, something happened to make me reflect on those days I was running around doing things I wasn't supposed to. It made me think of risks we took for fun.

The crew of graffiti guys I hung with from 144th Street liked to go down to the subways to tag-up. One of our favorite spots was the number 3 IRT train station on the Lenox Avenue line. The last stop for the number 3 was at 149th and Seventh, directly below the Dime, where we went to school.

The next to the last stop for the 3 train was at 145th Street and Lenox. The stop at 145th Street had a shorter platform, so the train was too long for it. This meant a few cars were still in the tunnel portion of the station and couldn't be seen from the platform. If you were in the two back cars, you were in the tunnel, and the doors wouldn't open. Since no one could see into the car from the outside, this could turn into a dangerous situation.

The 135th Street stop was the same way. There was usually no one waiting on the platform of the uptown side at 145th Street because the last stop on the line was less than four blocks away at 149th Street. No one needed to ride such a short distance, so there was no tollbooth clerk to get tokens on the uptown side at 145th and Lenox. If you weren't familiar with the line, you didn't know all this and could get caught riding in the back cars with the wrong people. People were robbed, beaten up, and a few girls had been raped in the back cars of the uptown number 3 train between 135th and 149th.

On March 19, 1978, one year removed from my graffiti-running days, Willie Bosket, a boy who lived in a rundown tenement on 145th Street near Lenox Avenue, shot a man to death on the number 3 train at the 149th Street station. The papers reported the initial story as an attempted robbery. Eight days later, Bosket shot, killed, and robbed another man on the number 3, at the same station. Bosket was fourteen, two months older than I was.

I didn't know Willie but could have run across him anywhere in Harlem. In the papers he was labeled "the baby-faced killer," in part due to his diminutive size. They didn't show his face in the papers, but the killer could have been a lot of fourteen-year-old dudes in Harlem. When I first heard about the story in the papers, I thought they might be talking about Baby Dow. I was certain he'd already killed someone.

Bosket was convicted of two murders in 1978. Later, people reported he bragged about the killings and attempted other robberies. One of the men Bosket killed was married and a father, yet Bosket was only sentenced five years, the maximum he could get as a fourteen-year-old. Willie had been in and out of juvenile facilities since he was nine. His father, Butch Bosket, was serving life for murder in Milwaukee. Like my friends LA and Cherry, Willie's destiny was scripted by circumstances. While I was finding my way through basketball, guys like Willie were trying to be the baddest and meanest dudes on the streets.

Some boys looked at violence in the same way I saw competition in basketball. They wanted to punch someone in the face just to get a rep for punching someone in the face. Their rush came from making someone bleed or stomping someone's head into the concrete. People would say, "Damn, that's a crazy mothafucka," and word would spread. Someone like Willie reveled in this kind of notoriety in the same way I did when someone told me I had a sweet jump shot. Their capacity for violence brought them a level of respect and esteem. Violence made them feel like men.

Willie's five-year sentence for two murders brought a public backlash sparked by Governor Hugh Carey that prompted a law change regarding juvenile offenders of violent crimes. Under scrutiny from his political opponents for being "soft" on crime, Governor Carey called a special legislative session and signed the new Juvenile Offender Act of 1978 allowing juveniles as young as thirteen to be tried as adults for crimes of murder and rape in New York. New York was the first state to enact the law, and Willie Bosket from 145th Street was the catalyst.

Willie would eventually get the rep he always wanted, as a notorious killer. He was released in 1983. Just ninety days later, Bosket was arrested again on a minor charge. No one was hurt or injured, and nothing was taken; however, Willie was arrested for aggravated assault after arguing with a sixty-seven-year-old neighbor in that same building on 145th Street where his mother and sister still lived. Of course, the police were interested in every move Willie made.

Once arrested, Bosket would never be a free man again. He began to believe the authorities would do everything to ensure he stayed in jail. While in lockup, he started assaulting guards. He nearly killed one by stabbing him in the heart with a shank. Bosket became known as the most dangerous inmate in the New York State prison system.

When I first read about Willie Bosket, and how he'd spent almost all his life in juvenile institutions, and how his father was serving a life sentence for murder, I thought about my life and how I was starting at Music & Art. When Willie killed the two men on the subway, he was awaiting paperwork for his legal adoption by a middle-class White couple living upstate. They were in their late fifties and took a liking to Willie after meeting him in a correctional facility in Troy, NY. Willie spent quite a bit of time with the couple, learning how to live out in the open, suburban environment. He was supposed to be starting a new life, one far away from the temptations and risks of urban city life in Harlem.

Like other troubled but charming boys, Willie was known for flashing a beautiful smile and exhibiting startling intelligence, while masking darker compulsions and inhibitions. Bosket wasn't supposed to be in Harlem when he committed the two murders. A lapse in the system due to his pending adoption granted him an unauthorized release from his detention center. He was never meant to be returned to his mother's apartment on 145th Street, where there was a violent criminal element.

In 1996, Fox Butterfield wrote a book about the Bosket family called *All God's Children*. He attempted to explain the random rise of violent crime as not only a phenomenon in places like Harlem but also a symptom of a culture of violence that has always existed in the United States. Fox traced Willie's family history back to the 1860s and found that in each preceding generation, a male Bosket had died a violent death. Willie's father was a convicted murderer but also a Rhodes Scholar who completed two degrees in prison. Like his son Willie, he spent most of his years institutionalized. Butch Bosket was eventually released after twenty years, but like Willie's stint of freedom, it was short lived. Within three months he was arrested again on a rape charge and died trying to escape the police.

• • •

The first time I walked through the hallways at M&A, I felt a little out of place. I had never been institutionalized, but I was navigating the same streets as Willie Bosket. In my new school, students sang in the hallways, wore jeans with holes in the knees, and it was no big deal. The teachers were extra polite, and there was no beefing in the lunch lines over people trying to skip. The cafeteria scene in my former school could be like a prison movie. If you didn't speak up or stand up for yourself, it could get ugly. And there was always some slick cat, or group of cats, trying to skip the whole line and get their lunch as soon as they walked into the lunchroom.

I'm not saying M&A was a utopia, but it felt less manic. Even the orientation of Black students was different. Some guys were nerdy, others glaringly eccentric, but people were free to be or act whatever way they wanted. The tension I'd known in school up until this point didn't seem to exist at M&A. If you wore jeans with a hole in the knee at the Dime, you were a bum-ass nigga. You could be a target of ridicule, humiliation, or even violence because of what you didn't have at the Dime.

The irony was that in the ghetto we had less, but we were compelled to desperately cover up the bad hands we were dealt. It was standard in the ghetto to front, and act like we had more than we did. I didn't want anyone knowing we were on food stamps or had been on welfare. Now I was going to school with people who had no idea what that life was like.

In ghetto life, things that at the end of the day meant little to nothing in terms of substance were ironically the things that got enhanced and blown out of proportion. We were honed to a laser-sharp, quick-fix mentality, completely enthralled by material wealth, appearance, and image. Living in poverty, we would die to avoid being categorized like that. Even the most ignorant, violent street-walking cat felt this way. Wearing new gear, earning a quick buck, no matter how you earned it, and coping in the streets was enough to make us believe, if only temporarily, in ourselves.

My new school not only encompassed a cultural shift but also a shift in my academic environment. The teachers at M&A were on par with those at some of the better specialized public schools in the city, like Bronx Science, Julia Arts, and Stuyvesant.

For the next four years of my life, I had the best of both worlds. At home I remained athletically focused and socially hard edged enough for the real world and supercompetitive basketball. But now there was another outlet and dynamic in my new school life. I could relax, explore my creative interest, and open up socially in ways I never had before or would have otherwise. It was a pivotal time in my maturity, knowing that on one hand I could deal with guys like Willie Bosket and on the other enjoy the psychological escape at Music & Art of knowing there were other ways to live.

CHAPTER 19
KENNY HUTCH AND RIVERSIDE

"**ICE, YOU HAD TWENTY-FIVE,** B. You wuz killin' 'em. Dem niggas couldn't touch you, Ice. Damn, my nigga. You wuz doin' yo thing!"

D-Smooth wasn't easily excitable. He was low key, on the quiet side, and didn't command a spotlight. But he was excited now. Smooth got his name because he was always in the mirror checking out his face, brushing off his kicks, and known for fading the latest fashions. He had an early interest in gymnastics for a while but didn't have the passion for basketball like the rest of us. This was obvious when he announced his favorite player was Doug Collins of the 76ers, from a few years ago.

"Twenty-five, huh?" I asked nonchalantly. I didn't need Smooth to tell me how many points I had. I already knew. I counted every basket in my head. I knew how I scored each point.

"Word, Ice, but bus this . . . !"

"What, Smooth?"

"You ain't miss one shot, B, the whole game. You ain't miss nothin', kid! That shit wuz crazy. You coulda had fifty, B!"

"Word?"

"Ice, I'm telling you, you ain't miss nothin', kid—not one shot!"

I didn't need Smooth to tell me that either. I knew I hadn't missed, and it hadn't been the first time. I had three other games I shot 100 percent from the field. I was eight for eight in a game at Mount Morris Park two weeks before, and nine for nine in another Rucker game. I also made all five foul shots in both games. I was an innately efficient scorer but knew I could do better. The day Smooth was at my game, I was twelve for twelve from the field, but only one for one from the line. My only trip to the line came on a scoop shot I completed after spinning away from one defender and scoring on another as I was bumped for the "and one." We won the game against the Sundevils comfortably, but maybe we could have put the game away earlier if I played more aggressively. I was shooting the ball well but didn't like missing. I knew I had to start taking more risks on the court.

Before my perfect twenty-five-point game, Kenny Hutchinson was *the man* on my 1978 Dykeman squad. A lean, lanky point guard who exploded on New York City's basketball scene, Hutch was from the South Bronx. The basketball gods blessed Hutch with a dynamic game early in life and a personality to match. When Hutch stepped on the court, he had a commanding presence and a big game like no one our age I'd seen. As a high school freshman, he held his own on the number one ranked team in the nation, Ben Franklin. I was just waking up to my talent, but Hutch was already establishing himself as one of the best high school players in the country.

When Hutch left our Dykeman team three games in to play with Riverside Church, it opened up an opportunity for me to show my ability. I was a starter before he left, but a role player. Walking into that void he left allowed me to emerge as a player in one of the hottest summer leagues running uptown, the Holcombe Rucker Tournament.

With Hutch gone, I became the go-to guy for Mr. Couch, the founder and organizer of the Dykeman basketball organization in Upper Manhattan. I never looked back. Playing with Hutch, I was a ten-to-fifteen-point scorer; once he left, I was scoring twenty or better in most of our games. The next time Hutch and I met on the court, it was as rivals.

At Dykeman tryouts earlier that spring, I was humbled by Hutchinson's irrepressible talent. Nobody was on his level that day. I was there with a few friends from my crew, feeling pretty good. Mike Poole and J-Mac were two of my closest friends, and two of the better players my age in my block. I had unique offensive skills of my own and was ready to take my talent up to the Dykeman tryout. I wasn't expecting to run into another kid my age I couldn't handle. But that was before I encountered Kenny Hutchinson.

The summer Rucker Tournament was the biggest basketball event of the summer for the city's best high school players. I missed the previous summer season, so playing this year was a big deal, and a breakout summer for me. This would give me the exposure and confidence I craved. It was time to up my game.

My offensive skills improved daily. I didn't think anyone could stop me, not even Hutch. My talent, outside of being long and lanky, was being able to see angles. I could score from long range with proficiency from all the previous years of shooting practice, and I liked to spin off a defender in either direction to get the separation I needed. I was also developing an innate nose for the ball, an instinct for getting into scoring positions conducive to my physical ability.

I had big hands and unusually long arms working to my advantage, so things looked easy, like I wasn't expending much effort. I also had excellent footwork that allowed me to stop and reverse-pivot using angles, possibly from years of playing neighborhood running games like Renny CoCo and Blackcrow, games requiring elusive running and juking maneuvers. My athletic ability enabled me to do things other cats weren't doing, at least not the way I was doing it. So, when I stepped away from the Dykeman tryout after experiencing the raw talent of Kenny Hutch, I learned another important lesson I would never forget. I learned to never stop working on my game because there could always be a Kenny Hutch out there.

I was primarily a park rat. Neighborhood parks were where I played, other than the winter Rucker season when we were playing in neighborhood rec centers. Not attending a credible sports school ensured I wouldn't be on the radar in city basketball. The best high school players were playing in the PSAL, or CHSAA (Catholic High School Athletic Association), or, if fortunate like Bruce Dalrymple, a private prep school somewhere upstate.

The High School of Music & Art was noted more for its soccer team than basketball. The only place I could make a name for myself was in the summer leagues, so I took it seriously.

Kenny Hutch was leading one of the best high school teams in history to a city championship. Gary Springer, Richie Adams, Lonnie Green, and a young Walter Berry gave Franklin a better starting five than most college teams in the area. People were literally scared to play Franklin. After his landmark freshman season, Hutch became a big commodity and quickly outgrew smaller community-based organizations like Dykeman.

Riverside Church, home of the Riverside Hawks, was one of the best-known religious institutions in the city. It was also the best-known

AAU basketball organization in the city—some would say in the world. Overlooking the Hudson at 122nd Street off Riverside Drive, its extensive list of contributors included John D. Rockefeller and families like the Carnegies. The massive, landmark church was in a quiet, secluded section of Harlem, rebranded as "Morningside Heights" to distinguish it from the ghetto stigma of Harlem. Nevertheless, along with Columbia University, Morningside Heights was surrounded by Harlem's ghetto on all sides. If you stood on 122nd and Broadway and walked one block east, you were in the Latin ghetto; two blocks east toward Amsterdam, St. Nicholas, and Eighth Avenue, and you were walking directly into central Harlem at its heart—Black, poor, and destitute.

Ernie Lorch ran the show for Riverside. He was head coach, general manager, and CEO of the Hawks' nonprofit organization that placed big budgets, contributions, and donations at his disposal. Anyone with anything to do with Riverside basketball went through Lorch. A middle-aged White man with black-rimmed glasses, he was known in basketball circles all over the city but still viewed skeptically by a lot of people working with community organizations in Black neighborhoods. Lorch looked like Herbert Stempel from the '50s game show *Twenty-One*, even though we were approaching the '80s. Yelling from the sidelines, he looked out of place in Harlem and the Bronx unless you knew who he was.

Some guys froze up playing against Riverside because they had so many good players. They didn't want to be embarrassed. Riverside Church established their program in the latter 1960s, and by the 1970s the Hawks were traveling all over the world. Hutch left Dykeman for Riverside because that's where the money was. He'd get to travel and attend Five Star camps and play against the best high school players in the country.

It was hard for someone raised in the ghettos of Harlem, Brooklyn, or the South Bronx to turn down money staring them in the face. Dykeman was still grassroots, an upstart program, so Hutch jumped ship.

Mr. Couch and Evander coached our Dykeman squad on a shoestring budget. Couch would often pay out of his pocket just to get guys to the games. They were critical of Riverside. Evander was a hard-nosed guy a lot of guys found it hard to play for and was responsible for bringing Hutch into the Dykeman. When Hutch left the team, Evander felt compelled to give us a speech about Riverside's organization.

"I don't know what it's gonna take for y'all to get the message. Those guys don't care anything about you at those other organizations. They don't care about your community, your family, or your education. All Riverside care about is you playin' ball for them, and what you can do for their program."

It was the same speech I heard from Mike Williams when I was playing for Minisink—the story about how we had to stick with teams from the neighborhood, and how organizations like the Gauchos and Riverside were only using us and didn't really care about us. There was a growing conflict over young Black basketball players in the city. For guys like Hutch coming out of the ghetto, living hand to mouth, it was hard to ignore the pretty gym bags, jackets, and winning personas bigger organizations like Riverside offered. When someone wore a Riverside or Gauchos jacket in the block, it was a statement to everyone that you had game. It separated you from other cats playing ball in the park.

College programs were networked through summer camps like Five Star, and consequently AAU organizations like Riverside and the Gauchos became vehicles of access to great players. The church attracted raw talent from ghettos in all five boroughs of the city. Scouts, recruiters, coaches, and sponsors poured into Riverside to get a look at players for their institutions. The recruiting paradigm flipped from when Black players in the '40s, '50s, and '60s were ignored by large, mainstream White colleges. A player like David Thompson, who played at NC State in '76, would never get the same look in 1966. My generation of ballplayers became the new commodity big colleges wanted to cash in on.

Riverside was trying to take over amateur basketball in NYC. Lorch refused to enter his teams into the Rucker Summer League, preferring instead to play in the Citywide League, a rival tournament Lorch used his Riverside Church connections, resources, and clout to form. Some people called it the "Riverside League" because his teams dominated the tournament. For a few summers, they ran three Riverside teams in a single division. A Riverside A, B, and C squad. It wasn't unusual for the Citywide championship game to be played between two Riverside squads.

Lorch may have looked at the Rucker in the same way Red Auerbach viewed the ABA—as a ghetto league of undisciplined rogues and showboating hotdoggers. What bothered many local coaches and community organizers about Lorch was his arrogance. They didn't like his "White savior" inference. A lot of the neighborhood coaches believed that without Riverside's deep pockets or the incentives Lorch dangled before us, he would be exposed as a fraud. Neighborhood coaches like Evander, Mr. Couch, One-Eyed Sam, Bob McCullough, and even Dave, who coached the Gauchos, were on the ground and in local neighborhoods. A lot of them still lived in the hood.

The Citywide Summer League was created, in part, to marginalize the Rucker Summer League. Luring guys like Hutch, Ernie Meyers, Walter Berry, and Alvin Lott into Citywide definitely diluted talent in the Rucker Summer League. The Rucker already had a well-established rep on the street, while Citywide was fairly new in the late '70s. Both tournaments played weekends and featured players ages twelve to eighteen. The rule was you couldn't play in both leagues

When Hutch quit our team, he was basically forced to choose. It was an odd rule since guys were always doubling up and playing in multiple leagues over the summer. At the height of my demand on the playgrounds, I played in six or seven leagues over the summer. You had to choose which game was more important when there was a conflict. The distinction between Citywide and the Rucker League were very clear, indicated by how far away Citywide sites were from Black neighborhoods.

After Hutch left Dykeman, I was curious about what was happening on the other side of town in the Citywide League, so I went over there to watch him play. Ernie Meyers, Alvin Lott, Kenny Smith, Bruce Dalrymple, and Walt Berry were all playing over there. If you made it to the championship in Citywide, the championship game was played at the Garden, another indication of the reach Lorch had. Who didn't want to play in the Garden? And one of the big sponsors for Citywide was Gulf & Western, a company with a market value of more than four billion dollars in 1970. Sponsors like that really showed the type of pull Lorch had and what resources he could tap into. The Rucker couldn't match those perks, so a lot of Black coaches working in the trenches resented Riverside getting *their* kids. They understood these same kids were the ones no one wanted to recruit not long ago.

The Citywide League promoted safety, order, and organization. The brand was shooting for having great basketball and control over their players. Lorch emphasized he didn't patronize "ghetto" tournaments like King Towers. The Citywide League would never get the same following from people on the streets, and maybe that was the purpose. People weren't taking the train down to 86th Street or over to 137th at Riverside Park to watch games. The Rucker still had the hearts and minds of people on the streets, and the fans reflected that. Nevertheless, the incentives Riverside offered were hard to resist.

If you weren't ready, it was a waste of time trying out for Riverside, especially for their A squad. Rep mattered at the church almost as much as skills. Some guys talented enough to play for Riverside didn't want to share the spotlight with two or three other high school all-Americans. Guys like that would steer away from Riverside and the Gauchos to play for other organizations in their neighborhoods.

The Hawks ran like a machine. Their teams had structure. For my age group, their A squad featured Kenny Hutch and Alvin Lott in the backcourt, two of the best young guards in the city, and rounded out a front line of Ernie Meyers, Bruce Dalrymple, and Walter Berry—a lethal starting five in any league. Coming up behind them were Kenny Smith, Ed "Bugeye" Davender, and Olden Polynice, all of whom would emerge as high school all-Americans while part of Riverside's family.

If Riverside ran like the Boston Celtics, then the Gauchos were the LA Lakers. In the South Bronx, the Gauchos had its own A-list of all-Americans with players like "Easy Ed" Pinckney, Jerry "Ice" Reynolds, John Salley, Chris Mullins, Pearl Washington, and rising young star Rod Strickland. Both AAU camps ran deep in talent, and each had an agenda for acquiring the best players in the city.

Riverside and the Gauchos wasn't for everyone. That was especially true for Harlem cats accustomed to doing our own thing and making our own choices. There were plenty of free-agent ballplayers in Harlem. I became friends with guys like Troy Roscoe, Richie Adams, Steve Burtt, and Dancing Dujii, who didn't fuck with Riverside or the Gauchos. Dujii had a rep and a special niche of followers notorious for playing in obscure venues. A guy with his profile probably fit into Lorch's "hoodlum" category, but he was killing it at Milbank, where both Joe Hammond and Pee Wee Kirkland got their start. Richie Adams was another notorious free agent. Big Rich was one of the best players in the city, but he played when he wanted and for whom he wanted. Despite sanctioned leagues like Citywide and big-money organizations like Riverside and the Gauchos, there was always a place for a street guy in Harlem, a guy on nobody's radar other than the wire running from block to block and through the parks.

Very few of us knew the full picture, but we knew some of how the system worked, especially the immediate gratification part. Once word circulated on the street about what you could get playing for Riverside or the Gauchos, a lot of guys dreamed of playing there. If Riverside took a trip to Hawaii, the Gauchos sponsored one to Vegas. Guys got money routinely for clothing and other things they either needed or wanted. If Rod Strickland was playing for the Gauchos, the Gauchos did certain things to keep him in pocket. They didn't want him going to Riverside. Guys were still playing for the love, but we were also following the cash. It wasn't business for us, but players in the ghetto had become "the business" in NYC basketball. Most of us didn't have a lot of spending money or disposable cash, and few were able to analyze how Riverside or the Gauchos benefited from our skills other than winning big trophies.

Most parents didn't understand the business model of AAU basketball either. All they knew was that someone thought their child was special enough to pay attention to. Players coming out of the ghettos of the South Bronx, Harlem, Brooklyn, and Queens were left to figure shit out on our own. "Steering" young players could start as early as fifth grade. When a player grew in stature, there was always someone like Ernie Lorch whispering in his ear about what he should do, where he should go to play, and what was best for him. Once you got indoctrinated by an organization, if you had never been out of your neighborhood, it was easier to be influenced. Getting your ego stroked made you more susceptible to advice about the direction you should take your career. At the end of the day, "cash ruled everything around us."

Riverside got young talents early in life and *helped* them access better school options. But it was never just about developing talent. A player like Ernie Meyers playing for Tolentine, one of the best Catholic institutions in the city, helped generate kickbacks to Riverside. This scenario was duplicated all over the nation, with city athletes like Isiah Thomas attending the predominately White, affluent, Catholic St. Joseph's, coming out of Chicago's Robert Taylor Homes. Myers lived in Wagner Houses, one of the most notorious public projects in East Harlem, and like Isiah he would get exposure to a good education and better options than he might if he weren't playing with Riverside.

But what were schools like St. Joseph's and Tolentine getting in return? And how were feeder AAU organizations like Riverside benefiting?

I was still under the radar in 1978. I didn't have to weigh options like Hutch, Al Lott, or Ernie Meyers. No one at the top of the food chain was evaluating me. I was playing block to block, tournament to tournament, earning my rep as I went. The guys taking risks on the street were the ones beginning to see me as a commodity. A lot of neighborhood guys were moving up in the drug trade as I moved up in basketball. Guys moving into this hustling life, living by their wits and guts, added color to basketball on the streets and became some of my earliest supporters.

Some of the street guys I began to associate with provided favors or hit me off with a few dollars when our paths crossed. Others hooked me up with arrangements they acquired through their affiliations. The smallest thing could be the biggest depending on the situation, like the day I was hungry and Gums, an older hustler from the block, sent me to one of his girls working at McDonald's to get free food. Wayne Davis, another rising hustler from the block, hit me off with fifty dollars because he witnessed me having a good game. Everyone knew Wayne was cheap. He didn't just give away money, so slicing me off fifty dollars, even though he had thousands, meant a lot.

When these guys reached out, I felt like they had my back. I wasn't down with Riverside or the Gauchos, but I was developing my own source of perks and supporters.

CHAPTER 20
MAKING OF A
PLAYGROUND STAR

AS MUCH AS I enjoyed playing in Harlem, I was never limited to its borders. There was something appealing about playing in other neighborhoods, particularly in front of hostile crowds. My early childhood was spent figuring out how to be more confident, but my adolescence was more about justifying why I had a right to be. There was nothing better than shutting up a skeptic about my game. And there were always doubters.

Forcing people to reconsider and reshape their opinions about my skills was appealing. Sometimes I'd have a game at St. Mary's Projects in the Bronx or at Roberto State Park, and there was always some neighborhood player, a guy with a nickname and his own local followers, who acted like they were God's gift to the game. I'd come in, dust the dude they idolized, and force people to acknowledge and rethink what being "good" really was. This was what Kenny Hutch did for me at the Dykeman tryout. I did the same to players who had never heard of me and didn't know what to expect.

It was even more gratifying if one of those guys happened to answer to the "Ice" trademark I was becoming known for. I wasn't looking to defend my nickname, but my rep went with the name, so there was no way around it.

I enjoyed facing players who weren't at my level of play but who nevertheless reveled in being called Ice. Their body language changed as soon as I walked into the park. Some of these "Icemen" melted right before my eyes. I'd start playing, pull off a few jumpers and spinning layups, attack the baseline and stop short to bank a few off the board, and someone from the crowd would yell, "Damn, the real Iceman showed up." I loved that shit.

I stayed silent on the Ice thing because I never really wanted it. I was on my way to being a pro, and there was already an NBA All-Star answering to Ice. I always turned down the jersey or shirt number 44 when offered because of this. As far as I was concerned, there was only one Iceman.

• • •

Riverside had not only a well-structured system but also the horses to make it run. And despite what everyone said about Lorch, and how he was using Black players, he knew how to orchestrate his system. In contrast, I was playing for a lot of upstart coaches who were less seasoned. I was also playing with a lot of teammates who hadn't found their loud game and sometimes struggled to perform in important games.

My twenty-five-point game against the Sundevils at Dykeman the summer of 1978 was a symbolic turning point in my life, initiating my transition from discovering and learning the extent of my talent to becoming a more confident competitor. Over the course of that summer, I went from being happy to compete against high school all-Americans to being discontented and frustrated when I didn't beat them.

One of Lorch's favorite players was Bruce "Moose" Dalrymple. Bruce lived in my neighborhood, in the first building on 142nd and Eighth Ave. He wasn't a "superstar" with the church, not with guys like Hutch, Myers, and Walt Berry on the roster, but he was just as valuable as they were. Very few people on the streets knew who Bruce was, but he was a key piece to a winning Riverside squad. Bruce rarely played in the neighborhood and wasn't out in the park on weekends or at local neighborhood venues. And since he attended a prep school in Connecticut, we didn't see him much during the school year. Bruce would become a high school all-American, and a lot of people in the neighborhood didn't even know who he was.

I got to know more about Bruce after losing to Riverside a few times. I called him the hardest-working player in basketball. He wasn't blessed with great athletic talent, but he was strong, could run the court, and was a great rebounder. Bruce was only about six foot three, but his game was probably 90 percent desire and heart. In the context of a playground game, few noticed his true impact. Then someone from the scorer's table would say he had twenty points and even more rebounds. He was the only guy I knew who could make thirty points look like fifteen.

If nothing else, Dalrymple was a winner who liked winning more than anything. You couldn't say that about a lot of other cats, even the ones recognized as being more talented. He did what he had to in order for his team to win, which made me wonder if he was learning this at Riverside. Maybe that's why he didn't mind kicking the ball back out to Ernie Meyers or Kenny Smith instead of trying to score. Maybe that's why he took charges on cement and asphalt without giving it a second thought. No matter how many stars were playing with Riverside, Bruce was always a starter because he was willing to do what others wouldn't.

I had something in common with most of the exceptional players playing for Riverside in my age group. We were hungry, hardened, and economically disadvantaged kids living in cycles of public assistance (welfare), public school, and public housing. Before you could understand anything about athletes like us, you had to know a little about the impact of that life cycle, and why seemingly inconsequential things meant so much to us. I guess for people coming from the poorest circumstances, trying to do something positive just meant a lot.

Ernie Meyers lived in Wagner projects. Walter Berry, Kenny Hutch, Bruce "Moose," and Alvin Lott were also "project kids." Alvin lived in so many different places and with so many different relatives I never knew where he really lived. He would spend many days right underneath me at my boy Mo Blind's apartment, without even having to call home. I am sure playing for Riverside helped fill some of the gaps in his life.

A strong player had options with teams like Milbank, Sloans, the Broncos, and Sundevils still out there. A lot of guys were leery of Lorch. There were rumors on the street he still lived with his mother, despite being in his fifties. He didn't have a wife or a girlfriend, so homo rumors circulated. Lorch was a practicing attorney and had no kids. He was also known for "paddling" players on their ass as a disciplinary action, something that raised a lot of eyebrows on the street. Few guys playing in Harlem were going to bend over and let Lorch whack them on the ass for missing foul shots.

On the other end of the AAU spectrum was "White Lou," the financial backbone of the Gauchos. Lou was from Argentina and drove a clean white Jag like he had a million bucks. He didn't have the same social stigma on the streets Lorch had, but Lou wasn't coaching for his organization. White Lou was like a franchise owner. His teams didn't boycott the summer Rucker Tournament like Riverside did. They knew most of us were from the neighborhoods the Rucker represented.

The way city basketball progressed in my era, it was hard to become a high school all-American if you didn't go through the AAU machine. The AAU thing was getting so big that if a player wasn't aligned with Riverside or the Gauchos and their affiliations, their opportunities for getting on that all-American radar were reduced, especially if they were attending a public school. To make the Street & Smith magazine coming out of New York in the early '80s, playing for a notable AAU team or a credible Catholic school was almost a necessity to get the proper national exposure.

CHAPTER 21
MY COUSIN KENNY SMITH

MAKING THE CITYWIDE ALL-STAR team was my first opportunity to play with Riverside Church guys instead of against them. The Sonny Hill Summer League in Philly selected their all-stars to play against us. This New York vs. Philly rivalry ran deep and was many years old by now. It was summer, but the game was going to be played inside the Palestra. Traveling to another city to play made me think about being a pro. Magic Johnson was just twenty years old and had scored forty-two points a month earlier in Philly, nearly single-handedly beating the 76ers. I wasn't too far behind Magic not to think about my own aspirations.

In our NY vs. Philly game, we had an impressive starting five. Kenny Smith was running the point, Byron Strickland was our off guard, and I held down the small forward spot. Walt Berry and Olden Polynice were our big guys. Lorch was the coach, and it was the first time I talked to him. He took the opportunity to whisper to me about playing for the church. He kept saying, "You got some ability, Wash. Get with a winner, kid."

Not sure if I could get recruited to big schools on the merits of a playground pedigree, I figured if I made enough noise, anything could happen. I was going head-to-head with some of the best players in New York City, but had yet to take any college tours. I received a few letters from schools like American University, Holy Cross, and Seton Hall, but none of them played on prime-time television.

We beat the Philadelphia All-Stars in the Philly vs. New York game, and Byron Strickland was selected as game MVP. He was high scorer, and some of the guys on our squad thought he "went nut," meaning he shot too many times. People mumbled about it, but it was an all-star game, and murmurs didn't bother Byron. I scored seventeen on less than ten shots.

When Byron was on, he was unstoppable and had no problem pulling up in the middle of a fast break to hit a shot from well beyond the top of the key. His younger brother, Rod, was a penetrator who was blessed with extraordinary body control, but Byron was one of the best in the business when it came to long-range bombing from the perimeter. He might drop four or five jumpers in a row because no one was prepared to defend so far away from the basket. Before you knew it, he was on his way to forty points. I guess what impressed me most about Byron was his confidence. The guy didn't give a fuck about what anyone said; he was a shooter.

During our road trip, I got a chance to talk with Kenny Smith from Queens. Smith was one of the church's future all-American prospects, on his way to becoming one of the best point guards in the city. I'd heard about him before our trip. Known as "Jet," he wasn't playing uptown as much as Alvin Lott, Hutch, or Berry, so I didn't play against him often. I never traveled to Queens, and it was more common to see guys from the Bronx playing in Harlem than to see guys from Queens and Brooklyn due to proximity.

After evaluating each other, we developed a mutual respect. He got to see why people were calling me Ice, and I learned why he was known as Jet. I didn't think he was as good as Kenny Hutch, but he was a little younger and holding down a starting spot in the senior division despite being eligible to play in a younger division. That said a lot about his game. Kenny was as quick as lightning and played a mature game. He didn't play around with the ball like a lot of other guys and made his move quickly. Jet also had very good athletic skills and a consistent outside shot. During the ride back on I-95 North, he and I talked.

"So where you live at, Ice?"

"I live uptown. You from Queens, right?"

"Yeah, LeFrak City projects."

"Word."

A few cats from Queens were playing uptown and making a name for themselves—guys like Tony "Red" Bruin and Kenny Patterson. Vern Fleming was playing uptown also, and people said he was a pro before he even signed with Georgia. Guys from Queens didn't have the big street reputations like some players coming into Harlem from Brooklyn or the Bronx in the latter '70s, but that changed.

Some thought guys from Queens were soft, or at least a little softer than those in the ghettos of Harlem, Brooklyn, and the South Bronx. There were always exceptions, like Kenny Patterson, who was as hardcore ghetto as anyone I'd seen.

Still, a lot of guys coming to Harlem from Queens to socialize were getting stuck for their cars, jewels, and cash. Stickup crews and wolves were out looking for opportunities, particularly crews from the South Bronx. Contract killers from the Bronx were growing almost as fast as Harlem bred young, flamboyant drug dealers. Many of the wolves operating in Harlem were capitalizing on the vibrant underground narcotics industry. Harlem was the central nervous system for a hustling economy in NYC, from as far back as when Bumpy Johnson ran the numbers rackets to the fading days of heroin kingpins like Nicky Barnes and Freddie Meyers. Uptown was where people came to get money, spend money, and hustle.

Since Jet wasn't playing in many of the Harlem leagues and I wasn't traveling to Queens or Brooklyn, our first competitive encounter came through Citywide. I could see he wasn't shy or timid, and he was certainly cool on the court in how he handled himself, but I didn't know much about his personal life.

"I got a few cousins livin' uptown," Kenny continued.

"Yeah, where?"

"Over near Lenox Avenue, not far from 145th Street."

"I live on 144th and Eighth; so what's your cousin's name?"

"Shelton Mosley, Wallace, and—"

"Wait a minute. What you say?"

"Shelton Mosley . . . ?"

Kenny looked confused as I stared at him with arched eyebrows. I was a little confused too. What was up with this guy? Was he trying to front on having cousins from Harlem? Some guys claimed a hard life when it benefited them and conveniently discarded their hard image when it didn't. If nothing else, Harlem was a trendsetting urban environment, a place Black America came to see style, fashion, and culture. Maybe Kenny, with his high-class Catholic school education, was one of those cats talking out of the side of his neck. I was skeptical.

"What do you mean Shelton Mosley is your cousin?" I asked.

"Shelton, Wallace, Delaine—those are my cousins," he responded.

"How are they your cousins when those is my cousins?"

"You know my uncle Mosley?"

"Know him? He's *my* uncle. He used to hang out with my pops on the weekends. Uncle James is married to my mom's sister."

"Damn, Ice, Uncle Mo is my mother's brother. My mom's maiden name is Mosley."

"Oh shit! I guess that make us cousins then. Had to be some reason for the skills!" We laughed at the situation. What made it even funnier in later years was people saying we looked alike even though we were not really related.

Ma and Uncle Mosley were never close. They didn't see eye to eye on most things, and Aunt Catherine wasn't the type to rock the boat. Uncle Mo was loud, brash, and as stubborn as any man I'd heard Ma talk about. But Uncle Mo also owned his own store, and had acquired a laundromat and a few buildings in the block of 142nd Street. He was the only uncle I knew that was an entrepreneur and independent. All of Ma's brothers got into trades and had gotten jobs, but Uncle Mo struck out on his own and decided to get a piece of the pie for himself.

He distanced himself from our side of the family, rarely attending family events or even allowing Aunt Catherine to do so. We rarely got to see her unless we went through 142nd Street. They owned a variety store on Seventh Avenue, so I would often stop in there on my travels chasing basketball games.

Uncle Mosley's oldest son, Wallace, was four years older than I was. He played a role in my life he never took credit for and probably didn't know how significant it was. When I was thirteen, I got into a fight in our back park with an older boy named Sam Williams. We were playing ball on the third court that day because the full court was packed with older, better players. Sam was at least fifteen and should have been on the full court with players like Imp, Ted Campbell, and Wendell Ramsey, but he was playing three on three with us because no one was picking him to play with the older guys.

Sam was a long, tall boy, an older version of what I was growing into physically. And since he was one of the taller boys in the neighborhood, a lot was expected of him on the basketball court. Unfortunately, Sam wasn't one of the better players in the block. He was routinely dogged by Imp and Gary Springer, and people started calling him soft, and I guess he was getting a little tired of it.

While we were playing, Sam called a foul, and I disagreed with the call. We argued. I think I called him a bitch and said he was soft, and that's when

Sam swung on me. We fought for at least thirty seconds against the fence before Johnny Mack managed to separate us. Had it ended there, the fight was at least a draw, and I might have come out on top since Sam was bigger and older and I managed to land a few punches. But I pushed the issue and we squared off again, this time away from the court. It was like fighting a taller version of myself. His arms were longer, and I was punching upward. With distance, he connected several times, and I fell to the ground. I wasn't out but realized I couldn't beat this guy, not this day. Pride made me push the issue, and now I had to take the long walk back to my building in defeat.

When I got home, Wallace was at our apartment, visiting his favorite aunt "Evee." I walked in dejected with a cut lip. Ma asked what happened, and I told her as best I remembered. Wallace didn't say much. He listened.

After a few days, I got myself together psychologically and went back to the park to play. I decided to provoke another altercation. I wanted revenge. I had worked out in my head what I'd done wrong the first time and figured if I couldn't beat him one way, I'd find another. Playing against Sam, I fouled and elbowed him, and stepped on his foot, anticipating a second fight. I was ready, but the dude didn't do anything. He acted like I won our first fight. It didn't make sense.

I found out later from Vee, who was always in someone else's business, that my cousin Wallace had approached Sam in the park after our fight. Vee said a lot of people watching were expecting another throwdown because of how aggressively Wallace stepped to Sam. Wallace wasn't as tall, but he boxed and looked like he knew how to handle himself. Apparently, Sam wanted no part of Wallace. Vee told me Sam was as quiet as a church mouse when my cuz told him to fight a man his own age. Wallace said if there was another problem, Sam would have to deal with him instead. After that, even with me provoking him, Sam never tested Wallace's words. He wasn't afraid of me, but he didn't want to fuck with Wallace. It was the first time someone older, who had more clout than I had, had my back in the block. Wallace never said a word about it, and I never asked why he'd done what he did. We just didn't talk about it.

Kenny Smith and I laughed about our common family and promised to keep in touch. As the years progressed, we ran across each other in tournaments, but neither of us made too much of our family connection. I was doing my thing on the playgrounds, and he was on his way to becoming one of the most sought-after point guards in the country. The way I looked at it, we would meet each other in college or in the NBA if he made it that far.

PART 5
1980–1982

CHAPTER 22
HIP-HOP AND JOHN LENNON

HIP-HOP WAS EXPLODING IN NYC among the young, poor, and brown in all five boroughs. A Drummer's Delight mix, Planet Rock remix, or the first few bars of Kurtis Blow's "The Breaks" kept things popping on the streets and court. Like basketball, hip-hop embodied daily life by 1980. Whether it was in Harlem, the South Bronx, Queens, the islands (Staten and Long), or on the streets of Brooklyn, New York's ghettos were the living expression of what would eventually become the multibillion-dollar industry known as hip-hop. We gave life to hip-hop culture with an attitude of defiance, creativity, and innovation. A culture bred from sterile, stone-bricked housing complexes manifested the day-to-day life struggles of New York City's ghettos. From meager circumstances, hip-hop and its trends, music, and attitude would become bigger than anything we saw coming. It wasn't about money, fame, or any of that in the beginning. It was about expression.

Most people over twenty-five considered it noise, but rap was part of the fabric of block parties, break dancing, graffiti, Kangols, and British Walkers. Hip-hop was a cultural phenomenon my mother's generation didn't have the time or patience to understand. Ma had bills to pay.

The general public's attitude about the rhythmic, repetitive drumbeats, and sampled melodies that comprised rap music was similar to how M&A examiners viewed my graffiti artwork the day I walked through the door in 1977. My artistic expression was junk in their eyes, but it was a part of this new hip-hop attitude that said "Fuck the rules, and fuck you too if you don't get it." That cultural attitude that began in the '70s had only grown stronger in the '80s.

I was three years into Music & Art, and hip-hop culture was letting its presence be known, much to the dismay of many school administrators, specifically our school dean, Mr. Cooney.

Cooney was a stickler for rules. My school crew didn't think he applied them objectively. There was a small group of punk rockers in school who were notorious weed smokers. They huddled up in various places around school, but never seemed to get the same scrutiny from Cooney as the boom-box-carrying, weed-smoking, hip-hop clans developing around school. Mr. Cooney's thinning, straight blond hair was graying at the ends. I assumed he was Irish, evidenced by his name and the green Boston Celtics emblem on his desk. The Celtics by now had traded Charlie Scott, so I had no love for the "Green Machine." Mr. Cooney supervised the blue-jacket security guards and maintained the status quo around school. He took his job seriously.

Music & Art's student population was still mostly White, and most of these kids and the teachers weren't from the surrounding neighborhood. As the demographics changed in school, so did attitudes, trends, and cultural influences. Not only was rap music emerging as an underground phenomenon in Black neighborhoods, but the student population at M&A was taking in this new cultural dimension.

With the infusion of new music, language, and fashion trends pumping through low-income neighborhoods, M&A during my tenure developed a special-interest group centered around hip-hop that didn't exist before. Kurtis Blow, Harlem's most famous rap solo artist, dropped "Christmas Rappin'" in 1979, and it became a best-selling rap hit that helped legitimize the genre. Blow had attended Music & Art before being kicked out and launching his solo rap career. In 1980, Blondie released a track called "Rapture," a song a lot of M&A students liked. Punk was big in M&A, and even though this song wasn't a rap song, it contained a "rap segment" that helped introduce a mainstream audience to the rap music bubbling in New York's ghettos as early as 1975.

White and Asian kids were curious about the new styles and language coming from the streets. New trends and attitudes were taking form in hip-hop and getting the attention of people who knew nothing about where it was coming from. The whole scene was part Malcolm X, part Gil Scott-

Heron, and part Black Panthers as we revolted against anything mainstream.

Mr. Cooney approached his job as dean as if he wanted to stem the tide of the new, alien hip-hop. When we were caught listening to beats by Spoonie Gee or the Zulu Nation in the locker room, it was an automatic write-up. White kids busted smoking cigarettes in the locker room or listening to Van Halen or KISS were getting warnings. The penalties were harsher depending on what you were into, but nothing Cooney did deterred us from trading mixtapes, bringing in our radios, or speaking hip-hop lingo in the hallways. Hip-hop simply became part of an assortment of eccentric groups already existing at Music & Art.

Our thing was so new and raw, it made some faculty uneasy. They didn't know where it was coming from or why it was happening, which only increased their level of apprehension. But hip-hop seem to fit at M&A. It was the most diverse place I'd ever been. The punk rockers sat around St. Nicholas Park, playing their guitars and smoking cigarettes, talking about rock legends like Jimmy Hendrix and Janice Joplin. Small Latin groups were into salsa and Cuban music. The heavy-metal cats had tattoos and piercing all over their bodies, green and purple hair, and wore leather boots even when it was hot as Hades outside. Some students were "Deadheads," disciples of the Grateful Dead rock group, and others liked the Stones or KISS, but everyone seem to have a place in M&A.

Rap music was the new thing. White people took note of our new slang and wanted to know what we meant when we said something was "def" or "that beat was dope." The truth was we were making up the script as we went along. Hip-hop, like most cultural phenomena emerging out of poverty, pain, and deprivation, was never planned.

• • •

Our school was an old building, not nearly as modern as many Manhattan public high schools. It fit right in with the gothic-styled campus of CCNY located next door. We had six floors, seven if you counted the single acoustic sound room at the very top of the building. The elevators required an operator and manual navigation. The first, second, and third floors had most of the art classrooms for art majors, painters, sculptors, graphic artists, and ex-graffiti artists like me. If you were an art major, you were required to learn about ceramics, and how to use charcoal, oils, watercolor, fibers, acrylics, pen and ink, and other techniques and mediums. Almost nothing was discouraged; even graffiti was acceptable to some of the instructors. Part of the curriculum included art history, which explored the concepts of Cubism, Expressionism, and Byzantine art periods. If you were an art major, you had to pass an art competency exam to graduate.

Nothing I learned or experienced in life prepared me for the academic regimen I encountered at Music & Art. From day one I was playing catch-up. Art was supposed to be the easy part, but it wasn't. A lot of students knew essential art fundamentals—how to mix and handle paints, canvasing, and using perspectives and technique. A lot of M&A students were guided and educated through years of previous instruction. I was learning as I went along, and not surprisingly, I fell behind in art courses pretty quickly.

The teachers at M&A were a little more stringent than what I experienced in previous public schools. To stay ahead at M&A required more discipline. I was a reader, so I read a lot on my own, but as a freshman, I was hit with more required reading than ever before. Getting good grades required rigorous effort. Previously, I passed classes easily with a lax approach to studying and turning in assignments. My junior high school academics evolved almost the same way I learned to play ball, on my own terms. By my sophomore year, that approach was catching up with me.

I kept my head above water for the most part. The experience brought me to a different level of perspective and understanding. I enjoyed *A Midsummer Night's Dream*, *The Old Man and the Sea*, *Siddhartha*, *Lord of the Flies*, *Animal Farm*, and *1984*. I liked Orwell's books the most and read *Animal Farm* twice.

In art history, I was exposed to funny-sounding names of White men from Western civilization like Raphael, Pollock, and Michelangelo. I silently wondered if there were any great Black artists because I didn't see any. Were White men like Leonardo da Vinci the only great painters, architects, and sculptors? Were there any great women artists other than Georgia O'Keefe, or any Black women artists at all? Maybe there weren't. Maybe that's why guys like me were doing graffiti. The whole art history scene turned me off. Where were *our* examples?

My art teachers covered Realism, Romanticism, and Impressionism, but it didn't take long for me to lose interest. There was no place to integrate this new information in a way that made my existence relevant, and that's what I was looking for: validation. Harlem was already marginalized and almost insignificant in the greater society, so I began to feel a natural disconnect with all this European art my teachers were pushing. M&A was a diverse school setting, but there was also a level of cultural isolation. I found art history interesting, to a point, especially the architecture. But I began to feel like most of it wasn't *my* history. It was *their* history, and that's how I looked at it.

It took me a year to relax and be somewhat socially competent in M&A. My academic discipline didn't improve. I attended classes I liked, but by my second year I was cutting class to catch jazz-band sessions or play ball. I was also making friends with some of the other eccentric groups around school, like the Deadheads. The freedom of making my own decisions contributed to laxity.

One day while cutting class I stumbled across a petite White girl sitting in a music room alone. She was delicately plucking the piano keys to a familiar tune, but one I could not immediately identify. I watched her from the hallway through the small window of the door. She looked up for a moment and noticed me watching her.

She smiled and motioned me to come over and sit where she was. I had become comfortable with this kind of friendly engagement, even from White students. I didn't recognize her, but I went in and sat down next to her anyway. Her name was Clarissa and she couldn't have been more than five feet tall and 110 pounds. She gave me the impression that despite her soft features and dainty appearance, she didn't scare easy. I tried to remember where I'd heard the tune she was playing. I wanted to surprise her by knowing it.

"Do you like 'Evergreen'?" she asked. I must have looked puzzled. "'Evergreen' by Barbara Streisand. She's from Brooklyn, you know?"

I didn't know the song, but then she said, "Have you seen the movie *A Star is Born*?"

Only then did it register. "Yeah, I saw the movie. I remember this song."

"Yes, and I remember you too. You're that basketball player everyone is talking about, right?"

"Yeah, guess so."

For some reason, this little girl reminded me of a book we read in freshman English, *Portrait of Jennie*. The story is about an artist who is inspired by a young girl he meets in Central Park. The young girl seems to exhibit a strange, old wisdom and is more mature than she appears. She ages several years each time the artist meets her over a span of a few weeks. My newfound friend playing "Evergreen" on the piano, Clarissa, reminded me of Jennie from the book. She seemed wise.

I was surprised Clarissa recognized me. How did my name reach her social circles? She didn't strike me as one for sports. Then she told me she was in my freshman gym class, and I remembered her. I noticed she always kept to herself. That year they had a three-on-three class tournament, and I caused such a buzz that students were cutting classes to watch me play. The gym teachers were so impressed by my ability it became something for people to talk about. Clarissa must have heard all the chatter and remembered me even though it was more than two years ago and we had never had a conversation.

Her face was innocent and reassuring, and I wanted to know more about her—how she learned to play so beautifully, where she was from, and how long she had been playing. But asking all of those questions would only interrupt the beautiful song she was playing, so I listened instead, preferring to marvel as her tiny fingers danced around the keys.

Small occurrences and pleasantries like meeting Clarissa were a daily routine at M&A. I socialized with different races and cultures that were far removed from environments like Harlem. I got to know a few Asians for the first time. Chan, who was in that same gym class with Clarissa, loved to play basketball, and he cut me in to a few of his Chinatown buddies. Like everyone else, Chan was impressed with my play and wanted to know how I practiced.

I didn't walk around on high alert like I did at the Dime, waiting for some crazy fool to buck or some other drama to jump into or avoid. If I wanted to relax and chill, I could. The days of gathering around the water hole and being unable to drink with a free mind due to watching for predators were gone. I belonged to Harlem but loved M&A at no sacrifice to my own interest. I felt entirely free for the first time in my life, like there was nothing I couldn't do. However, toward the end of 1980, something happened to once again put into perspective my school life and how different it was from what I experienced in Harlem.

It was Tuesday morning, December 9, 1980. When I walked into the front entrance of school that day, I saw Miss Lechner, my freshman English teacher, seated on the floor of the lobby, surrounded by students holding hands. Her long hair draped down her shoulders and back, she spoke softly, her head slightly bent. It was almost like she was praying. I had never seen anyone pray in school, so I wondered what was up. Why was a dead silence hanging throughout the entire first floor of the building?

Miss Lechner was one of my favorite teachers. Slender in stature, she wore brown, round-rimmed glasses and had long brown hair. I imagined she was a hippie and wouldn't have been surprised if she smoked a little weed, maybe some hash. She reminded me of women from the Billy Jack movies of the early '70s. A sharp wit, her youthful appearance and easygoing demeanor made her a favorite among students; people often came back to talk with her after moving on to higher grades.

A lot of White boys in school talked openly in the locker room about fucking Miss Lechner. The way she carried herself, she could make you think you had a shot at it. Justin tried once. Justin was a White boy who lived down near Eighty-Sixth Street. He started asking Miss Lechner to help him with this or that, always trying to get one-on-one interaction with her. When he got it in his head that she *liked* him, she dropped that "you're just a child" and "I have a husband" shit on him and let him know nothing like that was going to happen. Still, in the locker room, Justin tried to convince us and himself that it was just a matter of time before he banged Miss Lechner.

Today, for some reason there were teary eyes and hushed circles throughout the school. It took me a while to figure out what was up. Initially it felt like school was going to be canceled, so I looked forward to that. White girls hugged each other and said things like "It's going to be okay." I was five years old when Martin was killed and still remembered the mournful, somber atmosphere that seemed to be reinforced year after year on the anniversary of his death. I could see people were mourning today, but I just couldn't figure it out.

My homeroom teacher greeted us for the day and mentioned, "A lot of students won't be here today. They're holding a vigil in the auditorium fifth period. If you decide to attend, you will not be marked absent for that period."

I remembered thinking that whatever a vigil was, it couldn't possibly be good. Only then did it dawn on me that I'd briefly seen the news in question as I flipped through TV channels the night before. John Lennon had been shot and killed in front of his Manhattan apartment building.

It hadn't resonated with me even though it was a pretty big deal on the TV news. His death was all over television, and yet I treated it like any other homicide I heard about on a weekly basis. I guess if it were Stevie Wonder or Diana Ross, people around me would have been talking about it a little more. But I didn't know many people who knew much about Lennon.

I read a little about the Beatles and their experience, but I wasn't too interested in Lennon despite his radical lifestyle. It was hard to get into some rich people. Now that he was dead, I was more curious about why someone wanted to kill him. I listened and learned new things about Lennon I'd never heard before, like his extreme stance against war, and his antiestablishment beliefs. I heard that he didn't believe in God or religion.

The mournful expressions I saw from students and teachers alike provided another example of the bubble I was in. Nobody in my crew even bothered discussing John Lennon getting killed, and all Ma said about it was "He didn't believe in God." I guess she thought that would have saved his life. It hadn't saved Martin's.

CHAPTER 23
THE DREW CREW

MY NEIGHBORHOOD CREW WAS tight. We loved basketball and never passed on shooting dice. It seemed like everyone in Harlem was shooting dice when they had a little extra money. We got together for a game of cee-lo or chuck-a-luck so often that I walked around with dice in my pockets and basketball shorts under my pants. Cee-lo was the new dice game on the street. Old heads like my pop were still shooting craps, but 4-5-6 (cee-lo), played with three dice, was all we were into.

Ma found dice in my pockets a few times. I would lie and say it was from a monopoly game or that they were somebody else's. She had a severe hatred of gambling. It was one of my father's vices and contributed to the demise of their marriage—and to some degree, our family circumstances. She caught on quick and learned the difference between "street" dice and board game dice. So I had to hide my dice.

Our main hangout was Mo Blind's place. Mo and I lived the closest to one another. His apartment was 20F, and I was 21F, directly above him. Naturally, we spent a lot of time together and were in almost daily contact. Mo was a year or two younger, and his younger brother, Dee, two or three years younger than him. Both were like my brothers because I practically lived at their apartment after school. We listened to Richard Pryor records and sat around snapping on each other until something better came along.

Everyone in my crew was known for something memorable. Quarter, Mo, and D-Smooth were the stylish cats when it came to fashion. Warren also had some fly shit, benefiting from being an only child. Trendy cats either had two working parents or were hustling on their own to make money. The rest of our crew, when it came to popular trends and fashionable kicks (shoes), struggled just to be socially acceptable in most cases.

Mo was often free with his parents' food and resources. I guess he figured they could always get more stuff. Mr. White drove a city bus, and Miss Becky, Mo's mom, was a nurse. It was just Mo and Dee, and they lived well. I considered Dee as my little brother. I wouldn't let anyone fuck with Dee when I was around, so most of the hell he caught usually came from Mo.

Saturday nights were entertaining at Mo's place. Mr. White had his weekly card game, and he'd have a few drinks that night, and an assortment of friends, relatives, and colorful card players always showed up. Mr. White, who was at least six foot three, was often the most entertaining of them all, and it was quite a show.

One of the most animated characters was Uncle Charlie. I don't remember whose brother he was, Mo's mom or pop, but he was the one to watch when the drinks started flowing. Uncle Charlie would cuss and often pause to ask who all these "little niggas" coming through the house were. While Mr. and Mrs. White, Uncle Charlie, and Miss Mazee from across the hall were into their card game up front, we would be in the back playing chuck-a-luck or shooting cee-lo out in the breezeway.

Two of my closest and best friends, Mike Poole and J-Mac, had single mothers like I did. I'd known these guys the longest. Between the three of us, we didn't have the same resources as guys with two working parents. This didn't affect our status in the group because, as I said, everyone brought something. The stronger personalities in our crew were the guys with less material or financial resources. We all got into fights every now and then, but Mike and John were two of the better fighters in our group. I was the tallest guy and had the longest arms, and when trading hands with Mike or John, I needed that reach. The three of us were always mixing it up, seeing who the better fighter was.

We were also a little older than the other guys, and naturally set the tone, especially when it came to sports. I'd known Quarter and Mike since the second grade. Quarter wasn't much of a fighter but still held significant influence because of his popularity with a lot of older guys in the neighborhood. He brought levity to almost every situation, and I don't think anyone in our crew was more liked in the neighborhood than he was.

I liked most of the guys in my crew, even guys I got into regular beefs with. Mike Rich was a little older than we were, and he and I disagreed almost by instinct. I still respected how he handled himself. Mike was more independent and always seemed like he knew what he was doing, even when he didn't. Mike wasn't really a part of our crew, but he was an older influencer and a big part of our activities.

J-Mac, Mike Poole, Quarter, and I were tight before we had a crew. Everyone else formed later. Big Warren and I got tight because we were two of the taller guys in our group. He was big and tall, and I was long and tall. I got to know his cousins, Jeff and Lisa, from 150th Street, and met his grandfather, who lived in Delano Village. We mixed it up on the court because we usually matched up against each other. Warren was big and heavy handed and had a history of falling on people. I didn't appreciate him falling on me or tripping me, so we got into it every now and then. We called him Big E because Elvin Hayes was his NBA idol.

Sputnik was another cat in our crew. He lived on nineteen, same floor as Warren, and they were hanging out before our crew formed. Sputnik and I got into arguments for different reasons, even though he was a couple of years younger than I was. He had a level of arrogance and indifference I found irritating.

Most of us were arrogant in different ways. Sputnik's arrogance wasn't commensurate with his position in our group. If anything, he was closer to the bottom of the pecking order when it came to respect. He could be short tempered, and he was selfish and a hard guy to get a favor from. If you were short a quarter for something and he had five dollars in his pocket, you still might not get it from him. Since he was one of the newer and younger cats in our crew, he caught flak from time to time. But the one thing none of us could challenge Sputnik on was his school performance. His grades were off the charts, and he was taking advanced classes. Like me, Sputnik attended the Dime and became a pretty good ballplayer, but he was a great student with high test scores, good enough to get him into Choate. Choate, located in Connecticut, was no ordinary high school and known for having a superior academic program.

Sputnik could be very unintelligent in other ways. He was emotionally ignorant. He certainly wasn't smart to the ways of the street or human behavior. Warren told everyone a story about the day he and Sputnik were outside the Roosevelt Theatre on 145th Street. They were approached by

Ronnie Gailyard from 148th Street. Everyone occasionally went to the Roosevelt to see movies we weren't supposed to see, like *Foxy Brown*, *Shaft*, or *The Mack*. We were too young for these flicks but could get in anyway. At the Roosevelt, it wasn't unusual for a rat or two to run across your feet during the movie, especially if you happened to drop a few pieces of popcorn. But it was our only neighborhood theater, so people packed it like it was one of those fancy places downtown.

Ronnie Gailyard was a well-known extortionist with a rep for shaking people down for loose change. He wasn't the roughest young gangster uptown, but he was a part of a crew known for jacking cats for their money, and if you weren't willing to fight for it, you were a target. When I was at the Dime, I was walking with a friend to the Cards n Stuff store when he spotted Ronnie walking our way. He quickly took his money out of his pocket and hid it under his younger brother's hat. You didn't have to be the roughest or meanest dude to be a street extortionist; you just had to know how to identify the weak niggas unwilling to fight to keep their shit. Ronnie was an adept predator. He knew who to fuck with and who to leave alone.

The way Warren told it, when Ronnie confronted Sputnik as they left the Roosevelt, Sput immediately redirected the shakedown artist by telling him Warren had more money than he did. He told Ronnie he should check Warren's pockets first. Ronnie decided to take his advice. He and Warren struggled. Sputnik left Warren on the corner of 145th Street, fighting with Ronnie Gailyard to keep his money. As years passed, this incident was often told and retold, and it was enough to shade our perception of him.

Once I sized Sputnik up, his personality caused occasional friction between us, depending on the situation. He assumed he was smarter than everyone. I spent some time down at his house, but it was mainly because I liked being around his older sister, Nay Nay. Nay was pretty, but she was a tomboy and always hung out with us, especially Mike Poole. I believed she was in love with Mike, but he acted like he didn't know. Nay Nay was a little tougher psychologically than her younger brother, and more emotionally aware even though she didn't take shit from anyone.

Sputnik never seem to find his place in the neighborhood or in our crew in any significant way. Even before going to school in Connecticut, he was aloof, socially, and known for saying shit to piss people off. He always gave the impression he knew something you didn't. And maybe he did; it was the way he went about it that got under people's skin. He hadn't earned the right to express a superior posture, so he and I occasionally clashed.

I would jump on something Sputnik said and go out of my way to aggravate him, especially if we were playing ball. It was easy to do on the court because I held a distinct advantage. I'd block his shot and taunt him, or I'd make him look bad instead of letting certain things slide. If we were just sitting around talking shit, he would occasionally talk about things he thought we didn't understand, and someone was always compelled to let his arrogant, punk ass know he wasn't as smart as he thought he was.

The fact was, nobody in our crew was a dummy in school or otherwise. Sputnik had a way of distancing himself intellectually as if he had the better mind, but no one bought in. I wasn't a bully, so I didn't provoke him too much, but I wanted to. Having been bullied in my early elementary school years, I hated people who beat people up because they knew they could. Sputnik and I got into it once on the court, and I smacked him around a little, but it was never much more than that.

Two later additions to our crew were T Gator and Tone Wop, two brothers from the tenth floor. I knew Gator from the Dime before he moved into our building. He was a good ballplayer, one of the better ones at the Dime back then. He fit in well with our ball-playing clique and became one of the more notable members of our crew before hooking up with his girlfriend Poopie. Tone Wop had recently come back from living down south. Wop was getting into trouble when they lived on 148th, and Miss Jackson sent him to live with relatives in Georgia for a while. When I got a little out of line in school, Ma threatened to do the same. I was very close to being sent to my grandparents' place in South Carolina to finish school. Had that happened, I doubt I would be writing this book.

It was like Wop had never been away. He wasn't the athlete Gator was, but he was flamboyant. Despite being smaller in stature, Wop was older than Gator and good at snapping (telling jokes) on people. He had a comedic gift for highlighting another person's misfortune and exploiting it for maximum effect. In Harlem, this was an art form. When a person could turn the tragic aspects of ghetto living into a public show for everyone to revel in, people wanted that kind of person around. You either became tougher or weaker if you happened to be the target, and all of us had been victims at one time or another. If you were consistently the brunt of ridicule, you could lose a lot of standing in the neighborhood.

We were all thoroughly aware of each other's weaknesses and strengths. Playing basketball was my greatest strength. And since we played a lot of basketball, my ability to stand out was acknowledged and respected. I wasn't an All-City player or an all-American because I didn't play for an athletically focused high school, but I faced off with all-Americans and All-City players regularly.

It wasn't the same when the conversation switched to social activities. I wasn't known for having girls or for being on the party scene. A lot of girls liked Mike Poole. Some of the older ones talked about turning him out. He handled it well, like someone older than he was. Mike was the middle brother of five and had already assumed the role of family leader for his mother and siblings. He was aggressive when it came to sports and competition, but not so much when it came to the girls, something that probably worked out for him in the long run. Mo, Quarter, D-Smooth, and Johnny Mack were chasing girls whenever they could, but no one other than T Gator had a steady girlfriend.

Mack was having sex more regularly than most of us, especially since Miss Jackie worked nights. We called him "Johnny Mack" after the movie *The Mack* because he had a rotation of not-so-good-looking chicks he sexed on the low. It was easier for Mack since he had four older brothers who weren't going to snitch if he had a girl over.

Big E got a rep for being a big freak, but the truth was, all of us were just as horny and nasty. The difference was E wasn't too good at concealing it. I knew about E's encounters because I came to his apartment a few times when he had just finished. In our crew, if you let everyone know who you were fucking and there was no boyfriend/girlfriend situation, at least two or three other cats in the crew wanted to try to get some from your source.

Once, I came to pick E up, and a girl must have just left his room. You could smell the aroma almost as soon as you walked through the front door. He had the windows open, spraying air freshener, but that seemed to make it worse. Big E had a knack for finding girls willing to give him some, and he would only get better at it. If Mike Poole had been anything like E, he would have been a father by his sixteenth birthday. None of us were even talking about using "rubbers." She had to be a real nasty girl to take time and effort to buy a rubber. I guess you could say we were some sex-crazed teenagers.

When a group of us had money, sometimes we headed downtown, especially around the holidays. It was either to the Penn Station arcade or "the Deuce." There were twelve or more movie houses and a bunch of arcades around Forty-Second Street, but it was also sex-market central. We were all down for hitting the peep shows and live sex shops we were supposed to be too young to get into. Some of the shops had sex workers, and you could always see hands reaching through the partition window to fondle the assortment of naked women parading around. Some of the women would see how young we were and have us kicked out, but it was usually because they knew we didn't have tips to give them and were wasting their time.

My love life was nonexistent. No one ever saw me walking a girl home or talking long hours on the phone with some chick. I liked a few girls in the neighborhood—Adrian Knight on twenty, Michelle Johnson on ten, and Annette Mack from 144th Street—but I never got anywhere approaching any of them. When I was about eight or nine years old, I "played house" with Lena Ramos, who lived in 21J. Lena was Puerto Rican, and always tried to kiss me and slide her tongue into my mouth. I wasn't ready for all that. Because of Lena, it took another few years to not think kissing was nasty. I guess I just wasn't ready for a foreign tongue in my mouth.

Angela was my next girlfriend. She lived on the twentieth floor in the second building. She was also Puerto Rican, and since I was at least twelve by then, when we kissed in the basement laundromat of my building it was a little better for me. We turned the lights out, and I liked our little moments, but Angela only liked kissing, and so I lost interest. Then there was Pat, an older girl I'd known since I was six years old. Pat lived in Brooklyn and was four years older than me. She was the only girl in my life I was certain could kick my ass because she'd done it so many times. Pat liked fighting, and she was rough. Her younger brother June Bug and I were always fighting when they came to visit their grandparents, Mr. and Mrs. Tramble in apartment 21K.

Pat also took on the role of bully, and since I couldn't beat her, I wound up doing things I'd have no mind to do if I had control—like the first time Pat demanded to see my dick. No girl had ever seen my dick. She punched me so hard in the stomach that I let her pull my pants down. After she checked me out, she told me I had big, pussy-sucking lips. I didn't know what it meant to have "pussy-sucking lips," so I just assumed it was another hang-up about having big lips.

Pat also wanted to "play doctor" with me, which meant she was always the doctor, and I was the patient. She wanted to examine me, usually my dick and balls, but occasionally she'd want to look up my ass too and see what was in there. Sometimes we would go up to the roof of the building and she would tell me to kiss her and stick my finger between her legs. Once when my pants were down, she grabbed and squeezed my balls so hard I yelled loud enough for someone to hear me on the ground floor. A part of me liked what Pat was doing—the part that wasn't scared. But I always knew it would end with me getting hurt somehow. Of course, I got older and things changed.

I was nearly seventeen now, and Pat couldn't kick my ass anymore. I grew tall and she grew into a young woman. She had a nice round ass and a stackhouse body that got people's attention. We were cordial when I happened to run into her. She would joke how I was the "one who got away" from her, even though it hadn't really been that long ago. Now on her visits from Brooklyn, she came to see my neighbors, Daryl and Oliver, and it wasn't just on the weekends. Daryl and Oliver were brothers, and both were knocking Pat off, either together or one-on-one. I'd see her coming out of their apartment with one or the other when Miss Libby wasn't home. Pat and I never talked about the "doctor" game we used to play.

CHAPTER 24
DEATH AND 117TH STREET

BY 1980, MY CREW was my family. I spent less time at home or with relatives, even during holidays. I was all about my crew. I'd have a game at Mount Morris Park on 120th and Madison, only a block from where Pop, Nanna, Aunt Margaret, and Uncle Preston lived, but rarely found time to stop by to say hi. All I cared about was playing ball and hanging out. I was attracted by the respect I got on the street, chasing action wherever it happened to be, without much regard for anything else. Everywhere I went in Harlem, I was recognized and secretly began to covet the attention.

As a youngster, I spent a lot of time with Pop's side of the family. My first years were spent on the stoops, running back and forth to the store and being shuffled among relatives and friends around the Barrio. My father was known in his block. Someone was always stuffing a dollar in my pocket or asking me for a number to play. When Ma moved my little sister and I out of the Barrio and into the projects on the west side, we still went downtown on Saturdays to visit. Pop became the super of the building my grandmother and her sister and husband lived in on the corner of 119th and Madison. On cold winter Saturdays I watched as he shoveled coal into the furnace in the basement. "Super" was short for superintendent, and as the super of a building, you were responsible for making sure everything in the building worked. Watching him work the furnace was the highlight of my weekend.

The cast iron fixture, full of yellow-orange flame, had a smoldering smell and an intense heat that made me think about the power of fire and the sun. I was amazed by the spectacle but scared at the same time.

Pop was good at finding odd jobs. He always worked but was a full-blown alcoholic. He still hung out with his friends in the neighborhood, and it was still the center of his existence. In my own way, I was addicted to something too. Like Pop, I couldn't stand to be home. My social life away from home became the focus. I didn't smoke or drink, but my addiction became hanging out, playing ball, and gambling.

Pop and I had only grown further apart since 1968 after watching Martin Luther King's funeral on TV. We never talked about anything important and didn't make special efforts to see one other. The only time I even thought about Pop was when Ma brought him up. The most time I ever spent with him came the summer of 1977 when I was fourteen. Ma asked Pop if I could work the summer with him on the ice truck. He paid me forty dollars a week to run errands, but it did little to improve our relationship or communication. He didn't complain about giving up the forty dollars, but I could tell he didn't know what to say to me, and I didn't know how to talk to him.

That summer, we would jump in Brown's truck from the junkyard on 117th Street and head uptown to the Bronx to the icehouse next to Yankee Stadium. They loaded big, tall blocks of ice into the back of the truck, and he sold blocks and pieces throughout the day. I watched his veins bulge out of his forearms as he lifted and cut blocks of ice to sell to street vendors coming through 117th Street. All sorts of people came through looking for ice: people selling crabs, lobster, Italian ice, watermelon, pineapples, fish, sodas, and beer, out of their cars, on the block, or in a store. These customers came all summer long. On a good week, Pop took home as much as $600.

Every day at three o'clock, we took the remaining blocks of ice over to the fish market on 116th and Park Avenue. Over there the vendors converted the ice blocks to crushed ice to preserve their seafood. Park Avenue at 116th Street was a busy shopping district for the east side. It was a unique spot. Several storefronts were built into residential tenements up and down 116th. Pop told me Jews owned all or most of the buildings there.

When I wasn't sitting around watching him work, I was over on Park Avenue, looking for girls, or playing pinball in one of the convenience stores on Lexington Avenue. Sometimes I didn't show up for work, if you could call it work. Pop never said anything. I got the feeling he thought I was in the way. I didn't mind because I was done by four and none of my basketball games started before five during the week.

It wasn't the bonding experience Ma hoped for, but it kept me from running the streets all day, or worse, sleeping late every morning. I guess neither Pop nor I was expressive enough to learn anything about each other. We didn't talk about girls, sports, school, or society. Whatever I learned from Pop was from watching and listening as he talked to other people.

Sometimes when he was drunk, he'd try to teach me how to box, but he wasn't much of a boxer. I boxed at the rec center every now and then; so did a few other boys in my crew. We slap-boxed each other or put on the gloves to test our fighting skills. Pop held his hands awkwardly, so I could see he didn't know much about boxing. Maybe down south the style of fighting wasn't the same as it was up north. Occasionally he'd come up to the apartment when Ma wasn't home, and we'd slap-box for a few minutes, his beer stench permeating our living room. He'd get into his fighting stance and tell me to try and hit him, and I'd try to smack the shit out of him.

I may have been thirteen when I succeeded in hitting my father. I managed a stunning slap to the side of his face, hard enough to sting him. I instantly realized the big mistake I made. I went from feelings of elation to fear for my life in a span of a few seconds. I covered up to escape full-strength swings at my head. He resorted to pounding me a few times in the body as I tried to bury my head between my arms and elbows. Pop may not have been a boxer, but he was a very strong man. I had no chance no matter how good I was with my hands. People standing around the ice truck were amazed at how he wielded blocks of ice with grapplers in each hand, his lean, tight body straining in the heat. He hurt me that day. I had a headache after the pounding, and my body was sore the next day. Boxing with Pop taught me one thing. It taught me that soon I'd be able to whip my daddy in a fight, and to not to challenge him again until I knew I could.

My strained relationship with Pop was something I naturally grew into; my communication with Ma was just as difficult but in a different manner. In Pop's case, he hadn't put any time in. Children are like investments. Either you cultivate them, or you run the risk of bankrupting your life and theirs. I had a better relationship with my grandmother Nanna than I did with Pop. She was always there trying to fill in the gaps where he was lacking. She knew what everyone else knew. He hadn't been much of a father.

Maybe Nanna was trying to make up for the mistakes she'd made with Pop. There was always a Christmas present, some money for my birthday, warm meals, and love, none of which I could remember getting from Pop. Somewhere in my early life I decided I didn't need anyone else. I began resenting Pop, and to some degree I resented Ma for not being a father. I resented my little sister for not being an older brother. The way I saw it, none of these people could help me navigate in Harlem, not even my grandmother. If you weren't a part of my crew or didn't bounce a ball, it was hard to reach me as we approached the '80s.

• • •

I came in late one night from playing down at Riverside's gym near 122nd Street. Walter Berry had showed up unexpectedly. The school season had just started, so I figured he was there to hit Lorch up for some extra cash. I went down just to get a run with some of their winter-squad players. By now Berry and I had become antagonistic toward one another. We faced off a lot over the summer and in holiday tournaments.

On this night, we got into a few one-on-one games after talking shit to each other, with Lorch and a few others watching from the sidelines. We started talking about playing each other for money, but that was cut short. Lorch didn't allow this kind of talk in his gym. We were tied one to one and into our third game to break the tie. I couldn't stop Walt. He was left-handed, taller, and his arms were even longer than mine. He had exceptional footwork and quick springs off the floor. It seemed like every year he was shooting the ball better and becoming more proficient in his unorthodox ability to score. He was becoming unstoppable. He won the third game, but not really. We were tied in a game that had ten more points to play before Lorch yelled, "Next bucket wins." Walt ended it on a medium-range jumper.

Walt was no longer the role player he had been back in 1978 when he played alongside Gary Springer and Big Richie Adams at Franklin. Berry was a legitimate all-American now and capable of creating his own shot almost at will. He had become a legend in the PSAL and on the streets, but since he couldn't stop me either, I wasn't backing down. It was almost a waste of time to keep score since neither one of us could stop the other from scoring.

When I got home from Riverside that night, Ma and Prissy were in bed, and the apartment was completely dark. This wasn't normal. Ma usually left the kitchen light on, and if it was cold in the house, she left the oven on too. If I hadn't eaten, whatever was left for dinner was usually left on the stove top. Tonight, the kitchen light was off, and the house was dark and cool. I walked down the hall to my room, turned on the light, and lay back on my bed near the window, thinking about how I could stop Walter Berry.

Suddenly a bird flew up from behind the bed. I screamed loud enough for Mo to hear me in his apartment downstairs.

I got a good look at the thing. It was solid black, like the crows I'd seen in the movie *The Omen*. I opened the windows as wide as they went and managed to get it out of the room. But I noticed no one got up to see what I was yelling about, or why I screamed like a bitch. It was dead silent; then I heard Ma's voice. It wasn't the hard, direct voice I was used to hearing. This voice was soft and relenting, like there was no energy behind it.

"James."

"Yeah, Ma," I answered.

"James, Nanna died tonight."

The words sounded far away. I saw Nanna's face in my mind, her smile showing the gold crown, and her gray-streaked hair pulled back into a net. All I could muster in response to Ma's words was a feeble "Why?"

I didn't know what else to say. The week before, I spoke with Nanna on the phone, and she mentioned how she hadn't seen me in a while. It had been at least six months. Since that call, I'd played games at LaGuardia House on 116th Street, Milbank on 117th, and PS 96 on Second Ave and 120th Street. All of these venues were less than a ten-minute walk to my grandmother's apartment building on 119th Street and Madison, but I never bothered to stop and check in with her.

The last time I spoke with Nanna, I played her off, telling her I would make it down there that weekend. Several weekends came and went, and before I knew it the whole summer passed, and she still hadn't seen me. One night I walked directly by her building with a few of my basketball buddies and didn't bother to stop. It was after ten, but I knew she liked to stay up late, watching TV. She would have loved to see me even for just a few minutes, but I didn't bother.

The old Barrio neighborhood was where many of my fondest memories originated. Some of the worst, too—Aunt Sister died when I was in the old neighborhood. So had Martin, Malcolm, Dope-Fiend Danny, and the Kennedys. Now my grandmother, my mainstay during those early years, was dead at age fifty-seven. I would never find out if she lived the life she wanted to live.

The Barrio of the '60s wasn't the same Harlem that had attracted my grandmother when she left the South in the 1940s. Sitting on the living room floor, listening to Aunt Margaret and Nanna talk about Harlem's glorious days, the great jazz performers like Dizzy, Billie Holiday, and Cab Calloway, or athletes like Sugar Ray Robinson and Joe Louis, became part of their memories and mine. Listening to them talk about the old days made me feel like I knew things other cats my age didn't. Pop's family taught me all the things Ma couldn't teach me about Harlem.

CHAPTER 25
FRED "DISCO" BROWN

THE SUMMER OF 1981 was Fred Brown's summer. Every now and then, one or two players would capture everyone's imagination. People scampered from park to park, trying to catch whoever was hot or whose name was ringing out most. Each summer took on a life of its own. In '78, Artie Green was the man. The early '70s belonged to Joe Hammond. Different names rang out year to year: Sam Worthen, Richie Adams, Gary Springer, Kev Williams, or Steve Burtt. There was always a show to see and always a player at the peak of his playground prowess. In 1981 I guess it was Fred "Disco" Brown's turn. Disco had that street "flava," and was a six-foot-three shooting guard with supernatural ball-handling skills and a knack for making spectacular moves.

Some people on the street referred to Fred as a "pretty nigga." Grown men like my uncle Mosley would say Fred was a smooth, pretty mothafucka because of his trendy, stylish look. He was medium brown with Nordic features, a thin nose and lips, sharp facial contours, and always a glimmering, fresh haircut. Fred didn't bop like a gangster; he walked with calm reassurance, a ghetto swagger, like the world stopped on a dime for him.

On the streets, Fred was a Sugar Ray Robinson throwback without the conk. When he showed up to play or watch a game, he was flamboyantly fly. His box-styled fro was always perfect, glistening, and well preserved.

He usually had on fresh kicks, rings, and chains that were visible but never overdone, just enough to let everyone know he was that dude. With the look of a savvy street hustler, he had every angle covered. Even when Disco was just watching a game from the sidelines, as soon as he entered the park the murmurs started—if not from seeing him, then from seeing whichever fine Black, Puerto Rican, Dominican, or Caribbean bitch he had on his arm. Fred was one of those cats you expected to see in Harlem despite his living in the Bronx. He personified street culture.

Older guys who knew more than I did said Fred was tight with affiliates of Freddie Meyers and his crew from 116th Street. Meyers, also known as "Fast Freddie" in the early '70s and '80s, was probably the last of a dying breed of flamboyant, million-dollar-level narcotics traffickers in Harlem. Nicky Barnes, Pee Wee Kirkland, and Guy Fisher were all doing long prison sentences, leaving Freddie Meyers and his crew near the top of the food chain in the busy heroin market of Harlem.

I first caught Disco's show at a game in the Bronx in 1978. But he was a lot better in 1981. Whatever made him special was spilling out onto the playgrounds that summer. Fred improved his outside shot and was a very good shooter, but his ability didn't end there. Disco also developed a unique ball-handling style that mesmerized defenders and thrilled the crowds packing into the parks. Fred was coming up behind Wendell Ramsey and Dave Britton at JKF High School. Both these guys were All-City selections.

Disco had a style of flicking the ball back and forth between his legs or behind his back before stutter-stepping and making his move. It was the kind of thing you rarely saw in a college or pro game because it wasn't practical or fundamental. But Disco was shaking guys up so bad people came just to see the show. He'd stop, then go, hesitate, and flick the ball back and forth quickly before leaving defenders flat-footed. Fred was also a great leaper, and at six foot three he could dunk on anyone, but it was his ground game that caught my attention. His sequences of moves were so synchronized that everyone thought this was why he got the name Disco. He was dancing.

After watching Fred play several times, he made enough of an impression that I tried some of his moves in a few of my games to show I could pull it off. These were mainly fancy, crowd-pleasing moves only someone with a nice handle could even attempt. I didn't know Fred, but I liked how he handled himself and felt like I could learn something from the guy.

CHAPTER 26
SLEEPER SCOUTING REPORT: RIVERSIDE HAWKS

"WASH, YOU MISSED YOUR last foul shot today."

"Yeah, I know."

"You gonna be a man or a wimp about this thing?"

"I'm gon be a man regardless," I said as I cut a cold eye toward my newest and most experienced basketball coach, Ernie Lorch.

"I don't know about you, Wash. You come in here from that pansy art school and play like you own this place, but we have rules here, kid."

"Yeah, Coach, I know. I know all about da rules."

I planned to break some of Ernie Lorch's rules, at least the ones I didn't trust. Some of Lorch's rules I'd heard of before, like the ones about keeping your grades up. But Lorch never asked to see my report card even though he cut a few guys for low grades. Some rules were obviously subjective. He also had a rule about missing a certain number of foul shots. If you missed too many, you had to bend over and get the paddle in his nearby office located not far from the locker room. Some guys wanted to be down with the church so bad that they bent over and let Lorch pat that ass, an old Catholic discipline and school tradition. Some even pulled their shorts down to get whacked. But I wasn't a Riverside kid. I think we both understood he wasn't smacking my ass even if I missed every foul shot.

Lorch was known to hit certain cats off with money. The guys who got special privileges from time to time also got rides home in his nice, comfortable Audi. I came into the church with a few rules of my own, and bending over wasn't one of them. The bottom line was I didn't trust Lorch and probably never would.

I'd spent several years trying to get over the hump by beating his summer teams, something I was never able to do. I had only come out on the winning side against Riverside two or three times in four years. But in the fall of 1981, I was playing for Lorch, something I never saw coming. The Gauchos were closer to home, but I believed Riverside could do more for me. The three previous winters, I played in the B Division with my high school, Music & Art. I received a few letters from Ivy League schools like Princeton, Brown, and Cornell and others from Holy Cross, Saint Bonaventure, and U Mass. It was a big deal since few B Division players got letters from a D-I school unless they were playing soccer. Unfortunately, none of these schools were playing on national TV, and that's where I thought I belonged.

I would catch Lorch peering at me sometimes in practice through his black-rimmed, bookworm glasses. He sensed I wasn't grateful to be playing for his great Riverside Church AAU program. Lorch and I become familiar with one another because I had some notable games against his teams. I always looked forward to challenging his best "all-Americans." He also found out I was loosely related to Kenny Smith, one of his most promising prospects in the Riverside stable.

However, we were entering the winter season, which was less competitive than the summer in AAU. Guys like Pearl Washington, Walter Berry, Kenny Smith, Olden Polynice, and Ed Davender were playing for their respective high schools over the winter, which meant an exodus of talent. To compensate, Lorch scheduled games against JV college teams and junior colleges like Westchester Community. After three seasons with Music & Art, I became Lorch's main racehorse the winter season of '81 to '82.

Even without Riverside, I managed to get fifty letters playing at M&A. Almost all of them were smaller schools. The Ivy League letters had a lot to do with the type of school M&A was. Being in a specialized high school made me a more attractive athlete to programs like Columbia and Princeton, or schools outside the mainstream focus. Playing in the B Division, my name was almost always in the papers as the leading scorer for my team. We were good enough to beat schools like Printing, Gompers, Bronx Science, and occasionally Norman Thomas, but there were other teams, like Chelsea and Bergtraum, we never beat.

Riverside Church was on another level when it came to organization. Everyone talked about the church having deep pockets, and I didn't see anything to dispute it coming in. Lorch often commented on how he treated everyone the same, but I already knew that was bullshit. He didn't treat Walter Berry the same as Gary Voce, or Kenny Hutch the same as some B-squad player. I wasn't looking for special treatment but wanted to up my stock by using his connections.

The cutoff age for our senior team was eighteen. We played against the JV CCNY squad, Mercer Community, Westchester, and Fordham. The games didn't mean much, but I knew a lot of the guys I played against from the summer leagues. Mercer, a junior college in central Jersey, and Westchester Community College in Westchester, NY, routinely had good players, and Division I talent. Andre Slick, D-Mac, and a bunch of other guys I knew were playing for Westchester. From the beginning, I played eye-opening basketball with the church.

My first big tournament came on a road trip to Pittsburgh. Like in the summer, Lorch was running two teams that winter, an A and B squad. There was so much basketball being played in the city, and so many players, there was always a venue or somewhere for a guy to find a home. Lorch had his system locked in. If a guy on the A team got hurt or was unable to play, he upgraded a B squad guy to fill in. If for whatever reason a premium high school player couldn't play for his school due to a grade or discipline problem, Lorch had no problem making room for him on one of his squads.

Our A squad had talent but no superstars. I had a rep around Harlem but hadn't played big-time high school ball. I wasn't known in Queens or Brooklyn like I was in Harlem and the Bronx, and some of the guys I was playing with weren't known anywhere. They were good players, but I could see from the beginning more than half the team was just happy to be playing for Riverside and possibly getting a chance at a scholarship. Everything was a big deal. The gym bags, jackets, uniforms—it all meant something.

Greg Khaleel and Keith Dixon were our big guys. Khaleel had played for All Hallows alongside Troy Truesdale in the CSHAA the previous year. I wasn't sure how he landed with Riverside, but I speculated he either flunked off his high school team or didn't have any credible scholarship offers. Greg looked like a six-foot-eight Muammar Gaddafi, but he was a decent athlete who could run the floor and had a nice medium-range shot. If he played well, he could get a free ride somewhere on size alone.

Dixon had attended JFK and wasn't as talented as Khaleel. He was done playing at JFK but had no college prospects. Dixon was a good high-post guy and a role player who could shoot from the post but wasn't very athletic and was already experiencing knee problems.

Keith and Greg K. were the only guys I didn't know well. The rest I'd run across in the summer leagues. Andre Baker, Cedric Miller, and Rich Jones were going to be key players on the squad. All had played in the Citywide League. These guys were good, but not good enough to stand out in New York City. None of them were going to give you something you couldn't get better somewhere else. Two of my boys from my neighborhood crew, Johnny Mack and Mo Blind, were playing for the Riverside B squad. I thought they were both good enough for the A squad, but Lorch wanted his B squad to be somewhat competitive. It had been years since I'd played with my boys, after going my own way, and playing with the B team would allow them to shine a little more than they would if we were all on the same team.

Of course, the A team got more perks. We got to travel, and Lorch catered to us more, same as he did with his summer teams. A lot of times he didn't even coach the B squad. He'd hand it off to one of his assistants. If you were on the B squad, you weren't going to get the same exposure or scholarship opportunities.

In Pittsburgh we finished as the runner-up. We were supposed to win it all, but I could see our issues moving forward. I was the only Riverside guy to make the All-Tournament team. Some thought this was determined on one single play in the first game. I grabbed the rebound from the guard position of our three-two zone and flipped the ball behind my back in a fluid motion to avoid an immediate defender. Another guy reached for the ball, and I avoided him with a slick change-of-direction dribble between my legs, making sure to keep the ball low. Eyebrows and anticipation began to rise, and a low hum escaped from the spectators as I eluded two disoriented defenders in rapid succession.

I was off to the races. There was one player to beat as others pursued from behind. I charged toward the remaining defender like he wasn't there. He backpedaled, trying to set me up for a charge, but I took flight beyond the hash-mark area, at least one foot in front of the foul line. There wasn't time to take a charge. Floating to the rim with the ball in one hand, cocking it back behind my head, I slammed it through the rim, leaning sideways as the ball rippled the net. I saw guys on the bench leap up out of the corner of my eye, but for some reason I decided to look directly at the opposing bench, glaring at the head coach. My face said, "What else you got for me?"

My adrenaline was pumping after the dunk. I went on a tear and scored the next three baskets, one off a steal and another floating slam dunk, then a long bomb from the center of the court followed by a running one-hander coming across the middle. That sequence alone was enough to make people take notice. I was the only guy to come back home with two trophies.

After Pittsburgh, our next trip was Fork Union Academy in Virginia, where high school all-American Chris Washburn was the star. I didn't know Washburn, but Cedric Miller, our starting point guard, made sure to point him out in a Street & Smith magazine. Washburn was supposed to be a beast, a man-child on the level of a Daryl Dawkins or a Roy Tarpley. Maybe he was good, but I figured he couldn't be that much better than Walt Berry, Ed Pinckney, or Richie Adams, so what did we have to worry about?

For the Fork Union tournament, Lorch brought in Alvin Lott, who wasn't playing for Cardinal Hayes, his high school team. I had a good idea why Lorch wanted him. With Alvin on the squad, Cedric, our starting point, would come off the bench. Ced and Alvin were the same size, about five foot eight, but miles apart when it came to ability. Like most of the guys on the team, Ced had trouble handling the pressure of the spotlight. The word was out about the organization, so wherever Riverside showed up, people expected good performances. A lot of guys playing ball didn't perform as well when it was most important, and it usually didn't take long to see who they were.

The fans at Fork Union were dedicated basketball junkies. These were military-oriented gym geeks who supported their academy team with fervor. The games took place in an armory, a giant space equipped with a cafeteria and a full-scale gymnasium. The fans employed little mind tricks to rattle guys they singled out. They isolated a specific player by clapping and stomping their feet and jeering at him whenever he touched the ball. If the player missed a shot or committed a turnover, this process intensified; they clapped louder and made so much noise it seemed like the entire gym was focused against that player.

I looked forward to fan hate and was happy to play with my old junior high school friend Al Lott. I was a legit six foot six and hadn't played with Alvin since the eighth grade. I respected Al as one of the best but wasn't in awe like I was back then. He still had the confidence and skills of a warrior, but I was a different player now.

Prior to the trip to Fork Union, Lorch talked about how important it was to have a good showing. He talked about guys getting opportunities for scholarships. He said this was the tournament to "show your stuff" if you were serious about getting a free ride to a school. This meant a lot for guys with no offers on the table. A variety of scouts and coaches from all over the country were going to be at the Fork Union tournament. All we had to do was play our best and show people what New York basketball was about. It was also a lot of pressure to perform, but not everyone was looking at it the same way.

Alvin and I were in similar situations. He wasn't playing high school ball due to academic problems but was already well known as a great high school player. He was on top of his game and so was I. Our pressure was in showing the world no one could fuck with us on the court. Between the two of us, our mindset gave us enough firepower to compete with Washburn and his team of high school all-Americans. We weren't even thinking about any other team in the tournament. This was my first experience playing with the church, but Al had been all over the country with Lorch. We were like two little boys at recess, anticipating the Fork Union tournament.

Unfortunately, we didn't get the job done. We lost to Fork Union, and Washburn didn't even suit up. The house team turned out to have quite a few good players other than Washburn, who was being disciplined for breaking curfew. Listening to all the talk about his propensity for petty crime, academic liabilities, and disdain for authority, he sounded a lot like Richie Adams.

Our games at the field house were packed with active, motivated fans who were not content to just sit in their seats. They took part in the game. It was probably the biggest crowd I'd ever played in front of, making it feel more like a college atmosphere. There was a nice high scoreboard with our names in lights, and we got formal introductions with a loud microphone, and they had a nice hardwood floor.

Being the only team from New York, we added buzz to the tournament. People expected the Riverside Hawks to show them something different, but again we failed to win the championship, something none of us were happy about. I was a little surprised. It was probably my New York arrogance. There were quite a few legit Division I guys out there.

As in the tournament in Pittsburgh, I made the All-Tournament team. I adapted instinctively to Alvin's penetrating style, and he was looking for me on the break. We managed not to disappoint anyone looking for a show.

Without most of his summer superstars, Lorch was vocal about losing in these out-of-town tournaments. He talked about "honoring" the Hawks uniform. He expected to win and didn't want his program embarrassed.

The bottom line was Riverside had a rep and brand to maintain. We were winning games back home in the city leagues, but these out-of-town tournaments were the big events, and the stakes were a little higher because of the number of scouts.

No one knew this better than Big Hank. Big Hank lived in Harlem on 123rd Street and was our team manager. Hank used to be a ballplayer who was half in and half out of the streets. He really wasn't a street guy but was known to hustle to make a few extra dollars. He knew how high the stakes were for people trying to get a scholarship, so one day he and I discussed what was wrong with our team and why we were losing in the bigger out-of-state tournaments.

I'd known Hank for a few years. He was tight with Neal Hawk and Kool Moe Dee's crew. I got to know these guys when I was playing in the Entertainer's tournament at Mount Morris Park. Hank had a gap between his two center teeth and talked with a lisp. He blew out his knee and wasn't playing seriously anymore. He came up in a rough block on 123rd Street, so when he had something to say about how Lorch was handling things, I usually listened.

"Ice, you got to play yo game and carry these cats. They ain't where you at right now. They play like they jus happy to have a uniform, jacket, and a fuckin' Riverside bag."

"You might be right, Big," I would say. I always tried to sound concerned, but I wasn't.

"C'mon, Ice, you know what I mean. Some of these cats just happy to be out there, just happy to be playin' for Riverside. Some cats is like that. They all about the image and shit. These niggas go home and tell people they been on a basketball trip going out of town and that's all they need. Not everybody built like us."

Even when Hank was talking about something not so serious, it could morph into an intense conversation. He got angry watching our big guys play. Greg Khaleel had decent offensive skills, but he rarely showed intensity or aggression. In the beginning Lorch treated Khaleel like his top racehorse, even catering the offense to his benefit. He was treated like a guy who could help the church shine. But Khaleel wasn't helping himself shine. Lorch wanted him to play harder and bigger. Before our Fork Union trip, Lorch told him if he didn't play better, Chris Washburn was going to destroy him. He even let Walt B. run in a few of our practices, trying to get Khaleel psychologically prepared, but it did more damage than good. Walt was just too good. It got so bad I started trash-talking Walt to take the pressure off Greg. But Berry would spin off Khaleel on the baseline and dunk it. Or he'd throw a hip fake, drive by him to the hole, and slam it in on a reverse. He treated Khaleel like I treated some of my ball-playing colleagues at Music & Art—not too seriously.

I didn't know where Greg grew up, but he didn't act like a city guy. I thought he was Puerto Rican until someone told me he was from Greece. I should have known; Puerto Ricans typically weren't that tall. Khaleel wasn't drawn to confrontation like Lott, Walt, or I. His pride didn't seem to suffer from the drubbing he got from Berry, but it had to affect him. If Lorch had invited Kenny Hutch or Ernie Meyers to play opposite me, I would see it as an immediate threat and feel the need to challenge and outplay them.

Khaleel was already being recruited by small area colleges like Wagner and Seton Hall. I didn't look at him the way I looked at Ed Pinckney, Walter Berry, Richie Adams, or John Salley, but he was still a good player. A lot of practice time was spent trying to get Greg to box someone out. He ran the floor and could hit the outside shot from fifteen feet. But when you put him on the floor with someone like Berry, his game shrunk. He was six foot eight, and people wanted to see him tear the rim off and be an animal like Richie Adams, but it wasn't his way.

Our other big man, Keith Dixon, struggled getting up and down the court. Keith's problem wasn't so much lack of heart as it was lack of physical capability. With his knee problems, he did his best, but anyone big and able to move would give him problems. The good thing about Keith was he didn't shy away from contact and knew how to set a good pick. He could also hit the foul line extended outside shot. At least you knew what you got with Keith, and there were no false expectations.

Before his knees gave out, Big Hank was a banger. He was only six foot three, but he played the big-heart role to the max. Hank was only twenty-one or twenty-two, and you could tell he was simmering because he couldn't play anymore.

Big Hank was 100 percent in my corner. He had been following me since my first year in the Entertainer's tournament. I got a lot of love from his crew and the group he associated with. Nappy Red, Neal Hawk, LA Sunshine, Moe Dee, Tooch, and his crew gravitated to my game, and I got to know them over the years. This was how a player's rep grew organically on the playgrounds.

If I went to get some water, he was right there with a towel. It threw me off because he wasn't in character. I saw Hank knock a cat out on 127th Street with one punch. The dude never saw it coming. While he was beefing, Hank was swinging and caught him flush. He was a cat who was more likely to say, "Fuck you. Get your own fucking water," even if it was his job to do so. It wasn't his style, but Hank was jocking me—like he saw something in me and wanted to stay close.

After the Fork Union trip, I found out Hank wasn't the only one who saw something special in my game. At the tournament, everyone's name was displayed in lights on the scoreboard, and mine read, *Washington – 10* in red lights. In the consolation game, when the game was tightest, I scored on a string of five consecutive baskets that temporarily mesmerized the animated crowd at the field house. As they say on the streets, I went into my "bag of tricks."

After the game, a few young White fans approached me, holding their programs and Street & Smith magazines, asking for an autograph. People didn't ask for autographs in Harlem, even for the greatest players. Initially, my back was turned, so I didn't see these White kids coming up behind me.

"Hey, Pearl! Pearl Washington!" I turned and there they were, smiling. "Are you Pearl Washington?"

Al Lott was laughing.

"No, that's not me. That's another guy."

I didn't look or play anything like Pearl. I had my own version of a leaning, low-dribble crossover that didn't resemble his. Still, I was shook by these kids. I was also amazed at how big Pearl's name was on the national level. He was a high school junior and had virtually taken over New York City basketball. People speculated he could go straight from high school to the Knicks. They said the Garden would sell out. Al Lott, who was still considered an elite point guard himself, did not take all the Pearl talk lightly. Al spent the rest of the summer chasing the Brooklyn star down in tournaments to show everyone he was a better point guard. In 1984 he caught up with him, when Pearl was at Syracuse and Al at St. Bonaventure. Though Syracuse won the game, Al was not only the high scorer in the game with nineteen, but he also had six steals.

After the two big road trips with the church, my relationship with Lorch became inescapably more personal and consistent. Previously, every now and then I'd let it slip I needed forty or fifty dollars for this or that, and he'd reach into his pocket. I knew other guys regularly got a lot more money, but I wanted to keep Lorch at a distance, so I didn't ask for much.

I cashed in on the small fringe benefits whenever I could but instinctively knew not to get greedy.

After Fork Union, it became a little harder to keep him out of my business. The scouts, recruiters, and coaches began calling full throttle after the tournament. I was put on the "sleeper" scouting report and was talking regularly with guys like Tom Konchalski, a well-known and connected high school scout. Konchalski, who was at least six feet six, had seen me play a few times, and his word along with my road-trip performances put my name into blue-chip circles. I was an official top recruit with low exposure and a Division I prospect.

Lorch was aware down to the minute of when my name was put on the sleeper scouting report. It was his business to know, and his program provided the platform for exposure. He was connected to Garfunkel, Marty Blake, and Konchalski and began buffering inquiries on my behalf. Before the sleeper scouting report, I got calls and letters from smaller programs, but shortly after Fork Union, letters were coming from Georgia Tech, Maryland, NC State, Georgetown, and Syracuse. Every major college conference on television, from the Big Ten to the ACC to the Big East, was filling my mailbox. The more love I got from recruiters, the more Lorch wanted to know where my head was.

"Wash, you need a ride home?"

"Yeah, Coach. My man Mo and John need a ride, too. We going to the same place."

"No problem."

Johnny Mack and Mo Blind were both starting for Riverside's B squad. I liked busting their asses in practice and looking down on them for being on the B team. We were brothers, but it was pure joy humiliating them and letting them know I was the big dog and there was nothing they could do about it. Mo made big improvements in his game, but it seemed like Mack had reached his ceiling. Mack was the same size as he was two years ago.

Other than me, Mo was probably the most improved player in our crew and had grown to over six feet. Just three years earlier, Mo was shorter than everyone, and now he was taller than most of the guys in our crew. He was also a better athlete now, and able to dunk on anyone if you gave him a step. Mo was a much more confident player. John was still heady, crafty, and smart on the court and was a better playmaker than Mo, but he found it harder to keep up athletically as we got older.

The rides home always gave Lorch time to get a little more out of me, something he could gauge and perhaps use to his benefit. I didn't know his plan, or even if he had one. I just knew I didn't trust the guy.

"Wash, you're playing really well, kid. If you play your cards right, you'll be in the big-time. How are your grades in school?"

"They're good," I lied.

"That's good because that will almost ensure you can get a scholarship for college. You do want to go to college, don't you?"

"Yeah."

"What schools do you like? I can get you in to see whoever you want to talk to."

Our conversation usually led back to what schools I thought about, or what my plans were. As Lorch tried harder to get into my head, I grew more intent on keeping him on the outside looking in. During this time, Cedric Miller was consistently letting Lorch whack his ass with his paddle. Lorch said it built character and tried to explain to me one day why this was important for me to accept.

"It's about discipline, sacrifice, and trust, Wash. Those are the cornerstones of what we build here. You need to learn these things."

"Yeah, I'm learning as we go."

"You're on the top scouting reports now, kid. It's time to knuckle down and make some hard decisions. So, who's been calling you?"

"Everybody."

"Listen, kid, we can help you navigate through this thing. It's not something you have to do alone. That's what we do here."

"Yeah, I know, I know."

The Rucker Winter League ran through February. When it was over, the Easter tournaments at the Kennedy Center and the Wheelchair Classic kicked in before the summer season. The Governor's Cup ran in November and the LaGuardia House tournament shortly after that. This, along with the summer leagues for the past five years, had become my basketball diet. And now that I was on all the scouting reports, it seemed like it was going to pay off.

Once I became a Division I recruit, Lorch wanted to let all the big fish at the college level know that I was his boy, a product of his program, while at the same time demonstrating to me how much juice he had. He started taking me to high school games to watch *his* regular guys, like Olden Polynice and my cousin Kenny Smith. After discovering Kenny and I shared family, we became a little more aware of each other's careers, but we didn't get to dig deep into each other's skills because he lived in Queens. I rarely went to Queens for anything, and he and I hadn't crossed paths in any of the Harlem tournaments I played in.

Lorch took me to Seton Hall, Providence, and St. John's games, and each time I wound up talking with either the head coach or an assistant after the game. These informal visits weren't official school visits where you got a tour of the campus but were just as important. They gave me access. I started envisioning playing in the Big East with Mullins, Ewing, and Ed Pinckney, because it was the "city boys" basketball conference and I wanted in.

"Boy, he's a big one. A guard?"

"Yep, you betta believe it," Lorch chimed, answering St. John's Lou Carnesecca.

They talked as if I weren't there, and I saw no need to rush in and say something when I didn't know what to say. We were in St. John's locker room, surrounded by sweat-laden players, two of whom happened to be Billy Goodwin and Kevin Williams. I knew both guys through reputation. I felt like I was rubbing shoulders with the big-time, like it was just a matter of time before I played in the Garden.

As Carnesecca and Lorch talked, I walked over to get a closer look at Chris Mullins, who had just given Villanova all sorts of problems. Attending St. John's meant facing off against not only Goodwin and Kevin Williams but Mullins in practice as well. I wanted to see how I measured up physically. He was bigger and a little thicker than I thought he'd be. Watching him play, I thought he was slow, too slow to guard me, but he was already a Big East star, so I was most interested in talking to him. Our conversation was brief.

"So, you thinking about becoming a Redman?" he asked.

"Maybe. You like it here?"

"Yeah, it's cool. You'll like it. They know how to treat city guys like us. I see you came down with Lorch," Mullins remarked.

I'd heard a few stories about Mullins from friends who lived in Brooklyn, guys like Ed "Bugeye" Davender and John Johnson. They told me how Chris would go into some of the roughest parks of Brooklyn with Jerry Ice Reynolds and other streetball players to get a run. Chris had played for the Gauchos. I didn't know if he ever played for the church, but I respected him a little more for having the sense to stay away from Lorch. A White boy hanging around parks with Jerry Ice and playing for the Gauchos told me something. Either he had a big heart or a filthy nasty game.

"Yeah, I'm playing with the church right now, tryin' to figure out where I'm going next year," I told him.

The college letters kept rolling in. Soon I was getting phone calls from top-notch coaches like Bobby Cremins, Jim Valvano, and Rollie Massimino. All this activity escalated almost as soon as Fred Brown's inadvertent pass to James Worthy sealed Georgetown's fate against North Carolina in the 1982 NCAA championship game. In that game, Michael Jordan hit the shot that would forever change his life, a wide-open jumper to put his team ahead one final time. I imagined myself hitting a shot like that with the world watching.

CHAPTER 27
FIFTH-YEAR SENIOR, 1982

WITH MARCH MADNESS AT an end, the house phone was ringing so much that my little sister stopped answering it. I'd run to the phone, hoping it was a girl, maybe Felicia or some other girl I gave my number to, and it would be a coach, recruiter, or a scout. Nearly all of them talked fast and had stories to sell. An assistant at the University of Georgia told me I was a perfect complement for Vern Fleming. Ray Meyer, DePaul's coach, told me I could be good with Kenny Patterson. I spoke with Lefty Driesell and Bobby Cremins. I'd look at the pretty brochures with the campus life of fairytales and daydream for a few hours, wondering who to believe. I received a nice package from Southern Illinois and examined it longer than a normal person with letters from nearly every Big East and ACC school might. The Salukis weren't a big-time basketball organization in any regard, but Walt Frazier had gone there, and so seeing a letter from them meant a lot to me.

Everyone had a story or a reason I should attend their school. I drank it in, read through the material, and fantasized about playing in the NBA. I didn't acknowledge these fantasies came with potential detours and U-turns. The most immediate potential detour was my academic performance, or lack thereof, something Syracuse assistant coach Brendon Malone quickly and painfully pointed out to me in late April 1982. Brendan watched me play several times and thought my game was good for Syracuse.

"James, it doesn't look like you can graduate this year unless there's something I don't know. We may have to look at other options."

"What other options?"

"Options like junior college or perhaps a prep school like the one in Fork Union."

"Man, I don't really want to go to a junior college. And I ain't goin' to no military school. I ain't exactly a dummy. Music & Art is a hard school, and we got some hard-ass classes. Don't that count?"

Malone chuckled before he responded.

"It only counts if you graduate, James, and we both know the chances of you graduating this year are very slim. There's a mandatory art competency test you already flunked once, not to mention you are behind in a few other art classes. You really don't have much of a choice unless you want to do another year in high school and come out next year."

The thought of another year in school shook me up and brought me back down to earth. Another year in high school would make it my sixth. Not even Brendan knew that I was in my fifth year of high school. I had failed the art competency exam last year and couldn't graduate without it. Lorch didn't know either. Like Alvin Lott, who was also a fifth-year senior at Cardinal Hayes, I was eighteen, and eligible to play for Riverside in the senior division. A lot of guys started school late for one reason or another, so I could have been one of those. Lorch didn't probe much because of where I went to school. I was an anomaly to Lorch, and he never even bothered to connect with or call my coach at Music & Art.

Music & Art was so far removed from the athletic scene that it didn't exist within the city basketball landscape, so no one knew about my academic standing. My reputation was built on the playgrounds, and over the summers, where the only question worth answering was if you could play.

I put junior college out of my mind. The very idea vexed me. In four years, I managed to play my way into potential scholarship opportunities to almost any school in the nation. But was I ready to handle it? My single-minded focus on basketball pushed my game to the top scouting reports, but along the way I neglected many other responsibilities in my life. I was convinced I was smart enough to avoid the pitfalls of all those great Harlem players who fucked up opportunities, and yet here it was, right in my face: failure.

Despite the above-average education I received at Music & Art, it was primarily received on my own terms. The freedom I felt at Music & Art had been a gift and a curse. I was comfortable and content to live my life the way

I wanted to. It was no different in basketball. The freedom I exhibited and felt playing basketball had little to do with discipline, structure, or sacrifices I was not in control of.

I cut classes when I wanted. I could be home in less than fifteen minutes, and often left school early. Sometimes I cut class to spend hours in the library, reading about whatever interests I had. I read history a lot, mostly biographies, and sports magazines, but often they had nothing to do with class. I would commit to making up the schoolwork, and sometimes I did, but it was never enough.

The classes I struggled most with were the ones requiring greater sacrifice and discipline. I refused to knuckle down, and no one could convince or force me to do otherwise. I don't ever recall talking to an academic advisor; I just kept playing ball, going to school, passing enough classes to stay in school, and falling enough behind not to graduate.

I was probably in the most unique situation of anyone who had ever attended the high school of Music & Art. How many other students had been recruited by top basketball programs in the country? How many received letters of interest from Ivy League schools like Princeton, Brown, Columbia, and Penn State? But none of that seemed to matter after my reality moment with Brendan. I was burning the candle at both ends, elevating my basketball game to the highest level at the expense of my academics.

Brendan Malone was a Brooklyn native and knew New York City the way most of us knew it, from the inside. Almost immediately he knew how to make me feel comfortable and speak in a way that gave him insight into my personality. I had known Lorch a lot longer than Brendan, but Lorch didn't have a clue about how to reach me. Brendan convinced me he was sincere, so it was easier to relate to him.

But attending a JC could easily lead to a dead end. The rumors of good players with legitimate Division I talent squandering it and turning sour at the wrong junior college was common street folklore. A few guys from my block had gone to JCs, and few came back with better options.

With more than seventy letters in my apartment, ending up at a JC was a personal embarrassment. I kept my mouth shut about school. Other than Mo, few people in the block knew the kind of recruiting attention I was getting.

The truth was, many of the best players in Harlem or in New York City in general had some kind of academic problem. Some guys just didn't have cognitive education skills, but almost all of the best of the best ended up sacrificing academics for basketball. There were very few Kareems, who were supremely talented AND great students. This just didn't happen often. What made me successful on the playground was my own version of unique innovation, creativity, and spontaneous unpredictability. These characteristics were a distraction to my academic discipline. They consistently overshadowed practicality, discipline, fundamentals, and structure. I got away with these characteristics on the playgrounds, but it was never going to work in a rigid academic system.

I guess I started to believe basketball was more important, and all I had to do was keep playing and I would get into the NBA. All the practicing, in various conditions and circumstances, put me in a position to live a very different life. Yet, something was missing. Like so many other Harlem athletes before me, I was on a road to somewhere without a clear roadmap on how to get there.

Ironically, my biggest academic problem was something I once thought I loved almost as much as basketball: art. I flunked several of my art classes. As an art major, most of these courses were required to graduate. I may have fared a little better in a school that concentrated on graphics, but Music & Art wasn't that kind of school. I wasn't big on painting, sculpting, ceramics, and many of the other things we were doing. I lost interest and didn't work hard on this stuff.

The closer we got to the end of the school year, the more Brendan dug into my academic situation. He talked to one of the academic advisors in school and found out my situation was desperate. The academic standards at Music & Art weren't going to bend or waver like they might for a star athlete of a city school. It didn't matter how good of a basketball player I was. Brendan said the advisors told him that the peaks and valleys in my grades along with consistent attendance suggested my situation had nothing to do with aptitude. There were academic variances all over my record. I had high grades in some classes, and a few Fs in courses not as difficult. I passed English 3 and 5 with no problem, but had to repeat English 2 twice. Mr. Walsh taught English 2, and I hated his boring, droning style. No one ever suggested a tutor, so my case must have been viewed as one of willful neglect.

Things moved quickly toward the end of the school year. Once my situation was circulated on the recruiting wire as a potential risk not to graduate, letters started coming from Daytona Beach, Indian River, Allegheny Community, and San Jacinto junior colleges, basketball chop shops all offering full scholarships. I was amazed how quick the turnaround was. And this was when Brendan, who was a seasoned recruiter, went into his bag of tricks and started throwing out alternatives.

"James, we can set you up on a program to get you into Syracuse, but it's going to take a commitment from you. The program works like this. You agree to go to Pensacola Junior College, one of the college programs we work with down in Florida. You stay for one year and maintain a 2.0 GPA. Once you get the 2.0, we bring you up for a red-shirt year with us the following year in the '83 to '84 season. You'll be able to work out with the team, but you can't compete until the '84 to '85 where you'll be classified as a sophomore, not a junior. From what I hear, your playground friend Walter Berry is working a similar situation out with St. John's, and Kenny Hutchinson might be doing the same thing with Arkansas. Aren't they friends of yours? What do you think?"

"Yeah, I'm tight with Hutch, but I don't know Walt too well. Why can't I come up to Syracuse this year and get the 2.0 as a red shirt? Why do I need to go down to Florida?" I asked.

"That's a good question, James. Quite frankly, it's not just your academic situation that concerns us. You need a solid year of organization, structure, and orientation. You have a lot of potential and can really score the ball, but you've been playing on the playgrounds, doing your own thing for quite a while, and it might be best to go down to Florida and prove to yourself you can get it done in a structured system."

In other words, I was too big a risk. Brendan always knew how to put his words together, to make it all sound reasonable. I could tell he had probably talked to my high school coach and Lorch about my situation. I had made Lorch a believer. He'd seen me all winter and knew what I could do. If any coach called him to ask about me, he was like a gold-level referral. I had a feeling everything was going to be okay, even though I didn't know a thing about Pensacola, Florida. I only knew I was ready to play on television, and against anyone. Brendan made me feel like everything was going to work out and I'd be on TV in a few years, playing in the Carrier Dome and in Madison Square Garden.

I didn't mind being red-shirted and figured I'd use the year to work on my game and any weaknesses and be ready to play in 1984. I'd have three years to develop my skills with a national basketball program, and had no doubt I would be ready for the NBA by 1986 or '87.

"So, all I have to do is go down to Florida for a year and get good grades?"

"Yep, but you'll need to be more disciplined than you've been here in

New York. You're going to have to pull a decent grade point average and learn to play in an organized structure while you're down there."

I didn't even bother asking who the coach in Pensacola was. I didn't ask about their program, record, the school, or anything that would indicate what awaited me in Florida. I didn't know where Pensacola was on the map, and I never asked. I wondered, with all the JCs in the tri-state, why the same deal couldn't be worked out with Westchester CC or Mercer Community, closer to home. Maybe Brendan wanted me as far away from the city as possible. Pensacola was a trial, inadvertent or deliberate. If I passed, I would be playing for the Orangemen in a couple of years, and if not, it was probably back to the streets.

"Yeah, I'll have to discuss it with my mother."

"Does your mother still like Georgetown?" Brendon asked.

"Yeah, she talked with John Thompson for a long time and she likes him. She thinks he can keep me straight."

"Well, we can keep you straight too, kid. Tell her not to worry; you'll graduate with us."

I didn't say what I already knew, which was that guys like me rarely graduated from college. Most of the exceptional athletes coming from similar circumstances, demonstrating exceptional basketball skills, typically did not go to college to graduate. We went because it was the next step toward getting into the pros, and everyone knew the large White colleges were only interested in our athletic ability. College ball was just another level of competition for us. We weren't thinking about guys who didn't make it. I put the work in, and I was getting the results on the court. I believed it was going to stay this way until I decided otherwise.

Ma didn't care much for basketball or sports in general. From her perspective education was all that mattered. I played in some big games by 1982 and brought home a lot of big trophies, but Ma had yet to see me play. She even missed my game at the Garden my junior year. I dropped twenty-five points at Madison Square Garden against one of the better B Division schools, Mary Bergtraum, and she missed it.

Brendan knew how to talk to Ma. He talked about education and scholarship, as he probably did with most parents trying to help their kids out of the ghetto. It was the only thing she was concerned about and one of the reasons she hadn't given up on me.

I decided pretty quickly Syracuse was where I wanted to be. I scoured the literature on the Orangemen. I read up on the history of Jim Brown and how the Carrier Dome was built. I read the write-ups on Erich Santifer, Leo Rautins, and Gene Waldron, their best players. I knew I could play with those guys, and I was confident no one at Syracuse was as good as me offensively. I read Jim Boeheim's profile and his philosophy on basketball, what kind of players he recruited, and immediately saw where I fit in.

Bruce "Moose" Dalrymple was on his way to Georgia Tech along with John Salley. Olden Polynice was being recruited by Ralph Sampson's University of Virginia. Gary Voce was going to Notre Dame, and Ernie Meyers was already at North Carolina State. Three of the best guards in the city, Pearl Washington, Mark Jackson, and Kenny Smith, were going into their senior years, but all were rumored to be signing early, probably to the Big East. And there were a few all-Americans not going straight into big colleges, like Walter Berry and Kenny Hutchinson. Alvin Lott was headed to Saint Bonaventure to play in the Atlantic 10 conference.

It was Brendan's idea for me to take the GED as a precaution. There was a very good chance I wouldn't pass the art competency exam. Though I wasn't worried about passing the GED, I was embarrassed to take the damn test. But Brendan said it was a good insurance policy, in case anything went wrong.

"James, this whole plan means nothing unless you can graduate this year. As a backup, do you think you can pass the GED if you had to?"

"Yeah, I could."

"Will you make time to study for the exam?"

"I can pass the GED, Coach."

Brendan was patient. He was also covering all the angles. What if I didn't graduate? He knew I lied about my academic situation and kept pushing. I began to feel like he cared. Other than Bobby Cremins, Pat Kennedy, and Bob Zuffelato, Marshall University's coach, and a few other coaches from smaller schools, Brendan was the only guy who saw me play multiple times. He had a better understanding of my game.

Brendon wasn't manic like some of the other recruiters. Bob Zuffelato drove up from West Virginia to watch one of my practices at Riverside and brought a letter of intent with him for me to sign. After practice he bought me a cheap hamburger, and I lost interest in him very quickly. He never bothered trying to talk to Ma and tried to pressure me into giving him an answer before he left New York. Brendan, on the other hand, knew I didn't have a father around and spent more time running the street than I should have, so his mode and approach was calculated in a way that made him more relatable.

I took the GED a month before school graduation and passed. I looked over the exam prep materials in one day. Now I had my insurance policy. I still wanted to graduate from M&A but was unsure about passing the art competency exam. I knew I had to move out of Ma's house if I failed. Her language was changing, and my days were numbered.

"I didn't move all the way from South Carolina to have my children flunk out of school," she would say. "You mean to tell me I can graduate in the segregated South, where they not even fair to people, and you can't graduate from high school in New York?"

"Ma, I—"

"James, you lazy, and that kind of laziness is gon have you out in the street. I ain't gon take care of no grown man. I didn't do it for your father and I ain't gon do it for you."

My only solution was to avoid talking to her since I couldn't justify my behavior. I had to take the humiliation and learn from it. Getting the GED out of the way, I could rest a little, knowing I was going to college one way or another. At least I wouldn't be stuck in the house with Ma threatening to kick me out every week.

I finally decided not to bother taking the art competency test. Summer was coming, so I began to focus on what was important, basketball. I was on my way to Syracuse, taking the long route via Pensacola, Florida, and that was good enough for now.

PART 6
1982

CHAPTER 28
PENSACOLA JUNIOR COLLEGE

IT WAS SUNDAY EVENING when Coach Boes and who I took to be his son met me at Pensacola's airport in August 1982. I had never been to Florida, and it was hotter than any night in New York that summer, with air thick enough to cut. The air was not only heavy, it was burdensome, reminding me of the thick, still-air summers I spent at my grandparents' home near Charleston, South Carolina.

Boes was five foot seven and looked like he might be in his mid or late twenties. Another young coach. He and I talked over the phone once or twice but had never met. Boes was thin lipped to the point of looking as if he didn't have any. He had tiny green eyes and wore PJC school colors—green shorts, a white-collared Izod shirt, and a green see-through visor cap. His hairline was just beginning to recede, and his skin was red in some areas, and flaky pale white in areas missed by the sun. We greeted one another, and as we were leaving the airport, I noticed that at the slightest lapse in conversation, he resorted to biting what little of his nails were left.

"How was yer flight, Jim?"

"It was good."

"That's good. We had a hot one today—probably won't let up for a spell. Preseason conditioning starts tomorrow. You ready to git started?"

"Yeah, I'm ready." *Just show me to the court, White man,* I thought. The heat, lack of light, and small country roads made me think about the bright lights of Harlem and all the action I was leaving behind.

"Brendan told me about your summer leagues. How many you play in this summer?"

"Six."

"Six! Good lord, six basketball leagues in one summer. I ain't never hear'ed such a thing. How you find time to play in six leagues?!"

"That's all I do. I play ball every day."

"Well, that's something for sure. By the way, this is your teammate, Smitty. He's a local boy from down here, and he'll be a freshman like you." I had almost ignored the frail, small-framed boy up until then. When he introduced us, I said my usual "wassup" after re-scanning him briefly.

My brief conversation with Boes over the phone hadn't lasted more than twenty minutes, so after sizing up Smitty, I thought about how little I actually knew about Pensacola, Chip Boes, or the team I was joining. Smitty looked more like a high school freshman. He didn't look ready for college ball. He was five foot seven, and maybe 140 pounds. This kid wouldn't last two minutes in Harlem. If he made the cut, what did that say about the rest of the team? I hadn't seen him play, but his initial presence didn't impress me.

Brendan said PJC was a good place to pull my grade point average up and learn team structure and discipline before moving up and playing for Syracuse. But I was already questioning if I would get any better going up against players like Smitty in practice. He was no Rod Strickland.

Our apartments were twenty minutes from the campus, off one of the main city roads, with a bus line into town. Smitty explained how friendly people in the area were. He said a lot of players hitched rides to school rather than wait on the city bus. As I looked around, I was amazed they even had public transportation. Smitty didn't live in the apartments with the rest of the team but told me he spent time getting to know some of the guys when he was a senior in high school. One of his main goals was to be a walk-on at PJC.

From the moment I stepped off the plane at Pensacola's airport, I felt the South in a way I'd felt it before. The smell of fresh air and the dialect and slang wasn't alien to me. Having experienced my grandparents' farm in South Carolina made it easier to relax and not freak out about the lack of city conveniences. I was happy they had a city bus. I was a product of NYC subways and taxis, and I couldn't drive, so I liked the idea of having at least a little mobility.

My awareness of Deep South circumstances made the cultural and environmental adjustment easier than it might be for someone who had never been outside of the city for any extended time. In my block, a trip anywhere south of the George Washington Bridge for most cats was a trip to the country. I had a friend who spent one weekend in Trenton, NJ, and talked like he was in Selma, Alabama.

After introducing me to Smitty and feeling me out during our conversation on the way to the team's apartments, Boes left us to go home. Smitty looked like he was fifteen, but he had his own ride, the norm for a teenage boy in the South with means. Down south, a young boy got behind the wheel as soon as he could see over it. In comparison, the only driving I'd ever done was on the court. The only young teens behind the wheels of cars in Harlem were boys stealing them and young hustlers.

Our apartments were designed like a roadside motel—because it had been a roadside motel. They were single story, side by side, and according to Smitty, all the rooms on the left side of the lot belonged to the team. Once we got inside, I met Scott Petway and Ludwig Vita, two of my three housemates. They were both second-year players. Scott was from Chicago and Luddy from Syracuse, something that immediately got my attention. Luddy being from Syracuse didn't strike me as a coincidence.

Not completely paranoid yet about the racial complexity of my new team after meeting Smitty, Luddy, and Scott, all White boys, I began wondering how many Blacks were on the team. It was the first time I gave it any thought. I'd never played with White guys, let alone lived in the same apartment with them. I began to wonder if I was the only Black guy.

Racial diversity was abundant in high school, but it was a dynamic I didn't consistently encounter in sports. Whites playing in Harlem tournaments were a rare sight. When I was playing for Music & Art, it was a little different. White guys played for schools like Bronx Science, Printing, and Norman Thomas, but for the most part, almost all my stiff competition came from Black players.

As I lingered on thoughts of my new White teammates, Luddy mentioned that our fourth housemate hadn't arrived yet. Donnie Singleton was on his way from Miami, and he and I were sharing a room. With a name like Donnie, and living in Miami, I relaxed a little. No way this guy was White unless the world was coming to an end.

However, after talking with Scott Petway for a few minutes, I rethought my cultural perception of the guys I'd already met. Petway was a six-foot-five small forward whose flaming-red hair, charisma, and flamboyant personality were magnetic. He made an impression quickly. The night I arrived, despite the overbearing heat, he was rocking black leather pants and a silk shirt left unbuttoned to reveal an array of gold chains and other glittery adornments that would make Big Daddy Kane proud. His hair was cropped and cut short on the sides but teased on top. He looked like he belonged on a stage, or on *Happy Days*, not a basketball court.

"What's up, bro!"

"Wassup."

"Man, you really from Harlem?"

"Yeah."

"Damn, I know they play some ball up there!"

"Yeah, where you from?"

"Chi-town."

"That's cool."

"Yeah. I know you got some moves, man. I know it!"

Scott's smile was infectious. He had a lot of energy. Just talking briefly about the games in New York, I could see he was easily excited, and due to his colorful nature, you couldn't help but feel good around him. Once he put me at ease, we talked about Chicago greats Mark Aguirre, Clyde Bradshaw, and other Chicago stars like two old friends.

Ludwig Vita, known as Luddy, was five foot seven, but unlike Smitty, he was stocky and built like a wrestler. I found out later he was the nephew of Bernie Fine, another Syracuse University assistant working under Boeheim. It was further confirmation of a relationship between PJC and Syracuse. After talking and getting to know each other, Luddy, Smitty, Scott, and Zach, one of Scott's friends visiting from Chicago, invited me to hang out with them at a club in downtown Pensacola.

Even with Bernie Fine's nephew being from Syracuse, I wasn't comfortable. There was a lot at stake. PJC wasn't just a local community college; it was also part of a default farm system within the NCAA recruiting process. At least, that's what it was in my case. I didn't know much about the team but figured as long as there was a basketball court, I had nothing to worry about.

As my new teammates and Zach left for the club, I told them I needed to settle in. I wanted to be alone. There was no need to tell them I didn't have a pair of dress shoes. I took my bags to my room and sat out by the pay phone near the two-lane highway, watching cars stream back and forth until I went into trance. I thought about playing in the Big East conference, and possibly playing for Georgetown. I wondered if Big John Thompson's program was better for me. I thought about the street tournaments, not winning MVP in the Governor's Cup classic when I should have, and my promise to my city grandmother, Nanna. I realized how much Nanna tried to do for me. Now I was in college on a thin thread, the first from either side of my family to set foot on a college campus. As her only grandson, I felt like I owed her something.

After watching enough cars go back and forth, I made my way back to the bedroom and fell asleep amid all my fantastical imaginings, only to be awoken by loud voices in the middle of the hot and steamy night. Unable to immediately understand or distinguish what I was hearing, I got out of bed to find the source of the noise.

"Fuck me, you bastard! Don't stop! Don't stop fucking me!"

"Rock that bitch, Scott. Rock her world!"

Luddy and Scott's bedroom was across the hall from mine. I looked in and saw Luddy in his bed with the lights off, apparently drunk and ranting. As I peeked in from the short hallway, I had a full view of the living room, where I saw Scott and Zach half-dressed on the floor with a naked, sweaty, redheaded White girl.

Scott was behind her, hands on her waist, banging from behind while Zach was lying down, pants down to ankles, navigating her head up and down the sides of his pinkish-red penis. Time seemed to stand still for a moment. With Luddy in the bedroom yelling and throwing up, and Scott and Zach intensely engaged in their personal orgy, I'd lived in Harlem all my life and had never witnessed a live sex show like this one.

I focused in on the redhead. Gasping when Zach didn't have her mouth full, she was getting louder, saying even more outrageous things than drunk Luddy. Occasionally she looked back at Scott, who was sweating profusely, and yelled at him.

"Fuck me harder! Pound my pussy!"

She slammed her backside against Scott in a forceful rhythm that resonated throughout the room, her buttocks quivering from the force. Scott wasn't fucking her; she was fucking him. She had a shapely body and nice curves. Her breasts bounced frantically from the sexual exertion. Her hair was straight, saturated from the sweat and heat, and she was covered with moisture.

Scott noticed me standing in the nearby hallway and smiled as if to invite me in, but I couldn't move. He was sweating like a pig, and despite my urging, pressing erection, I couldn't budge from the spot I was in. I wasn't prepared to screw in front of anyone, let alone two White boys I'd met for the first time three hours ago. Maybe this girl was a prostitute, or a college student, but she was obviously some kind of intense freak. Perhaps Scott was being a nice teammate, offering me some college pussy to get me started. But it wasn't a risk I was willing to take. No one was wearing condoms.

The girl slacked up on Zach's blowjob enough to notice me standing near the doorway of my room. She was pretty and had a confident expression, like she was just getting started. My presence didn't disrupt her activity at all. Maybe it was the thought of having another person join the party, or maybe it was my brown skin and bulging dick under my sweatpants, but whatever the case, she became more animated once we locked eyes, slamming her backside into Scott even harder.

"You want some of this? Come give me some of that black cock, baby! Come over here and fuck me!"

She was looking directly at me.

Looking into her eyes, I was overcome with arousal and timidity, exhilaration and skepticism. I could only stand and watch. A smile crept across my face, a smile that implied I'd seen this shit before, no big deal, but that wasn't why I was smiling. What I was really thinking was *These are some crazy-ass White boys!*

The redhead got so wild I thought she was going to bite Zach before she was done. Soon he was yelling nearly as loud as Luddy in the bedroom. The only silent people in the apartment were me and Scott. Scott was too tired from pumping, and I was too stunned to open my mouth.

Scott and Zach swapped places and positions. I watched Zach upend the girl and pin her legs on his shoulders before driving into her at a frantic pace, her feet dangling like lifeless playthings in the air. I watched things that night I'd never seen at the Forty-Second Street peep shows we used to sneak into years ago. I watched until I got sleepy for the second time that night. The girl getting fucked in my living room was probably some father's little girl experiencing college for the first time like I was.

The very next week, Scott and Luddy couldn't practice. As a matter of fact, they couldn't do much of anything. They caught something called mono, a virus that rendered them virtually useless. I never imagined going to school in Florida, but my first night in Pensacola wasn't one I'd forget anytime soon.

CHAPTER 29
THE TEAM

When I was a young boy
Growin' up in the ghetto
Hangin' out on corners
Singin' with the fellas
Lookin' for the cute chicks
Tryin' to find me big fun
Lookin' for some trouble
From anyone who'd give me some . . .
I was young and crazy . . . in the ghetto
"Ghetto Life," *Street Songs*, Rick James

RICK JAMES DROPPED HIS newest album, *Street Songs*, and it hit the streets like a bomb. The funk king was hot the summer of 1982, and his soulful depiction of street life in the ghetto hit home with me and a lot of young cats of my era. For my new roommate Donnie and I, the single "Ghetto Life" became our theme song as an accurate portrayal of our lives.

Donnie Singleton was from Liberty City, Miami. From what he told me, Liberty City was the Harlem of the Deep South, and even more violent. His depiction of flat row houses with scaled-down living conditions and a hustling economy built around a cocaine industry sounded familiar. Donnie and I were the same size, six feet six. He played small forward, same as me. He was a little heavier, which wasn't saying much since I was only 183 pounds. I guess when you were as skinny as I was, even an additional seven or eight pounds was noticeable. Donnie was sporting waves, with a part down the center, like Dominique Wilkins. It took us about one day to become ghetto soul mates.

If Boes had anything to do with matching up roommates, putting Donnie and I together was a stroke of genius. We had similar backgrounds and personalities and hit it off immediately. Our common ground consummated around ghetto living. We commemorated people who lived by their wits and had something to show for it. His brother Cornell was in the drug game and, according to Donnie, took care of his whole family.

One experience we didn't have in common was Donnie having a girl and a two-year-old daughter back in Liberty City. We talked more about his brother, but I could see he was trying to figure out the daddy thing. I couldn't really relate to that. We didn't talk at all about our fathers and agreed that our mothers didn't understand anything going on in our world.

Listening to Donnie, I tried to imagine what it was like having an older brother looking out for you, someone you could trust. Maybe I wouldn't have done some of the stupid shit I'd done, like not graduating from high school, if someone like Cornell was on my ass. On the other hand, Donnie was down here with me, older brother or not, filling me in on what life was like for him and his family in Liberty City. But if not for Cornell, maybe he would have ended up in a worst situation.

"We got two Sevilles at da house. My brotha got his own El Dog [Cadillac Eldorado] and he don't let nobody drive that. That's how we livin' in da LC. I was fittin' ta be at Miami Dade Junior College where a few of my boys at, but Cornell wouldn't let me go there. He said I needed to get away from Miami."

"What's your little girl's name?"

"Shanna. She look just like me. Had her when I was in high school.

"What you know about Pensacola?"

"Nothin', but I know it's a lot of rednecks down here. We ain't far from Alabama. Man, if I was home, I'd be out on the strip right na, clockin' hoes, lightin' up trees and gittin' nice. In Liberty City, ova in the bottom, we ball till late at night. I miss that shit already."

Donnie didn't mind doing most of the talking and was comfortable with me not always feeling the need to talk. Some things he said to see how I would react. I'd talk just enough about Harlem and what my block was like to get him going, and he would start talking about Liberty City and how things were in Miami.

The only other players from a notable northern city on our team other than Scott Petway was Dennis Pope, a freshman from Baltimore out of Carver High School, and his homeboy Michael Tate, who was a second-year player from the same school. Dennis arrived a day after Donnie. I'd heard of Carver and knew they played good teams like Dunbar, where Muggsy Bogues played. Dennis was six-five and playing center. My first thought was that no real center was six-five, not at any college level. I also knew you couldn't underestimate a player coming out of Baltimore. I grew up watching some of their teams when they came to New York for the holiday tournaments, and they always had great players no matter their size.

Our team had five White and eight Black players, a turnaround from how I initially thought it might be. Our backgrounds defined preliminary boundaries in how we socialized. Donnie and I shared a room, and we liked the same music and had similar backgrounds. We understood what Rick James was singing about, and even though Donnie wasn't into rap music like I was, he liked Grandmaster Flash and the Furious Five's "The Message" and other popular rap songs I turned him on to.

Rap music was still a New York tri-state phenomenon in 1982. It hadn't fully penetrated the South or the West Coast like it eventually would. A lot of young cats in the South were listening to R&B mainstays like the Commodores and Earth, Wind & Fire.

Donnie, Dennis, and I were first-year guys from the inner city, so we gravitated quickly to one another. Jerome Davis and Andre Williams, both native South Carolinians, absorbed freshman guard Ron Green into their group. Ron was from Greenville, South Carolina. They were Black and heavy weed smokers, so their clique naturally formed around these circumstances.

Luddy, Scott, Dan, Smitty, and Charles Davis were the White guys on the team. They liked to drink beer and formed another subset group of teammates. The two team mavericks were Fast Eddie Aaron, a Black second-year guard from New Orleans, and Michael Tate, a second-year player from Carver. Dennis shared an apartment with Tate and Eddie, neither of whom hung out with anyone. As was the case anywhere else in society, people gravitated to and felt comfortable with what they knew best and didn't venture far beyond that.

My first few weeks in Pensacola convinced me I'd made a good choice. I could have gone to Daytona Beach, Indian River, or Allegheny Community in Cumberland, Maryland, on similar arrangements proposed by other schools like Georgia Tech and St. John's. Walter Berry was in Texas, as Brendon predicted, attending the San Jacinto junior college. In a year he would enroll at St. John's as a red-shirt freshman and have three remaining years with St. John's. My plan was to meet him in the Big East in a few years at the Garden.

Preconditioning started my second day in Florida. The track was made of black gravel surrounding the football field behind the gym. It was where aspiring men would become crying, whining boys. In August, any time before 6 p.m. meant running in murderous heat. We started practice at 1 p.m. when the sun was hottest. It took no time to hate this regimen. I hated idle running. The routine of mechanical, predictable movements aggravated my mind more than anything else. After a few days, my shins burned from sharp pains whenever I moved. There was no air to breathe comfortably, and the heat made you lightheaded. The only thing that kept me going was the rest of the guys. I wasn't going to be the one to quit.

Our first team goal was the six-minute mile. Every player had to run a six-minute mile as a qualifying preconditioning standard. If you couldn't make it in six minutes, you were assigned to the track every day before practice until you could. I'd heard somewhere that twenty-four city blocks constituted one mile in New York. I wasn't sure I could ever run twenty-four blocks in six minutes. I ran fifteen blocks once when I was eleven years old after being chased by an angry store owner. Even after I dropped the large bag of potato chips I'd stolen around block seven, this guy chased me for another two blocks before giving up. I ran another five blocks.

None of the first-year guys, aside from Smitty and Charles Davis, the two local boys, knew what to expect. Almost everyone predicted none of the freshman would make the six-minute mile the first time. And Jerome, who seemed to be the closest thing we had to a team leader, said there were guys on the team last year who never made the six-minute mile and owed penalty track miles the entire season.

This was the first opportunity for the second-year guys to play the situation up and mess with our heads if they could. They wanted us to know they knew something we didn't. I really didn't care what they said; I just wanted to get on the court.

"Don't eat nothing before you go out there," they told us.

"All you gon be doin' is throwin' it back up."

On our first day, Boes looked the part of a drill sergeant: His standard green-and-white school colors made somewhat of a military impression. He had a no-nonsense demeanor and approach.

His assistant, Wayne, who was from the Philippines, was a little more laid back both in appearance and approach. He told us he'd played with a professional team in the Philippines and had served in the US Army. I didn't make the connection right away, but I found out that Pensacola had an Army base. It was a military town, so that explained how Wayne and Coach Boes wound up coaching the PJC Pirates.

Scott and Luddy were the hard-partying guys, but before the mono kicked in, they finished the six-minute mile their first time out. A week later they would be sick with symptoms. Other than Eddie Aaron, Scott and Luddy were the only second-year players to make the six-minute mile cut on the first day. Dan, who was six foot eight and, from what everyone said, probably our best outside shooter, came in last. The first-year guys fared a lot better. It took me three days to make a time of 5:53. Dennis made it in ten seconds less his second day out. It took Donnie at least a week before he made it. Once you qualified, you didn't have to worry about additional laps unless you cut a class or committed some other team infraction. We were naturally competitive our first few days, but I could already see Donnie would only let himself be pushed so far. He didn't kill himself to make it until he was getting near the bottom of the non-qualifiers.

Preconditioning also included weightlifting. I'd done plenty of pushups and sit-ups but never lifted weights. Older cats in the block like Wendell, Phil Walker, and Ted Campbell, all college scholarship athletes from my block, talked about lifting weights in college, so I knew it was coming. I heard different things about weights. For an outside shooter with a soft touch, some said lifting weights would affect my shot, or change my game. Others said I needed weights, as many and as much as possible. They said I was just too skinny, and weights would only make me stronger and quicker and improve my outside shooting.

We used Nautilus, a fairly modern system in 1982. The weight room was a sweat box. The gym and locker area were also humid. There were fans but no air-conditioning. The weight room scene was a mixture of squeaking machines, light chatter, strains, grunts, and loud screams. It was a lot to take in for someone who had never "worked out." Some of the chrome-plated machines looked complicated, equipped with pulleys, steel plates, and chains.

Having never lifted weights, starting out on a Nautilus system was easier to adjust to than a free-weight system. Free weights forced you to control and balance the weight, which required more exertion. With Nautilus, the machine balanced the weight for you and made it a little less difficult. Either way, my body was so sore after my first session I didn't feel normal on the basketball court. I missed easy shots. Everyone was affected, but missing wide-open fifteen-foot shots and fumbling through my signature moves was frustrating since I wanted to make a big impression.

Starting out, it looked as if I was trying to do stuff someone my height and size shouldn't be attempting. I wasn't supposed to be handling the ball in traffic, splitting defenders, or trying to make spin moves and long jump shots. My mind was the same, but my body needed to adjust to the rigid physical regimen.

It took at least a week or two. The excitement and newness of the situation made me overlook any discomfort, pain, and exhaustion I felt. I wasn't going to let anything get in the way of making my mark on a new team. Everyone wanted to play and show what they had to offer. Every opportunity had to be taken advantage of to show your best stuff and therefore secure playing time. We were willing to endure whatever we had to the first two weeks. It was an alpha male–driven competition starting out.

New York City players had a rep for being cocky. I wasn't the typical outspoken New Yorker, but my game was arrogant and loud in other ways. I was coming to Florida after putting it down all over Harlem, so I was ready. I'd been highly recruited by some of the biggest basketball programs in the country, and I knew most of these guys were still looking for a place to land. My silent cockiness was useful on the streets where I let my game do the talking.

In the first few scrimmages, I didn't see much competition from the freshmen and only marginal competition from the second-year guys. I had already played against some of the best talent in the world in New York, so I wasn't expecting any surprises. However, as it was when I first crossed paths with Kenny Hutchinson, I was surprised once again by unexpected talent.

My roommate Donnie was the first player I scrutinized. We were close to the same size, and it was natural to see if he was a threat to my playing time. I liked Donnie, but it wasn't going to be a problem if I had to suit up against him. It didn't matter who I liked, because I *loved* the game. I figured Donnie and I would still be tight, even if he had to play behind me.

In workouts, he didn't work as hard to push himself. No one liked doing drills, but something in me refused to be at the bottom rung when it came to the finish. I might not be first, but I was not going to be anywhere near last. But this didn't seem to bother Donnie as much as it should have. He was too good of an athlete to finish near the bottom of a suicide drill. Sometimes he just didn't want to do it. He lagged in the drills, but then he would beat everyone and their momma downcourt, looking for the ball.

Early on, the conditioning and drills were mostly psychological. We watched to see who finished last in sprints, which guy quit on the track or gave up. All of that meant something in the beginning. It was how you could gain an edge on someone, particularly if they played your position. On a new team, teamwork was rarely the focus starting out; it was about proving your worth and making your mark. Who was going to start? Who was going to get more playing time, or less? Who was going to get a major scholarship to a four-year school? That was part of the real framework and dynamics driving us on the court. Time at a junior college was short if you were trying to get somewhere in basketball, and everyone serious about the game knew this. There was no time to waste or have a bad stint.

Donnie ran like a gazelle. He had a smooth, fluid glide in his stride. He wasn't "outburst" quick, but he was deceptively fast and had explosive athletic skills. He also had a soft midrange shot from the outside that was as smooth as his glide. I could bomb from long range when I had to, and though Donnie wasn't a long-range shooter, he was just as accurate from the midrange. He exhibited maturity on the court I did not always display. I was more prone to make something happen than let it develop. But Donnie held back a little and could bide his time and pick his spots better.

As a result, he made fewer mistakes than most of the first-year guys. He didn't try to do what he couldn't and let things come to him, a rarity for players our age. On the other hand, out on the break he was a freak of nature, finishing with some of the most spectacular dunks I'd seen. We started calling him "Nique" after Dominique Wilkens, who was finishing up his career at Georgia. Donnie ran the floor and finished on the break like Nique. Maybe that was why he wore that part in the center of his head.

Dennis Pope was a niche player who wasn't going to fit on most teams. At first glance, he didn't seem to have any outstanding physical skill or special talent for basketball. He didn't jump high. He was strong and solid but not quick or particularly fast on his feet. He had no unique offensive skills related to basketball. I didn't think he could even make a layup with his off-hand, but he added value immediately. He already presented himself as the hardest worker on the team. He was a six-foot-five relentless rebounder, a fierce defender, and also a consummate passer from the pivot and high post. He reminded me of Bruce Dalrymple, who was never a natural scorer but was a relentless defender willing to fight for everything he got because he had to.

There was one other freshman besides Dennis, Donnie, and I who had unique gifts that immediately got my attention. From day one, it was obvious who the team's best athlete was. I felt good having finished the six-minute mile in my first few tries. Dennis completed his mile on the second day, but Ron Green, a six-foot-three guard from Greenville, SC, finished the event the first day he hit the track with a time of five and a half minutes. He murdered it and had plenty of time to spare.

Being groomed for the point, Ron was built like Atlas and showed raw athletic ability no one on the team could match pound for pound. He was our fastest guy, jumped higher than anyone, and was one of the strongest guys in the weight room. With second-year point guard Jerome Williams ailing from knee injuries, Ron was being positioned as his replacement and had few challengers at the point able to match his athletic ability.

In his first few days, he dunked on anything in his way. Mike Tate, our six-nine center who liked to block shots, was his most frequent victim. Tate had a disability; he had a nub for one of his hands, with several fingers missing. He concentrated primarily on defense. Tate was a good shot blocker, but shot blockers at times paid for their gift by getting embarrassed.

Ron was a beast who adjusted to the weight conditioning a lot quicker than most of us. He played football in high school and lifted weights year-round. Not pushing up a lot of weight in the weight room was a battle I had no choice but to concede to nearly everyone other than Smitty and Donnie. I had unusually long arms, and bench-pressing heavy weight was a struggle. When I looked over at Ron and saw him throwing much more weight up than I was, I knew it was an area I couldn't compete in. I was used to playing against heavier, stronger guys, so I wanted to make my point on the basketball court.

As I struggled in some of our workouts, Boes paired me with Andre Williams, the strongest and most physical guy on the team. Maybe he thought lifting with Dre would motivate me, or maybe he thought I was mentally tough enough not to feel insignificant or insecure at being matched with an experienced weight lifter. Either way, he got what he wanted. I started working a little harder with Dre pushing me.

• • •

PJC's campus was pleasant, not like the stories I'd heard about barren, isolated, run-down junior colleges in the middle of nowhere. Pensacola was a small town, but there was a beach culture mixed in with the military that brought people in from the outside. PJC felt like a four-year school, with plenty of open space, trees, and red-bricked buildings. They had a golf driving range and a golf course where military retirees played. If you really tried, it wasn't hard to convince yourself you were still in a good situation, or at least headed in that direction. We had a full scholarship, and a fifty-dollar-a-week stipend that included free room and board, which made it even more convincing.

Study hall was twice a week at the library. Wayne, our assistant coach, served as the team chaperone responsible for getting us around for the necessities. Because he was Filipino, we wondered how much he knew about American basketball. It was funny to watch him during pickup games, particularly when someone dunked. He'd get excited more like a fan than a coach.

Once the team was settled in, it was easy to see who liked to get high, who liked to drink, and who was "fien'in'" to get out to the clubs. Donnie smoked weed, but when he saw neither I nor Dennis got high, he chilled and was cool just hanging with us. I hadn't brought much gear (street clothes) with me, and I was never big into the clubs, so I wasn't going out on the weekends either. I knew from experience that a lot of guys who smoked weed were trying to deal with anxiety. It helped take the edge off a new situation.

The White guys smoked weed also, but alcohol was their drug of choice. Scott, Luddy, and Dan, who was from Michigan, drank beer on boring weekends. Luddy drank sometimes during the week. Smitty and Charles Davis didn't live in the apartments, but they came over on weekends to drink with the other three.

I couldn't relate to getting high. I had been around drug addicts and alcoholics all my life. My father was an alcoholic and Aunt Sister was a smoker, drinker, and drug user who died before her twenty-sixth birthday. I'd seen dope fiends growing up in Harlem, on the court, in the block, in my family; and it just didn't appeal to me.

I also believed I had an edge on people who got high. I believed they were weak. To me, they were trying to escape the real world by indulging in a fake one. If my body was clean and I was living and eating basketball exclusively, I figured I would come out on top. Sometimes I reflected on guys like Kenny Hutch and how we met for the first time in 1978. I thought Hutch was the best young player I'd ever seen at that time. He was confident, talented, and unstoppable, and playing at a level I was trying to get to. Over the years I watched as Hutch occasionally went with guys to get a forty, or showed up to games with eyes fiery red from smoking weed. I didn't make time for these extras and thought this took away from his game. It was all about basketball for me. I was on my way to being a pro, and smoking weed wouldn't help me get there.

Donnie was basically a by-product of the drug life. His brother was a successful hustler and his most important role model. Part of glamorizing ghetto life, for him, was getting high. We would stay awake for hours, swapping ghetto stories about the streets and what it was like to be in "the game." He filled me in on the major hustlers in Liberty City, the cocaine cowboys and Griselda Blanco, and I told him what I knew about street legends like Nicky Barnes, Fred Meyers, and Guy Fisher.

My drug abstinence confused some of the guys. I was from Harlem, a place known as the underground drug capital of the entire world. With Donnie being from Miami, some of the weed smokers on our team thought about all the drugs we could potentially get for them. Guys like Dre and Ron were always coming at us with drug talk and ideas for getting good weed.

Race relations on our team were cool on the surface. Donnie and I lived in the most integrated apartment with Scott and Luddy as our housemates. Dre and Jerome shared an apartment, each with their own rooms, and Dennis shared with Michael Tate and Fast Eddie Aaron. Ron was in an apartment with Dan and Charles Davis but spent most of his time at Jerome's place, complaining about Dan and Charles. If I had to guess, I got along better with the White guys on the team than either Donnie, who was tolerant if not friendly, or Dennis, who was hard and distant with the White guys.

Sharing an apartment with Luddy and Scott often felt like a conflict was looming, waiting for an opportunity to present itself. Typically, we liked different music, ate different kinds of food, and had developed different customs growing up. But everyone was respectful starting out since we were just getting to know one another. This changed slightly as the competition on the court got more intense.

Scott, Luddy, and Dan loved rock music and were pumping a song by the Stray Cats called "Rock this Town." I was first-generation hip-hop and liked rap and soul music. Donnie was heavy into soul and funk. He and I were jamming to Marvin Gaye, Rick James, and Curtis Mayfield. Scott was the only White guy who got into Black music. He was also the only White guy from a major city, Chicago. The variance in musical taste was one example of how different things moved us. How tolerant and mature we were about respecting those differences would be tested through basketball.

On any team there are conflicts. In biddy league, high school, college, pro, corporate, or even church league teams some level of disagreement usually exists among its members. It could be over a strategy, or it might be personalities or something else. Some conflicts are ignited or fueled by class, personality, or culture. Competition was just the thing to bring it out. After a few weeks, people knew who they liked and who they didn't. If you decided you didn't like a guy, that dislike might elevate your motivation, make you compete even harder, but things could escalate, and sometimes tempers got out of hand.

It didn't take me long to realize I didn't like Ron Green, and it had nothing to do with his prowess in the weight room or the fact that he was the best athlete on the team. And it wasn't that he was good looking in a young O. J. Simpson kind of way. What I didn't like was his cocky and arrogant behavior. This cat couldn't stop talking about himself. There was little he didn't know or hadn't done in the world, and he was only eighteen. He was his own biggest fan. It became irritating after a few weeks, and I wanted to humble him on the court.

Ron told everyone he was offered football and basketball scholarships to Georgia and Clemson. But I saw weaknesses in his game. He was strong and fast and could dunk with the best, but his overall basketball skills needed work. He wasn't polished. He struggled to his left, and though I respected his extraordinary athletic gifts, I knew I was better in every basketball skill category. He didn't have an outside shot, and his handle wasn't disciplined or exceptional, so despite his prowess physically, and his Ali-like trash-talking, Ron wasn't the greatest. He was the first player on the squad I got motivated for.

None of the Black players cared for Luddy and questioned why he was still on the team. Not tall by basketball standards but strong for his size, he liked to mix it up. The rougher it got, the more he liked to get into the fray. He didn't do a lot of talking; people would be yelling and threatening to fuck him up, and through all the yapping, Luddy hardly ever said a word. Then he would go out and undercut someone while they were airborne and act like he didn't do it. Ron took a swing at him during one session and had to be restrained. In another incident Dennis stepped into an emerging confrontation between Donnie and Luddy, and slammed Luddy to the floor with incredible force. It was an impressive show of brute strength. Luddy was short and stocky but still pretty strong. He had a wrestler's body. Despite this, Dennis flipped and slammed Luddy like he was a rag doll. Luddy liked to get under everyone's skin, but he didn't fuck with Dennis after that.

Luddy got into it with guys because of his approach to defense. He'd tap people's elbows as they went up for a shot and stick his knees out when someone got by him.

The tension carried over off the court where Luddy's personality bordered on obnoxious. His living habits left a lot to be desired; add in the alcohol problem, and he didn't get along with many of the White guys on the team either. He got into a scuffle with Dan after calling him soft in practice. Dan was six foot eight, Luddy five foot seven. The only guy who connected with Luddy and tried to look out for him was his roommate, Scott Petway.

Like many of the other guys, Donnie and I were living on our own for the first time in our lives. We pooled our money every week for groceries. With four of us living in the apartment, we could have had a hundred dollars' worth of groceries every week. But Donnie and I didn't like some of the grocery items Scott and Luddy liked and vice versa. Scott and I were more accommodating to the situation, but Donnie and Luddy were on thin ice with each other after a few weeks. It didn't bother me. I would be moving on in a year.

CHAPTER 30
THE ICEMAN COMETH AGAIN

PRECONDITIONING CAME AND WENT, and formal practice began. The weightlifting soreness evaporated, and our bodies adjusted to the physical routine. Unlike high school, I wasn't skipping classes at PJC, especially since there was no place to skip to. Away from the city, it was easier to focus, and my basketball schedule wasn't as demanding, so I guess Brendon's gamble was paying off. Also, the classes at PJC didn't require as much concentration. I thought they were too easy, but I wasn't going to say anything.

Skipping classes meant penalty laps on the track, two miles for every class missed. Running the track was enough of a deterrent for me. But a few players didn't care. Andre from SC, who we called "Big Dre," immediately established himself as his own man, and was usually on the track before every practice, working off penalty laps he accumulated, some from the previous season. Dre was solid muscle and gave the impression he liked people to know it. He and Boes didn't see eye to eye on most things, and Dre seemed to prefer civil disobedience to arguing with the coach.

He accumulated fifteen miles of penalty laps for missed curfews, practices, and classes. By the time formal practices started, he still had to hit the track before or after practice to work off the penalty miles to keep his spot on the team.

Dre liked hanging out and smoking weed. Nothing Boes did short of kicking him off the team was going to change that. His hangout partner from the previous year, Reggie Hawthorne, was a heavy weed smoker and received a scholarship to Florida State. According to the legend, Boes had even more trouble with Reggie. Right now, he needed Dre. He was our best inside player.

When real practice started, Charles Davis and I developed a preliminary rivalry. Charles became my "showcase" victim almost by default. We were both first-year guys, and though I was almost five inches taller than Davis, Boes made an informal announcement shortly after our scrimmage sessions that I was playing the off-guard position. I towered over all the other guards, including Ron Green, so this probably raised a few eyebrows.

Eddie Aaron was six foot two, Jerome was six foot three, and super athlete Ron Green was six foot three, making the guard slots heavily contested. With Charles, Luddy, and Smitty all under six foot one, we had seven guards with me at the two. Boes wanted a big guard who could score, and this was enough for challenges to start coming once practice picked up.

I looked at Charles, Smitty, and Luddy as nonfactors and no threat at all. They were smaller, slower, and not as skilled. I shot the ball a lot better and could handle the ball under pressure. After assessing them in a few pickup games, I marked them off my list. When Charles challenged me early on, it was almost embarrassing. He saw me as one of his immediate obstacles to playing time, and as a big target. But he was out of his league. I was a year older, had played against a lot better competition, and enjoyed all the physical and psychological advantages. Charles became my personal "guinea pig" and gave me a platform to show the other guys exactly what I brought to the table. I had to give the guy credit: he never backed away from the challenge.

There were plenty of big guards in New York. It wasn't that uncommon, and I was a product of a growing trend that began long before Magic Johnson became the biggest point guard in NBA history in 1979. My childhood icons comprised a mixture of guys from the parks and NBA, guys like Sam Worthen, Pete, Maravich, George Gervin, and Charlie Scott, big guards who could score and handle the rock. But over the years, as I became a better ball handler, I discovered an unseen undercurrent brewing in some of the smaller guys' heads when a taller player was doing a lot of ball handling.

Smaller guys, especially point guards, didn't like to see bigger guys making things happen with the ball. If a six-foot-six guy could handle, pass, and shoot the ball as well as they could, what was left for them to do? It nullified the role of smaller guards. I was on several teams in situations where some guys attempted to get the ball out of my hands so they could "do their thing," but in a lot of cases I did their thing better than they did their thing.

In our scrimmages, people randomly reached, trying to steal the ball from me every chance they got, and this provided several eye-opening offensive opportunities. The worst thing you could do was reach on a skilled and confident ball handler. It made it a lot easier to make a move and get where I wanted to on the court.

Once people saw my handle and ability to make things happen, they started playing back and giving me the outside shot to prevent me from driving or making them look bad. These two factors alone allowed me to provide an offensive showcase. After the initial two weeks of training and conditioning, I was doing whatever I wanted offensively, and no one had an answer.

Soon defenders were skeptical about pressuring me when I had the ball. Some of what I was doing was typical flamboyant New York City stuff— crossover to elude a defender, reverse behind-the-back dribble, between the legs into a crossover, reverse pivot spins, and then, whenever the guy was playing too far back, I'd pull up in the blink of an eye and hit the shot from the outside. Despite being the tallest guard on the team, I was one of the best shooters we had.

Almost like clockwork, my childhood namesake followed me 1,000 miles from Harlem to Florida. I came to Pensacola as James Washington. After a few weeks, everyone on the team was calling me Ice.

When formal practice started, Scott Petway took his turn to see if he could put the handcuffs on me. He started challenging me in one-on-one drills, Chicago versus New York. Boes detected what was going on and started matching it up so we could go head-to-head. Even when I was playing opposite Ron Green or Charles or Eddie Aaron at the off-guard position, it was usually Scott who picked me up on defense, not the opposing defending two guard.

Petway had the reputation for being our best defensive player. He took charges, even during pickup games, played the passing lanes well, and was aggressive. He was the perfect team defender, and his defensive rep and work ethic had carried over from the previous season. Despite working his ass off on individual defense, he was probably better in a team defensive scheme than in a one-on-one situation because he lacked speed. After I exhibited my offensive ability, he wanted to test himself against me.

The few times I'd been matched up against Ron Green, he was quick and eager to switch off at any opportunity. This told me what kind of guy he was. I didn't flinch when it was time to guard him. Even Charles Davis showed more determination when he tried to guard me. He was small and outmatched athletically, but he never tried to duck the assignment the way Ron did.

To make it interesting, Boes set up some scrimmages with the first-year guys going against second-year players. He told us he thought we were the best freshman he'd had since getting the coaching job at PJC. It may have been a smoke job, just something to keep our competitive spirits going, but we believed him because we already thought we were better than the second-year guys.

Playing together with Donnie, Dennis, and Ron Green, we were formidable. We didn't have a fifth stellar first-year guy, but the second-year guys had a hard time keeping up with us because we were definitely the better athletes on the team. The only second-year player with noticeable athletic ability was point guard Fast Eddie Aaron.

Green was a constant open-court threat. He ran as fast with the ball as he did without it. It was one reason he struggled with ball control. Ron was a leaper and had dunked on everyone who challenged him around the basket, including me.

On one play, he blew by Smitty on a fast break, and I was the first one back on defense when he came at me. Typically, I was good for at least two or more blocks a game and thought this was in the bag as Ron attacked the basket. He went up on one side where I contested the shot, but to avoid me, he glided around the basket to the other side for a fingertip hook dunk. It was forceful and impressive enough for everyone to talk about afterwards. Never one for letting another player's moves stifle me, I was impressed how he got that one off.

One of the problems with Green's game was that he only had one speed. There were no in-between gears; it was either full speed ahead or nothing. No feints, hesitations, or pump fakes, just speed and power. He was the most out-of-control player on the team, so it made him the most explosive and reckless. Dennis would mimic the theme music from *Rocky* when Green was around and started calling him Creed because he looked like the actor Carl Weathers from the movie.

Donnie and I were good outside shooters, and we both ran the floor well. When we were teamed with Ron and Dennis, no other combination of players fit better. Dennis took care of all the dirty work and played the pivot with reckless abandon. He played the high post better than anyone we had and continued to surprise everyone with blind passes that were usually on point.

The skills and capabilities among first and second-year players were oddly split between role players and athletic and creatively versatile players. The second-year guys were role players; each had a special purpose or talent. Petway was almost all defense. Dan was a six-foot-eight sharpshooter who could hit from the outside if left open but gave you little else, and Dre was a scorer who couldn't pass or handle the ball well but was a force inside. Michael Tate was our best shot blocker and a good defender but had no offensive skills. They all had blaring limitations. All except Eddie Aaron. Eddie was from New Orleans. Fast Eddie could play the one or two.

Jerome, our ailing point guard, was a solid fundamental player but offered no glaring ability. He wasn't fast, was a medium-range shooter, and had trouble keeping up with everyone on defense due to bad knees. He seemed to be a thinking player but was usually a step behind, which could be exploited. Jerome's plan was to hang on and hopefully get a scholarship to a small college somewhere, maybe in South Carolina.

Once we became entrenched in our practice sessions, news circulated around campus about how bad the boys from the city were. Donnie, Dennis, and I began to feel like something because we were playing well and brought new style to the campus. We started hanging and rarely went anywhere without each other. The small town began to open up to us.

Campus life got more interesting once we got to know some of the local community residents. Some students were team supporters. Most were trying to escape or advance out of Pensacola. Some guys like Curtis, a freshman who lived in one of the Black sections of town, became somewhat of a groupie and an admirer and started hanging out with us in the café and student union center during lunch.

"You from New Yawk, huh?" he asked me.

"Yeah."

"What position you play?"

"Playing the two right now."

"Man, big as you is? How you playin' guard? You betta git yo big ass down low!"

"Come out there and find out," I told him.

"Man, I can't believe you play guard."

"Ice can handle that rock," Donnie confirmed.

"You play?" I asked him.

"Yeah, man, I played in high school, but Boes don't want no niggas from round here on the team. All the Black players down here is on scholarships like you big shots. He don't pick up Black walk-ons, and I know I can play better than both them sorry-ass White boys y'all got."

"Yeah? Maybe you can try out next year," I said, acting concerned.

"What tryout? Boes don't even do tryouts; he just pick the people he want. Smitty and Charles, dem boys ain't have to try out."

"Damn. That's fucked up," I said.

The truth was I didn't care. I figured if you made the team at Smitty or Charles Davis's level, you weren't going to get much court time anyway. I also understood that some guys just wanted to make a college team. Curtis seemed like one of those guys, and since I was curious and wanted to show him what I could do, I took him to the court to see if he could play.

Despite his physical limitations of being only five foot six, I determined in less than ten minutes that Curtis was a shooter with a quick first step that was impressive. For fun we played one on one, my six foot six going against his five foot six. Curtis lost the game badly but proved he was probably right about Boes overlooking him. After my evaluation, I thought he could add more value than Smitty, Luddy, or Charles Davis. On the other hand, I thought he talked too much, and that could be a different kind of problem. I was focused on the idea of playing one year and leaving Pensacola. Curtis could have my spot next year if he wanted it, but I decided not to be too cocky and tell him that.

Talking to local people gave us a different perspective. There were a few rumors, true or false, circulating about Boes. Some said he couldn't coach; others said he was a redneck. But I had to wait and see. My reason for coming to Pensacola was more about trusting Brendan Malone, not Chip Boes. I didn't know him. After hearing what a few of the locals had to say, I regretted not doing at least a little research.

Donnie, Dennis, and I were from notable cities, so it didn't take long for our popularity to rise around PJC's campus. The local students seemed interested in meeting people from different places, especially well-known places like Miami, Baltimore, and New York City. When we walked into the cafeteria, people seem to know we were the "new" boys.

Andre was the most well-known player. I got the impression he was expected to be *the man* this year. His popularity on campus was slightly enhanced due in part to his appetite for weed, which took him into social circles not everyone was drawn into. Perhaps Boes knew about Dre's drug habit but felt he was too valuable to lose. He knew Luddy had an alcohol problem, but I couldn't figure out why he was holding on to him. Luddy was on scholarship and in his second year, but it was obvious he wouldn't play, and it looked like he had no shot at a scholarship to a four-year school.

It was a little different with Dre, who, like Ron Green, was a physical athlete. When he lifted weights, he handled the entire rack of plates on nearly every machine. Dre had a future as a bodybuilder, and his playing style reminded me a lot of Adrian Dantley, an extremely effective offensive weapon but a land lover who monopolized the offensive end of the court.

My on-court rivalry with Petway heated up in practice. He and Donnie were going at it extra hard too. Both played the three, but some of their tension was a derivative of the intensity between Scott and I trying to outdo each other. When Donnie and I played opposite each other, he played me as if he knew he couldn't stop me, but it wasn't like that with Petway. Petway always approached me like he was going to shut me down, and I always wanted to make sure he knew he couldn't. All of us played the three, so whoever won out in practice would probably get more time. The way our team was shaping up, we would probably end up playing two or three different positions.

Once I showed everyone Charles was no threat, I looked forward to matching up with Petway, but I wasn't winning all our personal battles. There were days Scott played me smart and I wasn't as effective. However, even on those days I wasn't able to get my way on offense, I convinced myself it had nothing to do with how Petway played me.

I locked horns with Scott because he took so much pride in his defense. He took it personal. Crushing his efforts was the ultimate conquest. In our confrontations, I wanted him to give up, concede the obvious, and look forward to matching up with someone else.

I'd broken guys down psychologically on the court and knew what to look for. Some started out full of intent, passion, and determination to slow me down. They might foul hard, grab, or hold, and I learned to keep cool and keep coming, like Joe Hammond. I would figure out what they couldn't stop and how to break down their resistance. You could sense when a defense-minded player's approach went from being aggressive and hard edged to tentative and skeptical. I would block his shot, and the best he could hope for was luring or tricking me into taking a bad shot and hoping I missed it or setting me up for a charge.

When you were lighting a guy up offensively, sometimes he let himself get consumed by what you were doing on offense, particularly if you laid down a spectacular move, or something unimaginable. I'd seen a lot of guys get so concerned about what I was doing on offense that it affected their own scoring ability.

If I had learned anything on the streets, it was that some people couldn't be stopped individually. I lived and breathed the reality that good offense beat good defense most of the time. It took great defense to even have a chance against a good offensive player.

In the pros, basketball was often about matchups. Some players could only be slowed down by a good team approach to defense. You had to double-team Kareem or run two people at a player like Andrew Toney because one guy wasn't going to stop them. I was slowly convincing Scott that all those mornings I spent practicing in the park had potentially made me one of those guys. But his ego and pride were at stake. He was intent on unraveling the depths and levels of my offensive ability, and I was up for the challenge. Scott and I became two natural rivals, one gifted on offense, the other determined on defense, as the rest of the team watched to see who would come out on top.

CHAPTER 31
ORANGE DREAMS

I WAS IN PENSACOLA two months and hadn't heard one word from Brendan Malone and began to wonder why. We didn't have a phone in the apartment, but due to our consistent communication when I was in New York, I thought I should have heard something from him by now. I'd gotten used to his calls, and it felt even more important now, particularly since coming to Florida was his suggestion.

Luddy passed me a few messages from "Uncle Bernie," Syracuse's second assistant, telling me he said hello, or that he asked how I was doing. But I didn't know Bernie. I had never spoken to him, so I wondered why no one was calling to talk to me. Bernie Fine was obviously the reason Luddy was in Pensacola. I didn't know it then, but Boes had planned to dump Luddy after last season, partly due to his drinking binges. This was before Brendan promised him a potential blue-chip prospect. I was the prospect. Once I committed to PJC, Bernie used this leverage to convince Boes to keep Luddy a second year. Luddy's second-year full ride had a lot to do with my decision to come to Florida. These were the kind of basketball politics I didn't know existed.

However, my social instincts were somewhat keen. When Luddy started giving me updates from Uncle Bernie, I shut him down quickly. I didn't like him thinking he knew more about my situation than I did. It felt like he was trying to impress me with his special SU affiliation, like he was with the "in" crowd of Syracuse basketball. And maybe he was; I just didn't care.

Further complicating matters and contributing to my growing paranoia and suspicion of Boes was when he started talking more and more in our practice sessions about the future. He was giving long speeches at team meetings about how he expected his first-year guys to develop the following year. Boes wasn't saying anything about me not being here next year, and it began to worry me.

Confident about my prearranged agreement, I hadn't been so quiet about leaving Pensacola at the end of the school year. Other first-year guys were planning to be around for the full two years, so my talk about leaving before the season even started had most likely gotten back to Boes.

I didn't know I was supposed to be hiding anything. One year at PJC, 1982 to '83. One year as a Syracuse red shirt 1983 to '84, followed by three years' eligibility at Syracuse, from 1984 to '87. The way I was developing, I was certain I didn't need all three years at Syracuse to reach the NBA. However, I never talked about any of these details with Coach Boes. I barely knew the guy.

Not hearing from Brendan and never getting a clear confirmation from Boes, I got spooked the more I listened to his team speeches after practice. Also, I couldn't help considering what some of the local Blacks were saying about Boes. November was right around the corner, and it really began to bother me. Brendan was always good with writing letters or sending little notes of inspiration to try and keep a guy on track. Was Syracuse no longer interested? Was I set up to play for Boes two years rather than one? It was a big deal for me, and I got more and more paranoid and suspicious. I decided to do something about it.

Coach Boes's basketball office was across the hall from our locker room. We had open access to it in the mornings and usually just before practice at one. One day when it was clear, I went into the office for something and decided to rifle through the desk. Unfortunately, it took no time to find something that changed my life forever. It was almost as if I was supposed to find it. There were two letters from Syracuse with my name on them, both from Brendan. They had been opened.

It was fairly easy to put things together in my head after that. Boes handled all of our mail. If I got a letter from Ma, which I had, he or Wayne were the ones to give it to me, unopened. Routing our mail through the office seemed like just another way for Boes to maintain control of what came in.

After finding the Syracuse letters, I figured Boes was just another White devil. But what was his agenda? There was a certain sense of satisfaction in knowing my suspicions were confirmed, but it was tempered with an anxiety I now felt I had to do something about. I couldn't just let this shit ride.

For some reason it brought me back to my relationship with Ernie Lorch at Riverside Church, and how he tried to manipulate me into choosing certain schools. He was probably calculating what monetary advantage he could leverage for "delivering" me. Maybe Boes was trying to manipulate the system in the same way. After all, he didn't know me, and he hadn't recruited me. I was just another instrument or tool to get where he was trying to go. I'm sure he aspired beyond PJC. The best way to work his way up was to win. And for him to win, he needed the best players he could get.

The satisfaction I initially felt after finding my letters quickly turned into bitterness and confusion. On the streets when someone decked you, or did you dirt, you had to hit them back. Not only did you have to hit them back, you had to hit them hard enough they thought twice about fucking with you the next time. Biding your time and playing the shell game wasn't how you fought on the street. How was I going to hit back in this situation?

Boes having destroyed the limited amount of trust between us, it was a race now to use Boes before he used me. Staying in Florida two years severely limited my chances of establishing exposure and attracting NBA scouts. However, staying one year really didn't do much for Boes unless I could help him win it all.

I didn't confront Boes right away. Mainly because I didn't know what to say. If I approached him and he lied, he might screw things up for me because I knew the truth. What if he took me out of the rotation or decided to sit me on the bench? I came to Pensacola hoping I would learn something, or maybe get a coach I could trust, someone who could help me become a better basketball player. Finding those letters told me Boes wasn't that guy.

Without the thread of respect keeping our relationship civil, my sudden distance with Coach Boes made our communication strained, and he began asking other players what was wrong with me. The tension was building in me, so in my next talk with Ma, I let her know what was going on. I wanted her to get in touch with Brendan and let him know too.

"Ma, I think these people down here tryin' to set me up."

"How are they trying to set you up? Don't you have a scholarship?"

"Yeah, but this coach down here ain't giving me all my mail."

"You haven't been getting the money I've been sending you?"

"Yeah, I been gittin' that mail. I'm talking about the mail from Syracuse."

"How do you know they're keeping something from you?"

"Cause I went in and checked the coach's office and found letters from as far back as September."

"Well"—she paused—"how are they tryin' to set you up?"

Ma understood some things, but the recruiting process wasn't one of them. She still wasn't aware of the deal I was trying to work out with Syracuse. As far as she was concerned, I made it out of high school and I was being sent to college for free. That was the bottom line. After waltzing through high school, I was doing something no one in our family had an opportunity to do. To her, Pensacola and Syracuse served the same purpose. It was a big deal for a Black kid coming out of Harlem to be sent away for school.

"Ma, they tryin' to set me up cause I'm only supposed to be down here for one year, remember? I don't want to spend two years in Florida because it takes up two years of my eligibility to play ball on TV. Wit three years at Syracuse I have a much better chance for the pros."

"James, you need to settle down and concentrate on your schoolwork. That's why you had to go down there in the first place, isn't it?"

"Yeah, Ma, but—"

"Just settle down. Things will work out."

I knew Ma was probably just happy to have me out of the house and not running the streets. To her, nothing other than that seemed to matter.

Talking with Ma did settle me down—for about an hour, before reverting back to thinking about Boes and his motives. When I really thought about it, what good did it do his program for me to stay one year? I was talented, probably more talented than anyone we had, but it would take at least a year for me to mature physically and learn his system. The strength and conditioning alone was going to make me a much better player the following year. With a nucleus of Donnie, Dennis, Ron, and I playing two years, his chances for success were a lot better. I wasn't the only one trying to move up the line.

When I confronted Donnie with "the goods" I had on Boes, he didn't seem surprised. Maybe he was more seasoned than I was.

"Man, ain't it against the law to hold someone's mail? How can Boes do this shit!?"

"Ice, coaches do this shit all the time. These fuckas is crooked."

"Yeah, Don, but I can't let Boes fuck up my time here."

"I'm telling ya, Ice, Miami-Dade is probably tryin' to git to me right now to transfer down there, and damn they got a team!"

"Donnie, I ain't talking about Miami-Dade. I'm talking about Syracuse next year."

"But you killin' 'em in practice, Ice. You'll be there!"

Looking briefly at Donnie as though he was crazy, I tried to understand this young dude from Miami I had known all of two months. He already felt like a brother, a real brother. He understood me in a way that didn't require a lot of communication. We were so much alike, in circumstance and spirit, we became close in a very short period of time.

The thought of being in Pensacola for two years was probably the single scariest possibility in my life at this point. There was a lot riding on my coming to Pensacola, and I knew I was on fragile ground, having blown so many chances for going straight into major college ball, but here I was.

I thought Syracuse was not only the right fit for me but possibly my last hope. They were high profile, and Jim Boeheim was a coach who favored a more liberal approach to offense. I *knew* Syracuse was perfect for my style of play. The Orangemen, St. John's, and lots of other East Coast colleges seemingly understood New York City basketball players. All I could think about was the holiday tournaments and Big East conference games at the Garden and inviting all my boys down to watch me play. I wanted to rep Harlem on the largest stage the world had to offer.

Being red-shirted for a year made prospects even sweeter for the NBA. In 1983 I'd have a whole season to work on my game and feel out other guys on the team. A whole year of development at Syracuse—weightlifting, running, practicing, getting acclimated academically—followed up by three full years of playing eligibility was a yellow-brick road to the NBA. If I didn't get into the league with that kind of road map, it meant I was never supposed to be there in the first place.

Pearl Washington wasn't in the picture yet, but people were already saying he signed early with the Orangemen. This made things even sweeter. Pearl's rep in New York City by 1982 was on an epic level. He already had a national name. I knew from watching and playing against Pearl that our basketball abilities were extremely complementary. I could see headlines of Pearl and Ice in the newspapers. Chip Boes convinced me he could threaten these dreams.

CHAPTER 32
BOOSTING

I WASN'T THE ONLY player who had issues with Coach Boes. Donnie, who spent a lot of his time and money on the roadside pay phone, was homesick. He had never been away from Miami and felt he was forced to leave. We were the same age, and like me, Donnie spent extra time in high school. It was his hustling older brother, Cornell, who made him trek nearly 400 miles from Miami to Pensacola. If it were left up to him, he would be home, attending Miami-Dade Junior College with a few of his friends and near his girlfriend and daughter. Miami-Dade had one of the best junior college basketball programs in the country, and their football program was said to be even better.

Dennis, our inner-city comrade, wasn't too happy either. He didn't like the social dynamics in Pensacola. Dennis was from West Baltimore and thought Boes gave preferential treatment to White players. It wasn't far-fetched. Boes may have understood them in ways he didn't his Black players, and it could be easier for him to communicate with some of his White players than his Black ones.

The White guys weren't as athletic, but with the exception of Dan, they generally worked hard in practice, including Luddy, who tried his best to out-hustle everyone. It didn't mean the Black guys weren't working as hard, but with Ron Green and Donnie running and leaping like thoroughbreds, and me pulling off the occasional unbelievable move every now and then, it was glaringly apparent who had more natural physical talent.

Dennis thought Boes bent over backwards for Scott Petway. Scott wasn't an angel, but he had heart, was a consummate team guy, and usually played hard. He developed a rapport with Boes. I doubt any of the Black players trusted Boes or the system he represented to any great degree; consequently, many of us harbored individual ideas, or self-serving thoughts, despite being a part of the team. Trust existed on the thinnest of threads, especially when a team was just coming together.

A lot of athletes that ended up in junior colleges came with an assortment of issues. Poor grades, risky home life, underexposure, violence, drugs, and crime all came into play. There were also guys from stable families and good homes who hadn't been highly recruited, but who had decent grades and could really play. Junior college was all about trying to get a full ride to a four-year school. Dennis, Donnie, and I were already on edge about being in Pensacola. We weren't sure it was the right decision. Once I broke the news about Boes withholding my mail, it only made the situation more tense and suspicious.

It was during these negativity jam sessions that Donnie, Dennis, and I began stealing. There was a corner convenience store toward the end of the road near our apartments where we helped ourselves to things located in the back of the store. We copped Brut cologne, soap, lotion, wave hair grease, deodorant, and anything we could get our hands on. So much stuff from the shelves would be missing after our visits that the store clerk knew what was up within a couple of weeks. Soon, the corner store wasn't enough. We began venturing to the town mall.

Pensacola was a small town. It was nothing like Miami, Baltimore, or New York, and we knew it. Before long, our big-city personas were dictating our newfound criminality in a way that made us feel bigger and smarter, rather than feeling ashamed, smaller, or ignorant. Playing up the negativity toward Boes, our stealing became a bond between us. We reveled in our spoils and in depicting the slick, city hustlers we were supposed to be. Then, Dennis came up with another bright idea. He said we should start boosting to make a little extra cash.

Growing up, I saw guys boosting goods in the block all the time. They came through barbershops, stores, parks, and some of them even made house calls. Boosting was so prevalent in Harlem that some people put in requests and scheduled days to pick up their goods. This was part of the hustling culture, the getting-over syndrome you learned from day one in Harlem's streets, where you either got over or someone got over on you.

Usually when someone came through the block selling something, no one asked where he or she got it. Even hardworking, churchgoing, Bible-reading people bought stuff off the street if they could use it. There was a different code in the ghetto. The working poor, presented with an option of buying something that was most likely stolen or turning down something needed, would buy the stolen stuff almost every time. It was never viewed as immoral or criminal, but just another means of making ends meet.

The fact was, in Pensacola our ends were already meeting, so there was no need to steal. We had free room and board, and each of us had a fifty-dollar-a-week per diem for expenses. Add the fact that Ma would send me fifty dollars every now and then, and I wasn't wanting for much. There was no reason for trying to boost other than our own defiance to the real world and what we thought it represented.

We were amateur thieves at best, but our confidence was bolstered by how easy it seemed to be to get away with it. At the grocery stores we piled extra cold cuts, steaks, and cereal boxes into our gym bags. If we spent twenty-five dollars, walking out with fifty dollars' worth of food was likely. Dennis was the most demonstrative.

"Man, you see all the shit I got? This town is wide open. We can rob these crackas blind. From now on, all I'm eatin' is steaks, every night."

Taking life-altering risks somehow solidified the bond between us. The respect for each other's city lifestyle was the baseline for our understanding, but aside from that, we simply liked one other.

"Ice, that boy crazy. He ain't gon stop till he git caught," Don would say.

"Yeah, I know. When you gon stop, Donnie?"

"Probably after I git my little daughter some clothes. I wanna send her something. Whatever I can get, I'll sell and buy her some clothes or something. What about you, Ice?"

"Maybe jus some more clothes, probably something for winter—didn't think we needed winter stuff in Florida." I tried to grasp any justification I could for my larceny.

"Yeah, this ain't like Miami," Donnie confirmed.

I already knew boosting was a foolish prospect in Pensacola. We were highly visible, and none of us were the proficient thieves we thought we were. Still, the prospect of getting nice new clothes was an appealing enough prospect for us to forge ahead on our reckless, rebellious, and defiant path.

CHAPTER 33

BENCHED

OUR FIRST GAME AGAINST an outside opponent was against a team from Atmore, Alabama. It wasn't a league game, but it didn't matter since we were all itching for action and tired of beating up on each other in practices and scrimmages. Leading up to the Atmore game, we played a freshman versus sophomore scrimmage for the fans.

In practice, Boes switched the lineups often. We weren't really sure who the starting five were, but a few guys were consistently in the main rotation. Petway, Dennis, and Fast Eddie Aaron were almost always in the first rotation. I expected to start, but so did Donnie. Boes seem like the kind of guy who didn't start freshmen based on principle, but he had to discard that rule since Dennis didn't have a rival at center. He was definitely our best pivot player.

Our game was on a Saturday night. In Harlem, Saturday was always my favorite day to play or watch a big game. The streets literally came alive on Saturday nights in a way that didn't happen on other nights. The music would flare from the parks, turntables and speakers were plugged into the streetlamp post, and people were hanging out, anticipating the action. The adrenaline was tangible, and the animated crowds helped make those Harlem afternoon games what they were. I wondered how the Pensacola crowd would feel.

The PJC fans came out in full force, anxious to see their new team. Some came to see how the new city boys would play. There was enough speculation around campus. During warm-ups, Donnie and I scanned the crowd for girls sitting in clusters, going from cluster to cluster, looking briefly at faces and then conferring with each other about who was fine and who wasn't while running the layup line.

Ron Green pulled off tight dunks on the line, the kind of dunks that made spectators gape and cheer. Donnie and I were running a close second. Donnie had a dunk where he double-pumped and reverse-dunked it on the opposite side of the rim off a one-leg stride. It was an impressive statement. My most eye-catching dunk was a one-handed 360, a full rotation and extension before slamming it through. I had another where I tapped the glass with the ball before pumping the ball up from my knees and dunking it backwards. None of the second-year guys were dunkers, so Donnie, Ron, and I were the only guys pulling off eye-openers on the layup line. Dennis wasn't much of a dunker either, but his substitute for flair and style was raw power. Donnie glided like a gazelle, and Ron was jumping so high and dunking so hard that we had the crowd going wild before the game even started.

Looking down on the other end, the other team looked good warming up. They had some highflyers too, and nice uniforms and warm-ups. Since coming to Florida, I recognized that there were a lot of good players who simply didn't have the grades to attend Division I schools. Donnie, Petway, Eddie Aaron, Andre Williams, and Ron Green were all legitimate Division I prospects who, like me, were grudging it out in junior college.

Dennis was the only freshman to start the game. No one had beaten me out in practice, so I wondered why I was coming off the bench. Did it have something to do with my Syracuse letters? I tried anticipating how long it would be before I got into the game. It wasn't long.

The place buzzed with anticipation. Upon entering the game, I missed my first two shots right off the bat. They were easy ones, and not heavily contested. Nerves. My teammates gave me a few more opportunities to get on track. As fate would have it, good defense provided my first offensive opportunities. I blocked two shots and scored my first basket on a steal before I got things under control on offense.

Once comfortable, I started grabbing defensive rebounds and going the length of the floor to score or pass for an assist. Boes seemed to encourage my doing so. I had a slower guy on me and began making moves, changing directions, and reversing the ball quickly to create space. The guy had trouble reacting to sharp-angled moves, and I could get open almost every time. Donnie presented similar problems for his defenders because he was quicker than most power forwards, and though not a great ball handler, he was devastating on the break and able to outrun most guards.

The game ended without me on the floor, and we won easily. Eddie Aaron led the scoring with twenty-three points, with probably half of those on fast breaks. I was right behind him with nineteen despite playing less than half the game. Dre and Donnie were the only other players in double figures, and Dennis grabbed fourteen rebounds, something Boes was quick to point out after the game. He made a point of emphasizing that you can't run fast breaks without the ball. My six rebounds were somewhat insignificant; four of them were offensive. I got the feeling Boes didn't want to get too excited about scoring points and wanted us to know how important it was to rebound the ball and play defense. Dennis only had eight points, but his rebounding and defense was a key factor in the win.

The next day, Eddie, with his mischievous, boyish New Orleans grin, grabbed a newspaper off one of the tables at Shoney's. With no other academic colleges in the area, the PJC Pirates were the most important sports interest in the local scene. The write-up in the paper labeled me as a "freshman sensation from New York." My nineteen points had come in small binges but were more than enough to show ability.

My first college game was behind me, and my GPA was a 3.0, so I tried to be content with how I felt about Boes and getting to Syracuse. Two more weeks passed. Then one afternoon, everything changed again. Scott Petway walked into the apartment with a letter from Georgia Tech.

Of course, he was excited, and word circulated. It was early in the season, so it was a very good sign for his future prospects. Getting a letter now meant he was on somebody's list and had someone's attention at Tech. I couldn't help but feel good for him because he was the kind of dude you wanted to feel good for. I had a lot of questions of my own, but didn't ruin his moment, so I let him know.

"I spoke to Cremins a few times back when I was in New York."

"So, what's he like?"

"He's cool. I think he's from the Bronx."

"Yeah, can't wait to talk to this guy. ACC is a good conference."

"Mos def. So, Scott, when did you get your letter?"

"It came in yesterday. Boes left it in my locker."

Scott wasn't the only guy receiving college letters. I found out other players not named James Washington had gotten their college letters from Boes. Dan received a few letters from Michigan and one from the University of Wisconsin. Eddie got a letter from the University of New Orleans, his hometown. These were all second-year guys, but I knew for certain now that there was no chance Boes was doing right by me.

Boes genuinely liked certain players and perhaps he just tolerated others. He liked Petway and Smitty and even horseplayed with Luddy on occasion. With the exception of Jerome, who was a de facto liaison between Boes and the Black guys on the team, Boes tolerated a lot of other guys because he needed to.

When it came to talking off the court, about our personal lives, Boes had to rely on Wayne or Rome to get a read on his Black players. In some ways, he was never going to understand what made me tick, especially since I hadn't figured it out for myself. He didn't relate well to other Black guys on the team either, at least not in the way he did with Scott, Dan, or Smitty. It wasn't easy. Our life experiences couldn't have been further apart. Maybe it was too big of a jump for him to make.

On the other hand, we understood how Boes's world worked. His was the normal world, which in many ways excluded Harlem, Liberty City, and West Baltimore in a way we couldn't exclude his world.

Instinctively I suspected some of what bothered Boes most about me. I had possibly even contributed to his concerns. Even under the best of circumstances, I was naturally quiet and didn't like to show my hand, something that put most people off balance. Boes wasn't able to gauge what I was thinking or feeling. I rarely elaborated on anything, and people had no idea if I was inarticulate, uninterested, or pissed off. One-word answers worked for me, and I preferred selective silence among people I wasn't comfortable around. If I wasn't comfortable or didn't trust you, you weren't going to get much from me.

Another thing that may have concerned Boes was how we came into our coach/player relationship. I was an incoming freshman, planning to stay one year, and letting this be known. Maybe he saw me as a New York City hotshot, getting letters from Syracuse three weeks into the semester and using his program as a pit stop.

Like any coach, he intended to use my talent to win games. When Brendan presented the plan for attending PJC for a year, I felt no need to hide it from anyone. One year of structured discipline and organization was the only thing I came looking for in Florida. Staying two years might win more games for Boes, but what did it do for me? At the end of the day, I was little more than a business transaction between PJC—a smaller, less significant, farm system–conduit junior college institution—and Syracuse, a big, NCAA university within the NCAA Division I machine. I needed them to get to the NBA, and they needed guys like me to justify and sustain their careers.

To say I was eager going into our second game was an understatement. I was planning to have a huge game. I needed something to divert attention from what was really on my mind. Leading up to the game, my practice sessions were top notch because I wanted to start. Physically, I'd adjusted to our routine, and after scoring nineteen points in less than twenty minutes, I was looking to have a breakout game.

I learned a lot about myself playing against my natural rival Scott Petway. We also played a lot of one on one after practice. The more we played, the easier it was to play against him. I learned his defensive strategy, and then I'd beat him by doing something he wasn't prepared for or couldn't stop. After his Georgia Tech news, I was determined to step up even more, adding a few playground signatures, like looking him in the eye after shaking him up. Sometimes I pulled up for a shot in the middle of a play, launching it from an unreal distance with no hesitation and hitting nothing but net just to fuck with him and Boes. Dunking on a guy could embarrass him, but there were many ways to demoralize someone on the court. When I hit unreal shots, shots I wasn't supposed to be taking in the first place, it sucked some of the life out of whoever was guarding me.

It wasn't Scott's fault he got his college letters and I hadn't, but in practice I was sending a message to Boes and using Scott to do it. Pulling out all of the stops, I used everything in my offensive arsenal and played with more purpose leading into our second game. Offense was what I knew best; finger rolls, jump hooks, spins, half spins, fadeaways, crossovers, dunks, stutter-step dribbles, and hesitation moves were my offensive weapons. I wanted to show everyone why I was headed to Syracuse.

On game night, like clockwork, who was the main person in my ear making sure I was ready to go? It wasn't Donnie or Dennis, but Scott, letting me know he was ready to kick some ass.

The entire team was intense in this kind of way. They took mental preparation to a level I hadn't experienced. Some of them had come from really competitive high school teams, places where you lived and died according to the school colors and sang the school song. Boes promoted this kind of mentality, displaying a psychological routine of his own by staring you down to make sure you were ready. It felt as if he was searching for a certain look. I doubt I had it.

In practice he reinforced this "look" and the importance of playing hard. Sometimes I'd stare back at him momentarily and then go out and do my thing. It was nothing deliberate on my part—just another example of Boes not knowing how to read who I was or how to reach me. My game face was no game face. I'd learned how to keep myself under control by watching guys like Joe Hammond and how they handled pressure.

In some ways, Boes didn't know what to expect from me even on the basketball court. We had never gotten to know one another, and that was usually the way it was with junior colleges and highly recruited athletes. The JC was a last resort, an indication that I'd fucked up somewhere. Players like me only went to a JC when they ran out of mainstream basketball options and didn't want to be home on the streets.

I was used to picking up a ball, getting on the court without stretching, and playing with the best. All the looks, stares, and glares people were walking around the locker room with cracked me up. None of that shit mattered on the court. They were acting like they were preparing to go to war or to the South Bronx to play. Either way you might get shot. But what was at stake in Pensacola? I didn't have to worry about catching a stray bullet, or about some cat trying to cap me because he's pissed about betting a lot of money on a game. On this level, all you had to do was play, so where was the pressure?

When it came to fundamentals, and the basics of the game, it was easier for me to take them for granted. Even if fundamentals could help get me to the NBA, I didn't believe they would keep me there. Not leaving your feet to make a pass and setting up for a charge were things I learned but didn't always execute. Charles Davis and Scott were more fundamentally sound than I was, but it hadn't done them any good when they had to guard me. They were taught the game, but I had lived and experienced the game in my own way.

Anyone could be taught basketball fundamentals. I was used to seeing and doing things on the court that couldn't be taught. In my mind this was more significant. You couldn't teach a person how to fly like Connie Hawkins or shoot the rock like Joe Hammond. What kind of fundamental teaching could teach a person to run like Gayle Sayers, Earl Campbell, or Tony Dorsett? My game was hardwired to my inner being, and to who or what I was evolving into. I lived for opportunities to display the playground-honed skills that made me fall in love with the game. The love I'd developed, nurtured, and fortified in Harlem motivated my life.

Despite coming in on a high and feeling prepared for my second college game, the irony of life once again reared its head. This was a game where I wished I'd given fundamentals more consideration. I'd had bad games before, but I usually attributed my bad play to my own mistakes, rarely giving the defense credit for anything. This night was my baptism in confronting a structured college defense.

It was a game when you didn't risk dribbling on a zone or a press defense without tempered caution. It was a game you didn't leave your feet to block shots but played position defense. It was a game when you pulled up in the lane rather than driving further to the basket and risking an offensive foul. It was a game where you had to consistently position yourself for rebounds rather than relying on your jumping ability. This was a game in which I did very little if any of those things, leading to one of the worst games I played since acquiring my marketable basketball skills. When it was over, I had four points, nearly twice as many turnovers, three rebounds, and four fouls, three of which were offensive. I played five more minutes than in my previous game and had produced far less.

We trailed the entire game, and Boes kept putting me into the game at critical times, hoping I could spark the offense. Each time, my decisions became worse. I wasn't adapting or concentrating in a game that required both. I threw away passes, spun into double teams, and committed three charging fouls in the first half alone.

My performance was so contrary to the first game that Boes and Athletic Director Kearns wanted to talk with me after the game to quiz me about my social activities. Was I getting enough rest? Had I been drinking the night before? Was I following the curfew? My demeanor remained stoic. I guess they were reaching for anything to get a bearing on me. As was customary, I answered their questions with solemn, one-word responses, with little elaboration or emotion. This seemed to baffle them as much as my poor performance. I couldn't remember playing a worse game but didn't see the need to be remorseful about it. I felt bad, but I wasn't sorry.

I'd never used drugs, had never smoked a joint or cigarette, so the drug question insulted me. I was bothered more by how little they actually knew about me. I came in with a certain profile, having lived in Harlem and played most of my significant basketball on the streets and playgrounds, so maybe Boes and Kearny thought drugs wasn't such a big leap.

I didn't feel I owed them an explanation. Suspecting they were out to use and exploit me anyway, I didn't provide any specifics about why or how it happened.

I felt bad for letting myself and the other guys down. I knew I couldn't let it happen again. A good player did his thing in the game and practice. I wanted everyone to know they could depend on me in a game when they needed to. Since I had become psychologically detached from our head coach, I needed the support of my teammates even more. Dre was probably the only guy it would be difficult to win over to my side. I got the sense Dre wasn't on anyone's side, but especially not mine.

Dre and I weren't as close as people who had as much in common as we did normally were. He was from Columbia, South Carolina, where I had plenty of relatives. I knew the region. He also had people in Reevesville and Orangeburg, towns very close to where I spent many of my preteen summers. Despite this, we rarely talked to one another.

He didn't envy city life or the life of the Northerner and seemed to have a particular disdain for it. He occasionally made scant remarks about crime that implied people from the city were natural criminals and lacked moral values.

I figured Dre could influence others to not trust me or to suspect me of things I hadn't done. If something was missing, I was the nigga from Harlem, the slick cat always looking for an angle. In some ways, I was the typical suspect profile even among Black guys on the team, so I never played up my Harlem background. I proved to most of them I was good people who knew how to mind my business and get along. Donnie talked all the time about street life, but inside, he wasn't that dude either. Even as thieves, we weren't in it so much for the money as we were for being seen as hip and getting over.

This contradiction was one I wasn't completely aware of at the time. I was in Florida stealing but didn't want people to think I was a criminal or had criminal tendencies. I didn't mind the positive assumptions people inferred from my Harlem background, but on the other hand I didn't want the negative preconceptions I'd gone out of my way to reinforce. It was quite a paradox.

More notable than the city and country contrast between Dre and I was our contrast on the court. This made our relationship all the more contentious. Our styles should have complemented one another, but once our personalities were in conflict, it carried over into social life. The tension started during the first few weeks of pickup games in the gym. That's when I saw that Dre and I were probably the best scorers on the team. This guy could put the ball in the basket. As a freshman last season, he scored over forty points in a single game. He was big and strong and had a decent medium-range jump shot.

The animosity began when we had to play together. His methods irritated me. He demanded the ball in almost any situation, as if his matchup were always the best advantage. He was prone to go into his Adrian Dantley ball-monopolizing routine at any time. It slowed the entire game down.

In order for anything to work with Dre, it had to revolve around him. If it didn't, you might as well have been playing against six players rather than five. Like Dantley, he rarely forced a shot, and he was never in a hurry, which in a lot of ways was a good thing for a young player. I was irritated because it just took too damn long. Dre took such a long time to do whatever he was trying to do that it messed up everything else.

In comparison, I was a slasher. My moves were quicker and consumed considerably less time. There was less deliberation when I was on the attack. Either I was going to score or I wasn't, but it was determined fairly quickly in most situations. However, as was typical with a city style of play, there were times when I might dribble through one or two defenders and sometimes even a third to get where I was going. Dre hated that, no matter the outcome. He didn't like me grabbing the rebound and initiating the action either. But as far as I was concerned, it was what I was born to do.

When Dre created a vacuum on the court, everything and everyone stood still. Moving without the ball must have been a crime to him because he never did it. In our pickup games his team usually lost, but he never seemed to think he had anything to do with it. When I happened to be on his team, I heard his voice almost the moment I snagged a rebound: "Slow down, ain't no hurry"—code words to wait until he got downcourt to go into his one-man act.

What mattered most to Dre was that he had the ball in his hands. Even though I liked to score, it never mattered how. I didn't prefer scoring outside or inside. I scored off the dribble, right, left, off the ball, on a zone, or man-to-man defense. Individual practice and studying other players prepared me to score in most situations.

On the other hand, Dre was always looking for his comfort zone on the court, the place he liked to score, and consequently, he needed time and space to get there. He hadn't grown up on the playgrounds where it was essential to develop intuitive and creative talents if you wanted to get somewhere. He and I tolerated one another in the beginning, but he always had something negative to say if I didn't direct a pass in his direction or missed a shot that had a high degree of difficulty.

Despite this tension, Dre was the least of my worries now. By the time our next game rolled around, I had worked my way into Boes's doghouse. After my terrible game, a cold stare or sullen response in practice became intolerable for him. Soon, he took me out of the normal rotation. Determined not to let it bother me, I remained emotionless and expressionless over these actions. Boes face would get beet red as though it were sabotage.

Boes planned to get me in line. Our next opponent was Atmore again, this time at their gym in Alabama. Boes sat me the entire game, something even I didn't see coming. It was the first time in my life I sat the bench for a game I was physically able to play in. Even more crushing was when he put Charles and Smitty in the game in garbage time. Boes was trying to get a handle on my attitude. We won the game in Atmore, and the message was clear: "I don't need you to win."

My basketball talent overshadowed everything else about my personality. Something prevented me from showing emotion, especially when I didn't think it necessary. I viewed Boes as a phony and struggled to adjust my attitude enough to put him at ease. I hadn't learned to play the game away from the game.

I was so fucked up in the head after sitting the bench. I looked around the stands to see who noticed. As if I knew people in Alabama. I avoided looking directly at Boes because I wanted to sucker punch him. Obviously shaken I hadn't played, I didn't know what to say or how to act. My expectations for redeeming myself after my poor performance were extremely high. Donnie kept telling me not to worry about it, but even he didn't know what to say to me when I rode the pine the whole game. Scott put into words some of what I was feeling.

"Ice, you should be startin' on this fucking team, but you lettin' Boes fuck with your head. I mean, you do shit I ain't never seen before."

"Scott, this muthafucka is crooked. I think he out to fuck me over down here."

"Most of these coaches is crooked, Ice. That's the game. You got to play the game. I tell these mothafuckas whatever they want to hear as long as I can get something out of it, cause that's what they're doing."

But I never learned the game Scott was talking about. The game off the court was not often taught where I lived. You couldn't learn this game in Harlem's playgrounds, and I was late in my exposure to it. What we did learn was if a mothafucka hit you, then you made sure to hit his ass back. And Boes had hit me pretty hard.

Scott was quite a character. He really got fired up. I wouldn't trust all that passion in a policeman's uniform, but it seemed to work fine for basketball. Scott was probably the funniest guy on the team and played just as emotionally as Dennis did. We developed a mutual respect and rapport with one another in a way no other Black and White player on the team did.

Boes's gamble on benching me was meant to jolt me and it did. He thought sitting me down would light a fire in me he could see, something he could gauge. He was right, but the fire didn't burn in the way he expected. Playing ball was the only incentive I had for being in Pensacola. If I couldn't play, then everything else became blurry and distorted. Basketball had a drug-like effect on me, and withdrawal from it in any way was going to be a problem.

Boes used a singular incident in practice, a bad pass, to take me out of the normal rotation. With my rep for being a big-time prospect, he may have thought it was good discipline to take me down a peg. He wanted to see some sense of urgency and dedication from me.

But I had peeped Boes's hole card. What I saw was a coach whose ability was superseded by his talented players. I saw a man lying and out to use me for his personal benefit. I saw him as an enemy who was playing the game how it was set up to be played. And part of the game was to use me as best he could. I was supposed to be getting something I could use in return, but it no longer felt like I was.

I reacted like the years of socialization in Harlem suggested I would: I became negative and hostile. I resented his position, which enabled him to pimp my talent when he seemed limited in his own coaching ability. Several scenarios might explain his inexperience. Maybe he was a frustrated athlete looking to build a career managing players he could never compete with. Or maybe he was a glorified fan with big ideas for moving up the industry chain. It was obvious I didn't know who he was. I didn't know his history or his coaching track record. All I knew was that he was now firmly in my path for getting to Syracuse.

Maybe Scott was right. Maybe Boes was the industry standard. I knew most coaches and recruiters were liars. Bob Zuffelato lied to me so easily that he must have been living a lie. As the head coach of Marshall

University, he came to New York to fish in the big pond and catch a bigger fish. Zuffelato did everything he could to get me to sign, never bothering to meet my mother. He spoke about his program, about where I fit into it and what they offered. Then he took another job with the Golden State Warriors before the start of the next season. This was the business.

Most gifted players, particularly the ones emerging from the inner cities, weren't prepared to deal with recruiters. A lot of us were chasing short money, temporary fixings when it came to our basketball future. But the NCAA was about the long green, it was about CREAM. Nobody I knew playing ball was a businessman. We were athletes, so we weren't prepared to deal at this level.

Coaches and athletic directors, driven by this paradigm, were the ones in business. Some were better businessmen than coaches. And some were simply salesmen selling dreams. They needed to win to justify their careers, and they needed players like me to win. It was no different than a major corporation recruiting the most qualified employees to grow their bottom line.

CHAPTER 34
POP

OUR NEXT ROAD TRIP was to New Orleans, Eddie's hometown, and I was looking forward to it. We were playing in a three-day tournament, and I didn't think Boes had enough nerve to bench me again as he had in Alabama. I was hoping so, anyway.

The trip was a big deal because it was New Orleans. Second-year guys had been talking about it since I arrived in August. However, the budget only allowed ten to travel, and there were twelve of us. Prior to my rift with Boes, it could be assumed that Luddy and Smitty or Luddy and Charles Davis would stay behind. Now I wasn't so sure. I couldn't help thinking about Pistol Pete, one of my idols, and his career in New Orleans. I got excited just talking about Pistol.

"Donnie, what you think about Pistol Pete?"

"He's okay."

"You don't think he's one of the best of all time?"

"Hell no, Ice!"

"Why not?"

"He ain't done shit, ain't won nothin' since he left college."

"Done nothing? He dropped sixty-eight points on Clyde and Earl Monroe. That ain't nothin.'"

"Awww, Ice, that White boy ain't that good. If he was, he would have done more than he done by now."

"Man, you crazy. Pistol one'a the baddest mothafuckas out there."

Donnie was all the way wrong about Pete Maravich, so we argued nearly an hour about it, even though I had to admit Pistol's career hadn't been as explosive in the NBA as it could have been. He was never in a winning situation. It didn't stop me from believing in his talent. He wasn't the best player in the league, but when it came to pure talent, I still felt he was among the best. The New Orleans Jazz would eventually move the team to Utah, where Pete, struggling with injuries, would get traded to Boston, a city where the White basketball player was still revered. Larry Bird was revitalizing the Celtics, and older used-to-bes like Maravich and Bill Walton were welcomed into the fraternity in Boston even though their best days were behind them.

Donnie and I were still arguing about Pete when Boes, in an unexpected visit to our apartment, stuck his head in the door and asked me to come into the living room. He rarely came to the apartments, so I knew almost as soon as he asked to speak with me that I wasn't going to New Orleans. This time I was going to tell Boes "fuck you" to his face; fuck him and Pensacola, as far as I was concerned, and his mama too. My heart was beating so hard from anticipation it was about to pop out of my chest.

He sized me up, then got straight to the point. "James, your father died." My heart rate slowed as the words lingered. *Pop's dead?* I thought. What news to hear from Boes. Pop would hate him even more than I did.

Boes stood there, probably expecting some emotion, a question, something, but there was only silence and a stoned-faced glare. After my "Is there anything else I can do for you" expression, Boes mentioned something about a plane ticket before he turned and left the apartment.

I thought about Nanna. She died from a stroke last year in nearly the same exact month. Willie, her life partner, had died the year before her, also in the fall. Pop used to say Willie reached back to this world and took Nanna where he was. Maybe Nanna was reaching back for Pop now. I wondered who was going to reach back and take me. My paternal side of the family, who helped usher me into life in Harlem, was virtually gone before my twentieth birthday. My paternal grandfather died before I was born, my only paternal aunt, Aunt Sister, died when I was four, and now both Nanna and Pop were gone within a year of each other. None of them saw their sixties. The only one left was Aunt Margaret, Nanna's youngest sister, who lost her husband, Uncle Preston, to a stroke only a few years before. She was all alone now.

Pop died at forty-one. He was hospitalized over the summer and diagnosed as having liver damage. He may have left the hospital before full recovery since he disdained hospitals and probably had no insurance. The death certificate listed one of the contributing causes of death as cirrhosis of the liver. The truth was Pop ceased living in some ways the day Ma left him. When he lost Nanna, he was even more lost. He lost his father early in life, and a sister, mother, wife, and his kids in his short forty years. Maybe he started thinking he had more to die for than the other way around.

I saw Pop over the summer in the hospital, and in his eyes, I could see he'd given up. He'd always been thin, but there had been power lurking within his sinewy frame. He had big, strong hands and powerfully developed forearms from wielding blocks of ice with grapplers on the truck. But when we went to see him at Lenox Hill Hospital, there was no fire or spark in his eyes.

Ma told him I was leaving for Florida on a basketball scholarship, something she told people with pride. It should have been something he and I could discuss, but Ma literally had to drag me to the hospital to see him.

Seeing him at the hospital, I felt pity for him. He never looked directly at me. Maybe he wanted to say something important, but we hadn't developed that kind of relationship. Unlike my sister, my personality wasn't engaging or out front for people to gauge. Pop hadn't been a major part of my life for many years, and now that he was gone, I searched for feelings I was supposed to have a firm grasp on but had never developed. I was embarrassed I didn't feel something. Why wasn't I sad?

I flew home and we viewed his body in a funeral parlor on 132nd Street near Lenox Avenue. I dreaded funerals. We attended Nanna's funeral the previous year in South Carolina, and I vowed I would never go to another one. I experienced people dying early in life, but it never helped me understand how to deal with it. My cousins Lester, Donald Jr., and my aunt Sister were still fresh in my mind. Lester was fourteen when a brain tumor took him, and Donald Jr. was shot and killed in Brooklyn when he was seventeen.

When I looked at my father's body lying in the casket, I didn't touch him. I still remembered what that hard, cold stiffness felt like from years ago when we buried his sister. It felt like nothing. Next to me was Aunt Margaret, the last remaining relative from the old neighborhood. She'd buried her husband, sister, niece, and now her nephew, all while living in that same building on 119th Street and Madison. Looking down at Pop's plastic-looking face, his mustache and goatee intact, I wasn't moved to tears. I wondered what his last thoughts were. Did he know he was going to die?

Several people from my early childhood, people I hadn't seen in a decade or more, showed up at the wake. He associated with a cast of characters; some were distant cousins, others childhood friends from the South. Charlie, Roscoe, Uncle Jim, Bill Bailey, and Pope were all at one time or another drinking buddies and hangout partners of his crew. A few, like Roscoe and Uncle Jim, moved on after getting married and stayed away from 117th Street. But Pop never moved away from the block. The block was the most important part of his social life, similar to how playing ball on the streets had become mine.

That night at the funeral parlor, I couldn't cry, so I stopped wondering why and stepped outside to get some air. It was a cool night, cold enough to put your hands in your pocket. The funeral parlor was part of a tenement between Lenox and Seventh Avenue on 132nd Street. People who lived in the building were going and coming as usual. Life went on. I glanced at the faces, but I couldn't focus on anything until one brief moment of clarity came over me.

A child's laugh a few buildings away, adjacent to where I was, caught my attention. When I looked toward Seventh Avenue, I noticed a boy. He was six or seven years old. He was yelling "Daddy, don't git me," while playing with his father on the stoop of the tenement. The man was standing at the top of the stairs as the little boy attempted to dodge and run by him to reach the door behind him. It was a game I remembered playing with Pop in front of Aunt Margaret's building on 119th Street when I was five or six. He'd have a bottle in a brown bag in one hand while trying to grab me with the other. Since we hadn't been able to say our goodbyes or even exchange our true feelings, maybe this was Pop's way of reaching back to me.

It didn't matter what the message was; all that mattered was that it was being sent and I was receiving it. I was nineteen and didn't have a girlfriend. But I knew I'd have a son one day, and we would make up for some of the stuff my father and I got wrong. Maybe I would learn from his mistakes.

Time stood still as I watched the little boy and his father. Only then could I think of the good times I had with Pop. It was some kind of an awakening. As few as there seemed to be moments ago, the memories of Pop were suddenly clearer. I remembered him fixing my black five-speed Drag Stripper with the side mirrors. I remembered the cold Christmas morning he took me outside to ride my Big Wheel. I thought about the times he tried to show me how to shoot pool, daring me to take a sip of his beer. I could see him up on the ice truck on 117th Street, cutting and swinging blocks of ice to sell to customers.

Suddenly I felt closer to Pop than I had when he was alive just a few months ago. I hadn't been sure before if I loved this dude or not, but as I walked down Lenox Avenue toward 135th Street, teary eyed for the first time, I knew I loved my father and asked God to forgive him for his sins and maybe help me with my own.

CHAPTER 35
BACK TO THE STREETS

AFTER POP'S FUNERAL, I returned to Pensacola and nothing felt the same. There was no sense of renewed purpose. My mind was still focused on basketball, but I wasn't tolerant about my situation. I didn't want to be around Boes or listen to him talk.

There was a carnival in town the weekend I returned, and Donnie and Dennis were glad I was back so we could go scout the local honeys.

"Ice, Dennis got a new girl when you was gone."

"A new girl? I was only gone a week. Who is it?"

"Lisa Frye."

"Lisa with the red hair and fat ass?"

"Hell yeah, that's her. She actually fell for that ugly fucker."

Lisa Frye was a mature woman. She was at least twenty-seven and had caramel-colored skin. A part-timer at PJC, she worked a full-time job and was stunning not only because of her shapely figure but also because she had style. Lisa flashed jewels, rings, ankle bracelets, and silk blouses in warm and energetic colors. She had a confident wit and wore her reddish-brown hair short. She intimidated a lot of guys but not Dennis. He stepped up to the plate and hit a home run.

Most people agreed Dennis was somewhat hard to look at. No one was calling him handsome. He had raw emotion, however, and this attracted some and repelled others. When he pulled Lisa Frye, it created some buzz since she was one of the most coveted women at the college.

I was happy for him but had problems of my own to sort out. When I got back from New York, Boes informed me I wasn't going on the New Orleans road trip. I had missed a week of practices, and maybe he thought my mind wasn't right. When he informed me I was staying behind in Pensacola, I acted as if it didn't bother me, but it was all that could bother me. I needed to play to keep my mind off other things.

"James, I think it's best for you to sit this road trip out. We've had a few important practices while you were away, and I think it's probably best for you to stay here and regroup."

"Regroup from what?"

"Well, Jim, I don't know what it's like to lose a father, but it can't be easy."

"My name ain't Jim. My father hated that name too."

"Okay, James. I still think it best for you to take this time to refocus yourself."

"I am focused."

"You're out on this trip, James."

Maybe Boes thought I was a ticking time bomb since my passion wasn't detectable to an unskilled eye or the less intuitive. It was beneath any normal radar. Boes had no idea what made me tick. He wasn't sure what to do with me anymore. If losing a father didn't get a reaction out of me, what could?

After I came back from New York, Donnie was talking more about leaving than before. Maybe he knew I was thinking it, or maybe he was really homesick. Either way, he thought coming to Pensacola was a mistake and wanted to leave for Miami-Dade next year.

"Man, Ice, I can't take it down here for two years."

"I know what you mean, Don."

"Did you visit this place before you came?"

"No, you?"

"Hell naw. My brother came down to meet Boes. Nigga came back tellin' me this program was disciplined, that's what I needed and all that. He woulda sent me anywhere away from Liberty City."

I agreed with Donnie's brother. It was probably good for him to be away from Miami because unlike me, Donnie wasn't 100 percent focused on playing basketball. He had other things tearing at him. But it felt natural to gripe and marginalize our new rural experience under Boes.

Boes routinely got players like Donnie and I, guys he never had time to recruit or get to know because we decided on JCs at the last minute and usually as a result of third-party negotiations. PJC's program had to be rigid and machine-like because there wasn't much time to offer anything else. You could get bigger, stronger, and faster at a JC, but was it a place you could become a better player? By the time you got to know your coach, it was time to move on. Then you had another two years at a different school, to play for another coach who didn't recruit you as intently as his four-year guys. It was a duplicate two-year cycle all over again, one that made getting a shot in the pros even more difficult for guys coming out of junior college. Knowing this coming in was one reason I was frantic about staying a second year. A second year anywhere other than at a D-I was a nightmare reality I knew wouldn't work out for me.

Luddy and I stayed home for the road trip. Charles Davis, who I began to view with almost as much disgust as I did Boes, and little Smitty got to go to New Orleans. Boes may have been better off taking Luddy but probably didn't want Luddy anywhere near New Orleans due to his drinking appetite.

The team left early on a Thursday, and reality finally hit me. I'd thought perhaps Boes would change his mind. Maybe he was just fucking with my head, making me think I wasn't going and then taking me anyway. It was an odd feeling not to be in the mix, not being acknowledged, and sitting home like a reserve player. I was humbled, but no matter how much it hurt, I had to try and laugh it off.

"Yo, Dennis, bring me back one of those Creole hoes from the French Quarter."

"Shit, you know I will."

"No he won't," Donnie interjected. "Lisa got that ass pussy whipped."

"Man, I might not even be here when y'all git back," I lied.

"Ice, Boes just fucking wit your head. You know you should be on this trip. You got the least to worry about outta any of us. You know Syracuse want you. Shit, when I leave here, I have to start all over again," Dennis remarked.

I knew Dennis was right. He was in a different situation than either Donnie or I was. He was a six-foot-five center. On our team he was invaluable—he could rebound, pass, and play defense—but at the higher level he would struggle against bigger players. I was an inch taller than Dennis and playing guard. When Donnie and I ranted about leaving, Dennis wasn't as enthusiastic, especially after hooking up with Lisa Frye.

Some people did well with idle time. I always had until now. There

was too much time to think about the game, about Boes, and about all the
mistakes I'd made in high school. I had to think about how I'd landed in
Pensacola in the first place and about how long I would be kept out of action.

I had some success on New York City's playgrounds, against some of
the best young players on the planet. These were confident guys who played
with an edge of cockiness and demonstrated extraordinary abilities at young
ages. Everything I thought I was or would ever be had to do with basketball.
I wasn't brash or flamboyant off the court, but on the court, I'd developed
a swagger that was natural for someone who built his rep in Harlem. Boes
sitting me on the bench was an attack against every fiber of my being. What
was I going to do if I couldn't play ball?

We lost two of four games in New Orleans and failed to make the finals.
I viewed this more as good news than bad. The last thing I wanted to hear
was that they won the whole thing without me. Donnie told me that Dre
and Boes got into it in New Orleans, something Eddie predicted since Dre
had already asked him where to get weed.

"Man, New Orlins is a party town. A place to git 'on' and play the honeys.
Dre ain't gon listen to no curfew. He don't listen when he here."

And Dre didn't listen. For a guy like him, going to New Orleans meant
enjoying the city's nightlife. Like Luddy, he relished partying as much as he
relished playing ball, so with Boes trying to enforce rigid control over his
team, they clashed. After the road trip, Dre was in Boes's doghouse where
he seemed to stay quite often.

Our next game was against Mercer Community College at home. It was
the last game before the Christmas break. Mercer was from New Jersey,
near Trenton, and was ranked as one of the top twenty JCs in the nation. I
knew the coach, Howie Landa. He contacted me about going to Mercer late
in the summer. Mike Everette, an All-City point guard from Rice known as
"Mike Ev" on the street, was starting for Howie as a second-year player. I
knew Mike from playing against him in a few tournaments.

In practices leading into the Mercer game, I shut down emotionally, but
I sensed Boes wanted to lighten up on me and get me back into the rotation.
I was particularly hard on Smitty and Charles whenever I could be and tried
to humiliate them when the opportunity presented itself. I pressured and
hounded Smitty until he didn't even want to touch the ball, and I blocked
Davis's shots into the stands and exploded on offense like it was game mode.

When Boes put me back in the normal rotation, I was almost sadistic. I
wanted to destroy people's confidence, and it had little to do with helping the

team. I was playing harder, and specifically challenging more emphatically on defense. I wanted to psychologically maim anyone opposite me. If nothing else, I was reinforcing I was better than any of these mothafuckas. Seeing the new vigor, perhaps Boes started to think he'd done the right thing.

However, when game night came, I was dead inside. My mind was on going home for the holidays. The home fans came out in full force. I'm not sure when the thought of not playing entered my heart, or when I thought about it. Maybe I didn't want to risk Boes benching me again. Sitting the bench in front of the home crowd would further crush my hopes and any aspirations I had for getting back on the court. At some point I decided I didn't want to find out. I'd played well in practice leading into the Mercer game, but how did I know Boes wouldn't sit me again? Feeling helpless in Boes's hands, I decided to take things into my own.

Game night, I reported to the gym with the team but didn't go into the locker room. As the rest of the team got into game mode, I milled around outside, talking with some of the students I knew, making sure to say a few words to my homeboy Mike Ev and Howie Landa.

"How are things goin down here, Wash?"

"Pretty good, Coach," I lied.

"You still looking at St. John's?"

"Na, Syracuse."

"Let me guess, Brendan Malone, right?"

"Yeah, how you know?"

"I'm God. No one told you?"

Howie was used to city kids, as were many other New York tri-state coaches. He recruited north and central Jersey kids mostly but was known to scour New York's playgrounds to pick up a potential impact player or two. Like Brendan, he had his finger on the pulse of the city guys, which was why he could attract someone like Mike Everette, who despite knee problems was one of the best point guards in the NJCAA.

This game was important for three reasons. First, we were on a two-game losing streak. Second, Mercer was a ranked team who had been among the nation's best. And third, this was the last game of the year before the holidays. Beating Mercer could lay the groundwork for success when we returned.

Twenty minutes before the game, I was sitting in the stands with the fans. I was torn, but I wasn't going to show it. Part of me wanted to run into the locker room, get dressed, and join the warm-ups. Then there was the fear of not playing and sitting the bench. For me not to play against a former rival like Mike Ev and Coach Landa, people I respected, made me not want to take the chance. In one moment, I wondered if Boes would let me play, and in the next, I decided I didn't want to find out. Whatever consequences awaited me, I was no longer able to evaluate them.

Sitting opposite our bench in the school bleachers, I could see the team wondering what was going on. Donnie looked over at me, but even he didn't know what I was up to. Boes sent his flunky over to investigate, Coach Wayne.

"James, you not feeling well?"

"I'm fine, Coach Wayne."

"Then what's going on? Why aren't you dressed?"

"I'm not playing."

He looked at me carefully as if he didn't understand.

"James, I think that's a mistake."

"Yeah, Coach, I've made them before. Why didn't Boes come over himself? Why he sending you?"

"He's preparing for the game. You sure you don't want to change your mind?"

"Yeah, Coach, I'm pretty sure."

He looked puzzled, as if he thought he was supposed to do or say something, only he didn't know what it was. He sat there beside me for a moment, then got up and left to join the team on the bench.

I watched as he whispered in Boes's ear and waited to see a reaction. Boes never looked over at me, but my eyes were on him. Once the game began, I secretly rooted for Mercer to win. My stomach went up and down as the seesaw struggle ensued. If my team won, then my sitting out didn't mean as much. Landa was a Northerner, flamboyantly confident and an entertaining conversationalist, everything Boes wasn't. Losing to Landa might infuriate him even more, so that's what I hoped for.

Mercer pulled out a close game. Our team struggled from the outside and in transition, areas where I excelled. They played a matchup zone and forced Ron, Eddie, and Scott to shoot from the outside, and no one was hitting. I saw so many things I could take advantage of or would have done differently. I was happy I took some level of power back from Boes.

Immediately following the game, Wayne came over and told me Boes wanted to see me. I stopped to talk with Mike Ev for a few moments before heading to Boes's office. Boes asking to speak with me immediately was a good sign. It meant he wanted to talk even before he broke down the game to the team. That meant I was on his mind. Maybe I was pushing his buttons now, maybe not, but I was looking forward to finding out.

Scott, Jerome, and Mike Tate talked about Boes challenging players physically when he was the most upset with them. Despite being slightly built, he'd challenged Dre and Luddy to physical confrontations. I figured he was a dirty fighter and prepared myself mentally for anything. I was hoping he was angry enough for a fight. On my way to the office, Dre was hanging around outside the locker room, talking with a few friends, probably setting up a social encounter for later.

"Boy, you crazy," he said with a big smile on his face. I could see he identified with my open defiance. He respected it. Finally, Dre and I found some commonality, and a sense of camaraderie between us.

I entered the office aggressively, rushing through the door as though I had urgent news, like I had something pressing and important to say. Kearney, the AD, was sitting behind Boes's desk while Boes stood with his arms folded not far away. They were waiting for me, and I was glad I stopped to talk to Mike before coming in to see them. Boes cheeks were flushed red. Perhaps he was too mad to speak, so Kearney began.

"James, we've never had a player do what you did tonight," he said.

"You can take that in a lot of ways," I responded quickly.

"What the hell do you mean by that?" Boes snickered.

"Y'all never had a player do what I've done on the court either, so what's your point?"

Boes jerked his head up. "Who do you think you are, Washington? You ain't no better'n no one else."

"I know who I am. You don't."

They were dumbfounded by my approach and a bit caught off guard since I'd never been so direct in speaking with them. It seemed that my nonverbal communication was what bothered Boes the most. Now I was talking cocky, clear and direct, and it must have thrown him off. For the first time he may have seen me somewhat differently.

"Son, what is your problem?"

"I'm not your son, sir."

"Well, James, what is your problem?"

"One of the problems is y'all keeping my mail from me."

Boes blinked quickly.

"James, I don't think you're working out with our program. We have tried to work with you. If you didn't want to be here, you shouldn't have come."

Now I was angry. Neither said a word about my mail being kept from me. I wanted to shock them by revealing I knew what Boes had done and it was my only real issue. Kearney's silence implied he knew all along. He didn't even ask what I was talking about. I knew then my days in Pensacola had come to an end. Even a lame explanation might have been enough for me to have hope, but I knew now there was no way I could come out on top of this situation.

"Man, you finished? I asked.

"Yeah, and so are you," Boes said.

"Fuck you and this program!" I yelled at Boes.

"Pack your damn bags!"

I left his office as abruptly as I entered it. I thought about going over to Landa, maybe asking him if I could finish up the year at Mercer, but I knew that was out of the question. Once again I had fucked up. Maybe my homeboy Mike Rich was right; maybe I was un-coachable. I didn't know. All I knew was that my assets—like so many other guys who acted off the cuff and challenged traditions, structures, fundamentals—had become my liabilities. I had an inability to accommodate the system. I was unwilling or unable to "play the game" in order to win another day.

After I caught a ride back to the apartments with a few of the students, Donnie and Dennis sensed I wasn't coming back after the Christmas holidays. Maybe Boes had already told everyone. Scott avoided talking to me. He felt I was fucking up my career. And I was. But I couldn't stop myself. I guess if I came back to Boes and acted remorseful, apologized, and promised to do better, maybe I could go on, finish my year and perhaps reach my goal. But I already knew I wasn't going to do that.

"Ice, I don't think I can make it through down here wit'out you, man."

"Don, you gotta do what you gotta do. I mean, at least you're playing."

"Yeah, Ice, but it's boring and I ain't tight wit nobody else but Dennis, and that nigga be wit Lisa all the time now. I'm thinking about staying in Miami, transferring to Miami-Dade."

"Yo, Don, just stay away from the weed. I know you like to smoke, but don't let that be your life, B. You got to keep yo game on track."

"Damn, Ice. You really ain't coming back?"

"I don't know, Don. I don't want to. This cracker might sit me the whole year. How is that gon look to Brendan and Boeheim up at Syracuse? Then I'll be stuck here another year, playin' my heart out for this cracka cause I'm scared I won't get a good offer. A offer from a school with jus two years of eligibility left? Man, that shit would fuck me up even worse!"

"Yeah, maybe you right."

My last night in Pensacola, I fell asleep listening to Donnie talk about transferring to Miami-Dade, about how bad a coach Boes was, about his brother, his daughter, his ghetto, the same stuff I'd heard a dozen times by now. But I listened as though it were the first time. I didn't know if I would ever hear it again or if I'd ever see Donnie after this night. I felt like I was on my way back to playing on the streets.

PART 7
1983

CHAPTER 36
STREETBALL PAYS

IT WAS WINTER, AND I was home. The college season was going strong, and I was watching other New Yorkers playing on television. Mullins was at St. John's, Salley at Georgia Tech, and Meyers at NC State. The new three-point rule was being used in college ball, and the line was so close I knew I could kill that shot all day. That alone guaranteed a Division I player some TV time.

Being back home in the middle of the college season felt worse than anything. Ma and I were like her and Pop used to be, in total conflict. Prissy was fifteen and unwilling to give up her newly acquired bedroom, so I slept on the couch in the living room, living out of my gym bag. My trophies were still in the house, but most of my comic books didn't survive my mother's purge. Being home took on a whole new meaning. I no longer had a home.

While I was away, my family adjusted quickly. My sister didn't have to worry about me looking over her shoulder. Ma was working, attending choir rehearsals, going to school, and selling Mary Kay on the side, so Prissy was freer than ever before during the four months I was away. When I came back home with no job, no money, and seemingly no future, it complicated things.

At nineteen, Joe Hammond was conquering Harlem's playgrounds, living on his own, and making his own decisions, but I was considering calling it quits. I was a man—if not in practice, then at least in theory—and being home with Ma, doing nothing, meant I was a man who was a bum. I had to decide if I was cut out for school or the streets, since I was prepared for nothing else.

Playing ball in the streets and living off them were two very different things. In the same way not everyone was built to be a great ballplayer, not everyone was built for hustling. Things were different than when Joe Hammond and Pee Wee Kirkland dominated Harlem's scene thirteen years ago. Black ballplayers of my era were playing on national television and signing million-dollar contracts out of college. The incentive to leave the streets was much greater now because we saw another way to get paid.

Attending college on a scholarship made things easier for Ma. With me out of the house, she had one less mouth to worry about. Returning home to pursue a life as a playground legend was not going to happen on her watch. Choosing to leave Pensacola meant going it alone.

I was away from Harlem less than six months, but it was the longest I'd ever been away from home. It felt like it had been a year. Last year around this time I was rushing to the mailbox, opening letters from colleges, and fantasizing about my options. Now my future had taken a quick wrong turn. Unless I wanted to hear Ma's mouth whenever I walked into the kitchen, I had to figure out how I was going to make money.

I wasn't bred into a life of hustling. Playing ball for money and shooting dice was the closest I'd been to a hustling lifestyle. When I won money playing basketball, I often caught a string of dice games and could keep money in my pocket for months. Drug dealers and hustlers were always placing big bets that often led to shooting dice or other activities predicated on a hustling lifestyle. Even in Joe Hammond's situation, he was more of a gambler than a drug dealer. He loved to shoot dice, and since he knew all the major drug guys, their crap games ran into long-money games of tens of thousands.

I wasn't a hustler, but I was still enveloped within the fast-money culture of Harlem. Saturated with images of wealth, prosperity, and glamour, I knew none of it came without taking risks. People remembered legendary "money" basketball games almost as much as they did the performances of the players. They talked about the $100,000 bets Guy Fisher made in the '70s. In the '80s there were new guys running around emulating that lifestyle and pouring money into Harlem's underground economy.

It didn't take long to realize staying in Florida and taking whatever Boes had to offer was probably the best thing for me. I wasn't the only one disappointed.

"James, what is wrong with you?"

"Nothin', Ma. Ain't nothin' wrong with me."

"What do you mean nothin'! You mean you ain't doin' nothin'! Is that what you mean?"

"No."

"Then what does it mean!? Your lazy ass can't stay in school for free!? How many chances do you think you're going to get before you end up in the street like your father!?"

"Why you gotta compare me to him?"

"Cause you actin' like him, and you see where it got him. He's dead now. That's where you going to be if you don't straighten up!"

I could usually tell when Ma was at her breaking point, and one way was when she mentioned Pop and me in the same sentence. She rarely made these comparisons when he was alive because she was praying I didn't become like him. Now that I seemed to be following his trend of irresponsibility, I was going to endure the full brunt of her tirades.

"Ma, I ain't gon be in the street!"

"You not gon be here, so where are you gon live?! You're not staying here to run the streets! I refuse to take care of a grown man!"

"Ma, I told you, I got good grades in Florida, I got a B average. I can get into another school."

"You should take your ass back down there then."

"I can't do that, Ma. The coach is trying to jerk me down there. He's messin' up my whole career."

"Boy, what career you talkin' about?"

"Whatchu mean what career? Ma, I'm a basketball player."

Ma never saw it quite this way. She didn't have time for big dreams. She was about the practical, minute details from her Southern upbringing. Basketball was a game to her, not a career option. If I could get into college using it, fine. All she was really concerned about was that I had a chance to go to college.

"You need an education, James!"

"I won't get one without playin' ball, and I ain't playin' for Boes."

"You won't be playing anywhere but in those streets. The same streets killed your father, and they will kill you too."

"Ma, drinking killed Pop, not the streets."

"Fool! Where do you think he learned to drink?"

Ma was a worker and that's what she understood. She was a woman always on the move. After moving from South Carolina in 1963, twenty years later she had not only survived the transition but had done quite well for someone living in the projects, starting out on welfare and food stamps and with no supportive husband.

I saw guys coming back home from college or the service all the time and getting into trouble. Roy Spee and Don Johnson both gave the armed services a try before returning home. Now their main activity was getting high and living day to day. Tyrone and Jack from the twentieth floor were among at least five sets of siblings who were repeat offenders living in my building, going back and forth to Ryker's or "up north." It seemed like the only way to "make it" was to leave Harlem and to stay away. At least that way no one knew if you "made it" or not.

Ma just didn't understand how playing basketball made me feel. It was a feeling every boy eyeing the promise of manhood wanted to feel. My game validated my manhood. It gave me the confidence I needed to pursue and cultivate it. The playgrounds were like a woman who found me favorable and treated me like the king I aspired to be. She inspired me, kept me alive, motivated me to be brave, daring, and always looking forward to her graces. I was in love with basketball, and nothing was going to interfere with my love for it, not even school.

CHAPTER 37
PRE-SUMMER: THE MONEY GAME

APRIL CAME AND THE weather broke. I started shaking off my regrets. It was spring. The trees were getting their leaves back, birds were singing again, and a new summer season was on the horizon, offering new vigor for life and basketball. The previous winter had snatched my heart and left it like a dried prune in a desert, but my blood began to pump again.

I took a job washing and cleaning trucks at a U-Haul facility in the South Bronx, but as the weather got nice, I planned to quit. Michael Jackson's new album *Thriller* had something to do with my rebirth. The craze over *Thriller* sparked new dances in Harlem, along with new "hip-hop attitudes." Michael performed one of the most captivating performances ever captured on television when he dropped "Billie Jean" at Motown's twenty-fifth anniversary on ABC. People were talking about it all over Harlem.

Furthering my resuscitation was the developing hip-hop culture. The Rooftop on 155th Street was the newest Harlem nightclub on the scene, following hot spots like Harlem World, Broadway International, and the Latin Quarters. Rap music ran through the veins of Harlem's young people like heroin and soul music had back in the '60s and '70s. We were addicted to the culture.

As a result, hip-hop and summer basketball became inseparable. It all ran together. The guys I played ball with were listening to Whodini and local guys like Kool Moe Dee and KRS One. The summer block parties pumped mixes to "Play at Your Own Risk," "Planet Rock," and "Drummer's Delight," and there was always a basketball game nearby. The drumbeats and mixes were like a current running through us, forcing us to perform on the courts.

It seemed like every park I walked into at sunset was blazing music like Evelyn Champagne King's "Love Come Down" or Run-DMC's "Sucker MCs." When the warmer weather arrived, everything was out in the open again. That's when whispers in the neighborhood surfaced about me: "Yo, where James Ice going to school at?" "What happened with Syracuse?" "I knew that nigga wasn't college material. He got no fundamentals and no defense."

I could escape this talk in the cold months, but when spring and summer rolled around, people were in the streets, and nobody who meant anything wanted to be stuck in the house. The girls were out showing well-oiled legs, men were in 144th Street playing checkers and drinking wine, and I was ready to get back on the basketball courts to quiet down the whispers.

Most of my neighborhood crew were doing their own thing now. We weren't hanging out in front of the building or running around like before. While I was in Florida, Mike Poole was upstate at Purchase College. He came back with a steady girlfriend, Charlotte, and found different ways to spend his time. Mo Blind and his family moved to the Bronx, and Johnny Mack, who was always more independent, was taking classes at John Jay and working at Crazy Eddie's electronics store. Quarter-field, Warren E., and D-Smooth were running with a new crew, along with Tone Wop, Sherm Ice, Rick Dog, D-Ferg, and Mike Cock. These guys were more about the social scene—going to parties, running the streets, and chasing girls. Warren was still playing ball seriously and planned to attend college, but the rest of my crew didn't take the game as seriously as before.

With my old crew slowly dismantling, I took on a protégé and started hanging out with him on a regular basis. Anthony Poole was three years younger than I was but already showing more talent for the game than his older brother Mike, who was one of my oldest friends. Mike was playing for Purchase, a Division III school in the SUNY conference, but a lot of people thought Ant could make it to a Division I college. People were calling him "Ant Ice," another lanky outside shooter with a nice handle. Ant was starting for Rice High School's JV and already playing with older guys. Some even predicted he was going to be better than me if he kept his head in the game.

Ant and I started going everywhere together. If I had a game, he was on the sidelines. When I made my runs down to West Fourth Street park to entertain a different type of crowd, he came down too. When Rice had a game, I went to watch him and advised him on how to handle pressure and let the game come to him. He was starting beside Rod Strickland in the backcourt, and they were dynamic together. Rod was already dazzling people with his ball handling and uncanny body control. But Ant was the better outside shooter, and the two of them made an excellent backcourt.

Ant looked up to me in a way he didn't any of his older brothers or friends, and it was cool having him around. He was always independent minded and wasn't as critical of what I was doing with my career as some of the older cats in the block. I wasn't in school, but he respected that my name was still ringing out in parks uptown. Walking through any block, I was recognized by someone, and when he was with me, he was recognized too on some level.

Summer was coming, and even though I'd blown scholarship opportunities to Syracuse, St. John's, and Georgetown within a year's time, I was ready to rebound with a vengeance and take on any challenge coming my way.

"Ice, I got two Gs on the game next week."

"Two Gs?"

"Two Gs on Eighth Avenue, B."

"So what's my cut?"

"Nigga, all you gotta do is win and you git five hunnet."

"Five hunnet?"

"Five hunnet from me, nigga. If you smart, you can hit da other niggas for side bets!"

I knew "Vonn Zipp" when he was just Von, before the gold medallions and turbo motorcycles, or the late-night party binges with cases of Moet, fast girls, and even faster cars. I knew Vonn when he was at the Dime, where we attended the sixth, seventh, and eighth grades, back when basketball was just a game for me and street hustling only a dream for him. Now it seemed our separate interests had taken charge of our lives.

Vonn was a short, compact, slick-talking cat making his way in the streets by being as charming and as ruthless as any situation merited. He was with a drug-selling crew. He had a rep and propensity for violence, something he'd built up since I'd known him in junior high school. When I was at the Dime, people assumed Baby Dow would be the next Bat or Small Paul, local noteworthy gangsters in the mid-1970s. But Dow was shot and killed before his sixteenth birthday. Vonn was lesser known, but his rep had grown since then.

Another big game was being set up, and this time my neighborhood was in the center of it. My reintroduction to the playgrounds began with a pre-summer game between two neighborhoods. It was a street game in the purest sense—no tournament or league standards, no sanctioning bodies, just one game forged by a bet. Two of Harlem's more notable hustlers were the sponsors of the game. It was a Seventh Avenue versus Eighth Avenue contest, with me as one of the feature players on the Eighth Avenue squad. Wayne Davis, from our block, was Eighth Avenue's sponsor. And Chic, whose real name was Greg Rollins, was putting his money on Seventh Avenue. Other hustlers like Vonn, LA, and Rich Porter were making side bets. LA, who in the past placed bets on me or teams I played on, was betting against me.

Well dressed and usually sporting a fresh cut, Wayne Davis had charming, hustling good looks and a credible street rep that separated him from everyone else in our block. No one fucked with Wayne. He was a supplier, and a go-between for major-weight drug distributors and mid-level dealers known as lieutenants. Wayne wasn't bagging or handling product. Wayne also took college courses, and drove a low-profile vehicle, a Volkswagen Rabbit convertible. A lot of dealers at his level were buying luxury Benzes and BMWs. He had yet to do considerable time behind bars.

Our rival street sponsor, Chic, had been hustling as long as Wayne but until now hadn't been as successful. Chic was small boned, nonathletic, and his face was covered with pimples and skin blotches. When he looked at you with his widened, huge eyeballs and crooked smile, handsome was not the first thing that come to mind. But Chic was flossing, and guys with money could look however they wanted. Chic had a lot of admirers and got a lot of love uptown.

However, unlike Wayne, who you wouldn't suspect was as big of a narcotics dealer as he was, Chic was flamboyant, displaying an excessive collection of gold chains, rings, and routinely hitting people off with hundreds of dollars for the privilege of his audience. Chic was often neck-deep in a crowd of superstar ballplayers or hustlers and known for buying sneakers and sports equipment for athletes. In comparison, Wayne rarely if ever hung out in groups and rarely gave anyone anything they didn't earn.

Chic's new wealth was blowing up from Harlem's latest narcotic boom, known as "crack." Before crack even had a name, freebase or "base" cocaine was making its way to the street level. Only a few years prior, Richard Pryor burned himself up freebasing. Now Pryor's drug of choice was affordable to the mainstream. The average cat on the street could get a rock, and hustlers like Chic exploited this economic opportunity that coincided with the despair and lack of hope and education of their customers.

People knew Chic for what he had, not so much for anything he'd done. I remembered him at my Rucker games back when I was a thirteen-year-old afraid to shoot the ball. He was selling dime bags of weed and loose joints back then but was always a park-rat junkie when it came to basketball. If someone was putting up numbers and dominating games, he knew about it. As I became better and more confident, he became more interested in me, and soon we were on first-name speaking terms. Like Vonn, as the years progressed, he excelled in his world and I in mine.

Once the bet between Wayne and Chic was on, Wayne was in the back park getting his team in order. Almost all of the Eighth Avenue guys lived in Drew Hamilton Houses, and we all knew each other. Guys like Johnny Tucker, GE, and a few others from Wayne's building were playing. I didn't think we needed these guys. I ran circles around them in the park, so I was already irritated they were playing. My crew played tournament ball and were just better than these guys.

Aaron Allen, known as "Ap," was from the first building, and even though he didn't play in tournaments, he was good enough to. He had a deadly bank shot from the angles and would hit that shot all day long in the park. Most of my crew—John Mack, Mike, Warren E., and Mo Blind—were playing. Sherman Ice from 139th Street was also playing. Sherm was the only guy on our squad who didn't live in the block, but he spent a lot of time in the neighborhood.

"Ice, I need you to play with my senior team against Seventh Ave. You ready, baby?"

"Yeah, I'm ready, but you should put me in the second game with Dujii, Imp, and Mike Rich."

When I found out there were two games, one for the younger guys under twenty, and a separate game for the older guys, I wanted to show my game had stepped up and play with the older crew. It seemed like a bigger challenge. Wayne had other ideas.

"We don't need you for the unlimited team. You have to carry our senior team. And we need you to handle D-Mac."

When I found out Daryl MacDonald was playing in the senior game, it changed my perspective a little. D-Mac was on the rise in Harlem, like I was. Everyone wanted to see a matchup between us, including me.

Wayne was always cool with our crew. But we knew he had another side, the street side. Marky Rod thought Wayne was cool a few years ago, until they had a disagreement over a drug package. Wayne gave Mark a purple eye when he punched him with a ring on his closed fist.

Wayne didn't have to convince me to play for his team. I was dying to get back into the mix any way I could. The game he was putting together had nothing to do with college, recruiting, or scouts. It wasn't for a tournament, more for pride and rep, but that was all I had.

"I'm ready, Wayne."

"You win and I got three hundred for you."

"I git three hundred win or lose?" I asked.

"Whatchu mean lose, nigga? You betta win." He smiled.

His smile may have been genuine, and though the pressure was subtle, even sublime, there was still a push to perform because I was supposed to be the best player on my squad. Three hundred dollars wasn't a lot of money, but everyone said Wayne was cheap.

I was the "big dog" on our team but thought we could use some help. The first guy I thought about was Bruce Dalrymple. Bruce was a high school all-American and lived in Ap's building on 142nd Street and Eighth. He was a Riverside guy I played against several times over the years—a six-foot-four wrecking crew who hit the boards and played defense like a fanatic. Bruce was the type of guy who took charges without thinking about it. He made outlet passes as soon as he grabbed a rebound. With my offensive, street-laced talent and his workmanlike, Charlie Hustle approach to basketball, along with Sherm and my crew, I thought we couldn't lose. But Wayne didn't know Bruce. A lot of guys in the neighborhood didn't know how good he was because Bruce rarely played in the park.

Nevertheless, word got around, and I heard back Bruce "Moose" wanted nothing to do with a game being put together by two high-profile drug dealers. He was a scholastic star, not a street star, and these worlds only occasionally crossed his path. He'd attended a prestigious prep school in Connecticut and was a three-year starter with the largest AAU program on the planet. He had a full ride to Georgia Tech and didn't need validation from the streets. But I did.

Money games were common in Harlem. Money, power, and street prestige were part of a hustler's profile, and basketball was often involved.

Guys making a living in the street came up with new ways to entertain themselves. Sports in many cases became a forum to flex their exploits. A lot of guys would play two-on-two and one-on-one basketball games for thousands of dollars just to make life more interesting.

This sports-and-street mixture went on for a long time. Gangsters like Guy Fisher and Freddie Meyers were known to bet tens of thousands of dollars on basketball games in Harlem, while incorporating the basketball services of players who were as great as Tiny Archibald and Lloyd Free and as revered as Pee Wee Kirkland and Joe Hammond. It was nothing new in Harlem; people played for money in some of the most obscure and meaningless games over nothing more than street rep.

Once word was out about our money game, it was a hot topic in the block. Local hustlers like Peanut took immediate interest. Nut used to live on the sixteenth floor of my building. He put two Gs on us to win. He was a quiet guy, and strictly about his business of selling drugs. He was always clean and dressed to impress, and his girl, Puerto Rican Nelsa from the tenth floor, was considered one of the finest girls uptown. Nut kept a low profile, and didn't do much talking, but it was nearly impossible with a girl like Nelsa on his arm. He had a rep for that alone.

LA was the boldest, youngest, and most popular hustler on the west side of 125th Street. Only eighteen, he was already a folk hero in the streets, and despite being younger than Wayne or Chic, he was already better known. Everyone knew LA because he was always doing things to be remembered, like when he came to school in the fourth grade with two black eyes.

When I heard LA put his money on Seventh Avenue to win, I figured it must have been just to fuck with Wayne. LA grew up playing ball with us, not Seventh Avenue, so maybe this was his way of saying he was bigger and better, or the newest personification of a Harlem hustler. He was a lot closer to the guys on our team because he grew up playing with us. He was fairly tall now, almost six foot two, but his athleticism never took him far. LA wasn't overweight, but he was still slow on his feet and could never get up high enough to dunk a basketball.

LA flashed every possible fashion item. He drove a black turbo SAAB with a rear spoiler kit. A lot of us didn't know what a SAAB was. We had never seen one. He hooked it up with a futuristic design, gold rims, tinted glass, and fog lights, and had people buzzing in Harlem every time they saw his car on the street. There wasn't another one like it. People were talking about LA's SAAB the way people talked about Sugar Ray Robinson's pink

Cadillac back in the '40s.

LA also had an assortment of motorbikes. His turbo motorcycle was so quiet you couldn't hear it running even standing next to it. The trendy clothes, jewels, and pockets of cash were all things eleven- and twelve-year-old Harlem boys dreamed of. Above and beyond all the trinkets, what LA most enjoyed were the moments. He wanted to be in the spotlight and to command an audience.

He did that when he came through the block popping shit about how his Seventh Ave crew was gonna blow us out. I was trained by now to laugh it off and ignore him because this was just how he was. But ignoring LA only went so far.

"Who got money on Eighth? Put it up cuz you gon lose it. We got D-Mac, Ike, and Craig Sky. Y'all niggas in trouble. We gon lock James Ice up. Ice ain't getting shit on us. I got five Gs right now. Who want it?"

One of the biggest factors in a street game was the amount of propaganda surrounding it. There was a lot of talking, and if you listened to what everyone had to say, you'd better have tough skin. LA was a master at propaganda.

Rich Porter, another young and upcoming hustler from St. Nicholas Ave, was partnered with LA. Rich was always about money and the hustle. When LA and I were chasing basketball dreams, Rich was selling newspapers in our building and packing bags at the Pioneer Grocery store on 145th Street. He was one of those guys up early in the morning, walking up and down hallways yelling, "PAPERBOY, Sunday news!"

But now Rich was stylish. Unlike LA, he was never interested in sports unless it was about money. Rich was known for powder-blue velour sweat suits, thick rope chains, fresh white sneaks, and a pocket full of cash. He owned a 7 Series BMW by his sixteenth birthday. Seeing foreign vehicles driven by teenagers was surreal. It created a buzz on the streets. The crack trade took the narcotics game to a new level, creating a new underground economy being managed by teenagers.

Our neighborhood game was purely about two hustlers looking for a new and exciting way to entertain themselves, and consequently us, with their spoils. This wasn't about trophies, playoffs, or all-star games. It was about who did what to who. It was about the streets and who was going to walk with their head up and talk shit afterwards. It was about who was the better player, the better team, the better block. And essentially, who was the better hustler, Wayne or Chic.

Funny things could happen in a money game, especially when it came to emotions. A lot of cats had talent, but when money was at stake, that talent evaporated and disappeared. I'd played in money games before but never one with big stakes. The most I'd ever pocketed for my talent was $500, and that was for a game my cousin put together at Saint Mary's projects in the Bronx. I already knew the older and better you became, the higher the stakes were. Our game wasn't a one on one or two on two for a couple hundred dollars. Larger bets would be taking place over the summer because a lot of disposable cash was flooding the streets.

Someone told me Wayne put up $15,000 on our squad to win. If this was true, I thought he must not have thought much of my ability, just offering me $300. Most people living in Drew Hamilton didn't make ten grand a year. The average yearly salary for the entire country was only $13,000. Yet in Harlem we were playing basketball games for 15k. Side bets were thousands of dollars. In anticipation of the game, I thought of ways I could make this situation work for me.

Wayne told me, "Ice, all you gotta do is play yo game and I'ma look out for you. Whatever you need."

"We probably need another horse, somebody like Bruce Moose."

"Ice, they ain't got shit for you. Fuck Bruce; we don't need him. D-Mac can't touch you, and that's all they got over there." Wayne's street mentality didn't allow him to think about anything other than the mano-a-mano aspect. But I had questions about how the team was put together. The way he saw it, I could win the game by myself. I wasn't convinced. Sherm Ice was talented and had heart, but he was raw talent and not a tournament player at that time. Neither was GE, Johnny Tucker, or Aaron Ap. I didn't know what to expect.

Comparatively, Seventh Avenue had tournament veterans and guys who had played high school basketball, guys like Ike, Ed Boone, and D-Mac. Most of their team lived in Esplanade Gardens. They weren't streetball players. Nearly all of them, with the exception of D-Mac, played for Catholic schools like Power, Rice, and Cardinal Hayes. They knew how to play under the whistle and were used to organized regulation games.

A street fight gave us a better chance of winning. A straight-up game of running, picking, shooting, passing, and playing organized might not get it done for us. While they were running plays and having practices, we were playing freelance full-court games and talking about how we were going to blow them out and get paid.

A month after the college season ended, Ralph Sampson was named the college player of the year, and Jim Valvano's North Carolina State team won it all, beating Houston's Phi Slama Jama squad. Derek Whittenburg threw up a last-minute desperation shot from half court, missing the rim entirely, but Thurl Bailey was right there to catch the rebound and put it in for the win. Valvano, a New York native, took a seventeen-to-ten team to the final four and won it all. They were the Cinderella story; hardly anyone gave them much of a shot to beat Houston.

I watched the NCAA final four of North Carolina State, Houston, Virginia, and Louisville and couldn't overlook that just a year ago I communicated with coaches and recruiters from three of these four programs. I paid special attention to Milt Wagner, the all-American guard from Louisville. Milt was from Camden, NJ, and I thought I would get to face him in a King Towers game the previous summer. He never showed up for the game.

I started questioning if I was "coachable." There were few coaches in my basketball life I could say I trusted. My best and favorite coach was Mr. Couch from the Dykeman program. Couch had been a player himself, and whatever he lacked in experience or knowledge, he more than made up for with heart and consideration. You knew Mr. Couch cared about his players. After leaving Pensacola, I didn't hear anything back from Brendan and didn't make any attempt to reach him. I didn't know what to say. Sorry may have been a start, but I didn't know how to do that right either.

By the time the big street game rolled around, I was numb to any lingering criticism on my college status. Anyone paying attention could see my game growing, and Wendell Ramsey, one of my first mentors, was paying attention. Wendell was tight with Dave Britton, a JFK High School teammate. He said Dave might be able get me an audience with Texas A&M where Britton played two years after attending a junior college.

Dave was getting ten-day NBA contracts, and it looked like he might stick with the Washington Bullets. I always liked his game, watching him play in the Whitney Young tournament during the latter '70s with guys like Dave Crosby, Artie Green, and Jim Bosket. Britton was a six-foot-four guard with good fundamentals but could also be an explosive scorer. When Wendell said he was going to hook me up with Dave, I was all for it, even though Texas A&M had never been on my radar.

"So, Ice, where you thinking about goin to school?"

"I don't know right now, Dave, nobody callin."

"You went to a JC. What happened?"

"Had problems with the coach. He was tryin' to jerk me."

"They all gon use you, baby. That's the game. You got to handle that. I went to a JC myself."

I didn't want to go into a full explanation, so I didn't really open up with Dave. It was too painful to think about, let alone try to explain.

"Yeah, you probably right, Dave."

"Ice, you can play for Texas A&M."

"I don't know much about Texas; don't know if I want to go that far to play ball."

"I went there for two years. It ain't that bad."

"Yeah, that's cool."

I didn't see Texas A&M as a basketball school, and it was so far away from where college basketball was focused; I wanted no part of Texas. The coaches from the Big East conference had me hooked, and I wanted to remain on the East Coast, where the action was.

Unfortunately, I didn't seem to have any more choices, so I listened to what Dave had to say. At the end of the day, Texas A&M was still a D-I program.

"I can talk with the coach, Ice, cuz yo game has really stepped up. I wouldn't even be saying this if I didn't think you could play. You too good to be out here playin' in the streets."

The money game was set for 145th Street at Colonel Young Park, a catch-area park everyone from 140th to 149th Street on Lenox, Seventh, and Eighth Avenue frequented, but no one crew dominated. I knew a lot of Seventh Avenue guys played in 145th Street Park because it was the closest park with full courts. Other than my crew, our neighborhood guys rarely left the block to play. The backboards and rims at 145th Street were different. There were dead spots in different areas, and guys looking to make their typical shots would have to adjust. Colonel Young was a Rucker site, and having played there for several years, I knew where all the dead spots were. Also, Colonel Young had double rims, not the single rims my guys were used to. To me, these were difference makers. Certain signature shots my neighborhood guys were used to making weren't going to fall.

Walking down 144th Street toward Lenox Avenue on game day was one of the best feelings in the world. I remembered the first time I took that walk to a Rucker game and how nervous and excited I was the closer I got to the park. The walk could be long or short depending on your frame of mind. I saw familiar faces, people who saw me take this route a dozen times, people hanging out on the stoops of their tenement buildings, on the corners of Seventh and Lenox Avenues, young fans, store owners, garbage men, schoolmates, neighbors; anyone who spent any time in the block could figure out there was a game when they saw my crew walking toward Lenox Avenue.

"Yo, Ice. Wassup, B. Is there a game today?"

"Yeah, down at 145th Street."

"Word?"

"Yeah, we playin' D-Mac and his crew from Seventh Avenue."

"Oh shit. Yeah, I heard about that. I'll be down there, B, mos def."

Our game was on a Saturday at three in the afternoon. It was still spring, so it felt a little different than a summer game. Even so, I expected a good-sized crowd.

Vendors were always at Colonel Young, especially Mr. Armstrong selling his foot-long franks and hot sausages with red onions. Outside the main court were small cement tables and wooden benches usually populated by older men playing chess, cards, and checkers while drinking a little wine.

On the corner of 145th and Lenox, I spotted a group of guys in front of Kansas Fried Chicken. They had on gold rope chains, fresh white sneaks, bright and colorful gear, and were displaying ghetto-fabulous mannerisms. The scene reminded me where and who I was. Maybe they had a piece of the bet, or perhaps they were down with a crew with a stake in the game. The pizza parlor a few spaces down was packed, people spilling over onto the sidewalk and milling around, anticipating the game.

Wayne, our team sponsor, seemed to want to make the game personal. It was his money at stake. Some people were saying D-Mac was a better player than I was. But I knew D had nothing to do with it. D-Mac had always been a humble dude, not the type of guy who went around bad-mouthing friends. And we were friends.

I met Daryl MacDonald in the sixth grade when he, I, Alvin Lott, and Stan from 149th were playing games at seven in the morning on the courts behind the Dime. Mac was one of the few cats skinnier than I was, but like me, he was a park fanatic. Both of us were in the parks testing and pushing our game as skinny eleven-year-old kids. Now Mac was building a rep on the playgrounds like I was.

At the start of the game, the crowd was crazy, and everyone was a little nervous. I missed a few easy shots early. Sherman threw balls out of bounds with his typical flamboyant style, and the closest thing we had to running an offense was taking the ball out of bounds. I think all of us were trying too hard to impress and not make mistakes.

Seventh Avenue was running plays and doing something not often seen in a game like this—they were setting screens. Not blessed with exceptional shooters, they didn't need great shooting to beat us. They got opportunities due to the nature of the game and experience alone. My team hadn't practiced. We hadn't prepared a press or zone to mix things up defensively. We approached the game like it was just another game in the park. Next.

We switched from man to zone defense three or four times in the first half alone. It wasn't a strategy; nothing was working. By halftime we trailed by fifteen points, and D-Mac hadn't even gone into his bag of tricks like I knew he could.

The matchup between D-Mac and I didn't turn into the big showdown everyone expected. Their head coach, Jeff, had a game plan to match me up with Rodney Murray, who was a better defensive player than D-Mac and just as long and lanky as I was. I was six foot six, but Rod was nearly six foot seven. I knew him well enough to know I could get by him with my first step.

Jeff wanted to win and showed a lot of poise, not feeding into the hype between D-Mac and me. Normally in a street game if there was a big matchup, a showdown, then no one got in the way of that, not even the coach. Big matchups were encouraged by everyone. People wanted to see Pee Wee against Tiny or Joe Hammond against Earl the Pearl; it was always about the individual matchup on the streets. But Jeff didn't buy into it. I guarded D-Mac most of the game, but Rod was usually on me.

Rod Murray was a starter at Power his junior and senior year. He attended Daytona Beach Junior College and was a potential star in his own right. He was a big guard who could hold down the two or three position. He had a high dribble, but his handle was good enough to run the point. Rod's Achilles heel was his outside shot and his desire to be the best. I wasn't sure if Rod wanted it as much as I did. He was talented, but inconsistent on offense.

Seventh Avenue also had Craig "Sky" Ware, another former Power high school starter who was probably the best athlete on the court. He was one of the best dunkers I'd seen uptown and came up with dunks no one was doing, and he was only six foot one. People were waiting for Craig to explode because like Rod Murray, he was a consummate underachiever but still a crowd-pleaser. At times, he could do it all—shoot, pass, score—and he brought a level of excitement because he could pull off spectacular moves in the air. I'd played with Rod and Craig in the RYA tournament and knew their abilities.

Wayne was disappointed with the first half and singled people out for coming up short. I played well enough to escape direct criticism, but I felt I wasn't doing enough to cover for our lack of performance. I wasn't taking control. Wayne's input only made things worse. It made the guys who weren't playing well feel more pressure. But his money was at stake, so what were we going to do? Guys mumbled, but no one was going to say anything to Wayne.

If we had any pride or street bravado, it was time for it to kick in. With the exception of D-Mac, who lived in a tenement on 146th Street with his seven siblings, Seventh Avenue's team was primarily composed of middle-class Catholic schoolboys. We were the harder guys, the ones attending public schools, and whose parents had been on welfare at one time or another. We lived in the projects. We were supposed to be tougher and harder than any boys from Esplanade Gardens. These guys had swimming pools, patios, and security guards. They wore better clothes, went to better schools, and had better choices than my public housing crew. It was just a street game, but these little things said something.

In any street game for money, several things can potentially happen. There were always variables affecting the outcome of a game that had nothing to do with talent or skills. If someone was about to lose money, the game could get physical and lead to a violent confrontation. Some guys opted out or faked sprained ankles to get away from the pressure. In most cases, the person who stood a chance to lose money got desperate, and who that person was usually determined how violent or physical it got.

We were losing, so I wasn't surprised to see Wayne pushing for a more physical game. He wanted to win, and when it came to toughness, we had a big edge over Chic's team. Chic had plenty of cash, perhaps more than Wayne, but wasn't known for knocking anyone out. Wayne had some historic fistfights, most of which he won, and he was from our neighborhood. Overall, our team had a tougher demeanor and profile when it came to handling conflict because this was a main element in our block. We were always fighting over something.

With Wayne pushing for us to be more aggressive, someone on our squad had to step up and be the bad guy, the goon. Someone had to bring the street into the game. It wasn't my style. I wasn't going to take someone out deliberately. No one in my crew played like that. Johnny Mack, Aaron Ap, Mike Poole, Big E, and Mo Blind were all skilled players. Even though Big Warren had a rep for hurting people, he wasn't a goon. On the other hand, a guy like Johnnie Tucker had nothing to lose.

Johnnie wasn't really a basketball player, but I guess he wanted his day in the sun. His first order of business was to slow down Ed Boone, who was killing us from the corner, on the boards, and on the baseline. Boone was about six foot three and 200 pounds; Johnnie was six foot five and maybe 180. He tried going at Boone to get him off his game.

The crowd picked up on it immediately. So did the refs. But what ref was going to cross Wayne with so much money at stake? The game became a lot harder for Chic's squad, and before you knew it, we were back in the game and only down four points. The momentum swung our way, and offensively we got back on track and played with more confidence.

We started playing like we were in our own park. I was one of our tallest players but also one of the better ball handlers, so every now and then I took over the middle of the court, grabbing the rebound, splitting defenders, and going coast-to-coast. We were rolling, but Seventh Avenue wasn't out of it yet.

One move on the playgrounds can alter the events of a game. I'd seen it happen. I'd even done it once or twice. A spectacular move might single-handedly demoralize an opponent and invigorate your own team. Win or lose, it may be what everyone in the park remembers that day. Like the move Doc pulled off against the Lakers when he went around Kareem and outside the baseline with the ball in one hand to make a shot on the reverse side of the basket. Everybody saw the move, but there were thousands of different reenactments of how he did it.

I knew D-Mac could break open a game. I played him on defense because that's what I wanted to prevent. I was a good shot blocker, and I figured if I could get my hands on a few of his shots, it would throw his timing off and make it difficult for him to impact the game. I wanted Mac also because I knew people wanted to see me play against him.

However, on the best play of the game, Johnnie Tucker and I were caught in a switch, and he picked up Mac, something I was grateful for later. Mac caught the ball on the wing and simultaneously went into slow-motion mode with an exaggerated hesitation dribble as Tucker scrambled to get his footing. As was customary for Mac, he went into a series of high-dribble hesitations before transitioning into a smooth spin. The crowd was already mumbling at the grace of the move.

Johnnie was playing aggressively and reaching, the worst thing he could do against a guy like Mac. Mac lured him in, showing the ball, tempting Johnnie and throwing his timing off. He went into another spin, his back to Johnnie, and danced in slow motion as the crowd oohed and aahed. He shook Johnnie up two or three times before even attacking the basket. I guess this would have been a great time to help. But that didn't happen.

Mac wrapped his dribble around Johnnie with his back to him during one of his spins, meeting the ball on the other side of Johnnie's body. Johnnie anticipated the ball in the opposite direction and the crowd went crazy. But Mac wasn't done. Big GE stepped over to contest Mac's attack to the basket. Mac left his feet, and GE went up to block the shot, but even airborne, D-Mac was in vintage slow-motion mode.

Not known for being a high leaper, D-Mac was a player who, like Dujii, got the most out of a jump and could release the ball with uncanny precision on the way down from an ascent to the basket. Most guys shot the ball at the height of their leap into the air, or as they were going up, but Mac was one of those rare guys who could kill you shooting the ball as he descended. It was an odd skill, hard to defend and effective for getting out of tight spots because it threw your timing off.

As GE went up to block the shot, Mac in midair went into a half spin and shielded the ball from him with his lithe body. Switching the ball from his right to his left, he completed his 360-degree spin in the air and finger-rolled the ball into the basket with his left hand as he descended. The crowd roared.

That single animated move changed the complexity of the game. Before Mac moved the crowd, we had the momentum, but Seventh Avenue capitalized on the energy of the crowd and pulled away.

We couldn't match the excitement generated by D-Mac. Tucker, after being embarrassed, was subbed out. Sherman and I both tried to provide a spark, something on par with what Mac pulled off, but we couldn't manage it. We wound up losing the game by ten or twelve points. I had twenty-five, but it was a weak twenty-five. It felt more like fifteen, and I was disappointed because I was really looking forward to the money I could get if we won. A win with a great performance could jump-start my whole summer financially. The last thing I wanted to be worried about over the summer was being broke.

Our small-stakes game was only a preview of bigger games on the horizon the summer of 1983. This was obvious almost as soon as our neighborhood game was over. Chic got my attention and got straight to the point.

"Ice, who you playin' wit this summer?"

"What tournament?"

"In my tournament." Chic smiled.

"Nobody. You got a tournament now?"

"Yeah, I want you to run wit us. I like what you doin' out there. I think we can take the whole thing wit you on our squad."

I watched as Chic rifled through six or seven hundred-dollar bills wrapped around a large stack of twenties. His fro gleaming from a fresh cut and his extra-large rope dangling from his neck, he personified the early-'80s hustler. The message to me was clear. If I wanted some of the knot he was flossing, I needed to get on board.

"Yeah, I'll run wit y'all," I said. I didn't give it a second thought.

"R-ight, baby, walk me to my joint."

Chic's "joint" was a red jeep. He walked me to the back where he had a stack of sneaks organized like they would be in a store, according to shoe size.

"What size?"

"Fourteen."

"Okay, Ice, we got you. You and Mario Ellie is runnin' wit the team you played today. Same guys plus you and Mario E-lie, and my man Jeff 'to-the-left' is gon coach. There ain't no tryouts, and we startin' practice next weekend." He reached into his pocket where he'd separated $200 and handed it to me.

Mario didn't get as much hype as some other guys, but everyone playing in the main tournaments knew who he was. He lived further downtown, but he was always over on the east side or uptown playing in the best leagues. With Ed Boone, Craig Willis, another six-foot-seven Catholic school standout, Rod Murray, and Craig Ware, we had a damn good squad. Add in D-Mac and Ike Garrow, Alvin Lott's old backcourt partner, and we were good enough to make some noise.

"Sound good to me, Chic, and good lookin' on the sneaks, B."

"A lot more where that come from, baby, a lot more. We the house team. Y'all team is Young Boys Make Noise. Ain't nobody gon stop y'all young niggas this summer!"

CHAPTER 38

PRESSURE

"ICE, THIS YO GAME, baby. Take it to da ba ha! They can't stop you, kid. Ain't got nothin' for you, baby, nuttin at all!"

Words of encouragement flowed from the sidelines like blasts from a radio. It was colorful, profane, and animated language only a ghetto child understood or appreciated. People's faces pressed into the mesh fences, their mouths like bullhorns. I was in the middle of another grudge game behind Colonel Young Park as cars streamed back and forth on the nearby Harlem River Drive like pod racers—a familiar scene.

This championship game of a weekend tournament was another prelude to bigger summer games coming ahead in July and August. We were going against 149th Street and one of Harlem's biggest legends whose time was fast approaching its end. I was with my new crew, Young Boys Make Noise. And that's exactly what we were doing: making noise.

Some games, the basket felt like twice the size of a normal rim. I was having one of those games. I relished the natural groove I was in. A bank shot from the left was effortless, the ball floating like a balloon, displaying a high arch and rotating spin as people's eyes lingered on me long after the ball left my hand. The energy and adrenaline I pulled from the sidelines gave me a power I depended on. My idle mind languished on moments like these, one where the game, the opponent, and my performance were onstage for people to see and I was in complete control.

My demeanor rarely indicated the pure joy I felt watching a helpless defender trying to keep up with me, but I loved this shit. On one offensive possession, I pulled off a stutter step followed by a perfectly sequenced crossover, leaving Alex Hooper flat-footed, before flinging a one-handed, blind-bounce pass to Mario Ellie streaking toward the lane for a dunk. I showed no reaction, but the crowd did. You never had to worry if Mario was going to be there on the break. He was a machine, a relentless rebounder and fast-break threat who would pass it out and still beat everyone downcourt. You could tell how much fun Mario was having. He loved competition.

When you felt the game like I was feeling it today, anything was possible. I wasn't the best passer on our team, but I was delivering the ball perfectly on pure instinct. I wasn't the best defender either, but I was getting to the ball, picking up steals, and blocking (sticking) shots to the boards in dramatic fashion. On a day like this, my range and touch on the ball was off the charts. I could hit shots from anywhere on the court and was playing like I had something to prove.

This weekend tournament was perfect for establishing my role with a new team, a team I lost to only a month before in our neighborhood game. We all knew each other, and I had played with or against everyone on the team. This game was an opportunity to go up against older, more established vets, some of whom weren't convinced we were ready for top-notch competition.

The biggest incentive for having a big game was playing on the other team. Artie Green was at least twenty-four or twenty-five by now, old by playground standards. His career had probably reached its zenith, but he still had people's respect and did incredible shit when the opportunity presented itself. Last summer in a game at King Towers, Artie spun to the middle and went up high for an underhand shot, but the ball hit the back of the rim and bounced off. Artie landed on the ground and immediately sprang back up, one-handed the offensive rebound over everyone, and slammed it through the rim over outstretched hands before they could do anything about it. Only the Grasshopper did shit like that.

I'd known about Artie since I was a shy twelve-year-old playing on cut-out garbage cans and shooting tennis balls into door hinges in the hallways of the projects. I knew about his cousin Butch Lee, who played at Marquette, and his younger cousin Lonnie, who scored over eighty points in a junior high school game at the Dime. I'd watched Artie at the Whitney

Young tournaments for years, but all that didn't matter right now. I was the young gun, and today was my chance to shine against the legend.

Artie was selected in the tenth round of the 1981 NBA draft by the Milwaukee Bucks after playing two years at Marquette. I watched Marquette's team on television, wishing they would put Artie into the game, hoping he would do some of the things I saw him do on 139th Street. But Artie got limited minutes with Marquette and never became the big star I wanted him to be. We got word back home that he pulled off some incredible and amazing moves at the Milwaukee Bucks camp, but it just wasn't enough. Now he was home, trying to figure out his life, waiting for his next big shot to play in the CBA or NBA. Artie wasn't the big star he was back in '77, but he still had twice as many fans as I had. That made him a target for unproven guys like me.

He had been in the block a few times, and I got to play in games with him. I was nervous, not wanting to let him down, but now I dismissed those feelings. He was just another legend to be conquered. Since turning sixteen, I always looked for ways to play against older guys. I wanted to knock some of those big names off the mountain. There was nothing like doing your thing against a "name" because that's the way our culture worked on the street.

"Ice, you killin' 'em. Just keep doin' what you doin.' Ike, keep lookin' for Ice. He's hot."

This was the way Jeff coached. He was willing to scrap a play if someone had it going. We had a few plays and special defenses for certain situations, but Jeff didn't hesitate to throw in isolation plays and improvisations when he felt it necessary. On the playgrounds, coaching was based a lot on the personality of the game. In many cases, strategy was developed on the fly. If a guy couldn't shoot, you backed off him to entice him to shoot outside. If he couldn't go left, then you played him to his right. Once a weakness was detected, it was quickly attacked in real time.

We hadn't practiced how to stop Artie, but everyone knew his game and what he could do. He could jump out of the atmosphere, had dynamic dribble moves and spins to the basket, and could potentially embarrass you with his aerial fireworks that got the crowd, his team, and everyone else riled up. Mario knew this and played Artie tough on defense. He wasn't going to let Artie get to the rim. Other than an occasional fast break, he hadn't been much of a factor.

A small crowd of fifty-plus people converged over the backcourt at

Colonel Young. A few of my boys were there—Warren E., Mo Blind, Ant Poole, and Smooth, my die-hard crew, same ones who watched my game elevate to a level even they didn't see coming. And I was doing my thing in a mature kind of way. The half year I spent in junior college didn't hurt. Artie, always one to take a challenge, switched off to guard me toward the end of our game, and I couldn't have hoped for a better ending. By then my confidence was so high I was ready to take on Bernard King if he had been out there.

Jeff played me the whole game, and the crowd buzzed over many of the moves I pulled off. We were playing a veteran team who came in thinking they could run over us. They tried pressure, but we were quicker to the ball. They played physical, but our athleticism nullified any advantage of strength, size, or experience.

Even with a well-organized defense, pressure only worked against timid or reckless players, or those without skill or aptitude for handling pressure. None of our main guys showed problems with pressure; as a matter of fact, we looked forward to it. What we lacked in experience we made up for with effort. We were young, and even though there were no major college or pro players on our squad, we were hungry and had something to prove.

Most New York City players who excelled in basketball learned to love pressure. Georgetown probably had the best press in college basketball. They intimidated people by pressuring ball handlers, trapping and forcing people toward Patrick Ewing, who was a monster in the middle. But some guys performed better when pressed in this way.

In years to come, penetrating guards like Pearl Washington and, later, LSU's Chris Jackson showed how foolish it was to try to pressure players like that into making mistakes. Sometimes it was better to let a guy make his own mistakes rather than trying to aggressively induce them. Today wasn't the first or last time I made these words ring true. People ran at me all game long, and I adjusted, crossed over, reverse dribbled, and slashed my way to a forty-plus-point game. When in counterattack mode, overly aggressive defenders were like puppets on a string if you could see the angles, and I was seeing all the angles.

However, it was still a close game, and Artie, though not totally dominant, did enough to keep his team in it. He played alongside Alex Hooper, Big Lou, and Craig Singleton, all of them from 149th Street. They were experienced guys with reputations uptown.

Alex was a six-foot-four swingman playing at Hampton University, and the muscular Craig was mostly a street guy, and brother of gangster Small Paul Singleton, who was very well known uptown. Small Paul and Craig were also the older brothers of Stymie Singleton, who was at the Dime when I was there. Craig had a rep for stretching people out and looked the part. Big Lou was a very good post and midrange scorer. Lou was the older brother of Stan, another guy I played with while at the Dime.

It was time to put the game away, and Jeff wanted the ball in my hands. We were the *young boys,* so we weren't supposed to win against vets like Alex Hooper and Artie Green, who took every spare moment to let us know who the *men* were. After scoring a basket to put his team up by one point with about fifteen seconds left, I heard Artie's high-pitched voice above all the park chatter after my team called a time-out.

"Yeah, this a man's game. This is where the real men step up. Ain't no room for no boys around here! Let's see where these niggas' hearts is," he yelled in our direction, clapping his hands.

I was thinking about winning the game and being the hero. Brendan Malone had told me the best players always stepped up and didn't have to be told to do it.

Artie's perimeter game didn't improve enough for the NBA, but on the playgrounds, there was always a place for someone who could outjump and outmaneuver people in the manner that he did. Two years ago, Artie dunked on Ray Williams viciously up at Columbia gym, and people said it was the best dunk they had ever seen.

Coming out of the time-out, I readied myself for the inevitable. It was time for me to begin building my legend, and what better way than beating Artie Green, a Harlem legend everyone knew?

I thought it would be hard to get the ball in the final seconds, considering how I lit them up. But in the playgrounds, circumstances and events were often unpredictable. It was unpredictable how easy it was for me to get to the ball, but it was easy. Mario inbounded the ball to Ike, our point guard, who immediately looked for me breaking back to the ball where Ike hit me with the pass. Everything around me intensified as I tightened my grip on the ball. I eyed my defender to see how he was playing me. Was he off balance? Was he overplaying me?

I made my move to the right, just outside the top of the key. Alex Hooper was on me. Alex was known for his offense, not as a defender, but he was experienced. He was putting up good numbers at Hampton and had a decent rep uptown. Most scorers rarely got credit for playing defense, but

I was extra careful with him guarding me. I thought he might be a better defender than some people knew. When you could score, people rarely looked at the rest of your game. I was one of the better shot blockers in my neighborhood, and certain guys were still saying I couldn't play defense.

Weak team defense was customary in most playground games, especially in local neighborhood tournaments like this one. This wasn't the case in the bigger summer leagues, but in the smaller games, structured defense was rare. If I beat Alex, someone might step up and help, but you could usually count on the rotation being slow and someone getting an open shot somewhere down the line. We just had to make sure to play it that way.

After driving right toward the wing, I stopped quickly on a dime and pivoted off a spin back to the center of the court. The sudden spin took me away from the help defense and seemed to open the whole court up. I was one foot beyond the foul line extended with a clear shot, a shot I'd made a thousand times, and at least four or five times this day alone. I could hear the people at the stat desk counting down the seconds: seven, six, five . . .

When I released the shot, it wasn't rushed. It felt the same leaving my hands, even though my footing wasn't perfect. I was already thinking about the rush of winning the game and beating a legend. My teammates would probably mob me, people around the fences would admire me, Chic would pay me, and most of all, I'd get Artie's respect, whether he wanted to give it to me or not. Two, one . . .

It was a shot that looked and felt good until it no longer did. It couldn't have felt more right. Sometimes you knew when your shot had a chance of falling short or being a little off, and it would surprise you when it went in, but this wasn't the case. This shot felt like it was right on the money.

Had my eyes been closed, I would have known the outcome by listening to the crowd as my shot rimmed out. The distance between high expectations of being the hero and the disappointing reality of missing a game winner seemed eons apart yet instantaneous at the same time.

The people huddled around the park fences that day got more than they anticipated. This was supposed to be a small game and an insignificant contest on nobody's radar, just a notch above a regular street pickup game. There was no big buildup, and no hype surrounding it. We were in the back of Colonel Young, playing in a small, somewhat secluded park, but people found their way back to watch an otherwise inconsequential weekend tournament.

"That's r-ight, Ice, they still couldn't stop you," someone shouted from the sideline. Another I didn't recognize added, "That boy is bad. They couldn't do nothing wit him."

But Artie, the most respected player in the park, wasn't going to let it go so easily.

"He did all that shit and miss the game winner? That tell you where his heart is. Nigga was scoring all game when it didn't count. But you gotta be able to handle that pressure. That show you right there he ain't ready for nothin."

All the points I scored didn't seem to matter now. I think I had thirty-six, someone else said forty, but every move that excited the crowd, every breakaway dunk or spinning layup, drew nothing but blanks now. Artie was walking away the winner and let it be known I didn't do it when it counted.

His words stung and washed away the euphoria. They would ring in my ears for a good part of the summer as I played in other leagues around Harlem. The summer was still young, and I knew I'd see Artie again. If he were a peer, or someone younger, maybe a response to his criticism would be justified, just for the sake of my rep. But something in me respected what he said. Even though I was gunning for his rep, I would have liked for him to say, "Hey, man, you played a good game. Nice moves." But instead he was letting everyone around him know I wasn't ready. I listened even though I hated what he was saying.

We didn't know each other. I was still a kid to him, just another young nigga playing ball. I was unsure if he remembered helping me up the day Butter smashed me to the ground after I hit a game-winning shot in our park. That was five years ago, and five years was a lifetime on the street.

Maybe Artie didn't remember me, but he had to be hearing the drums on the streets. And the beat of the drum was saying I was an up-and-coming player. When people thought of Harlem basketball, I wanted them to think of James Ice. After the game, Artie was still shooting arrows with his postgame comments he was sure I could hear.

As usual, I didn't let on how I was feeling, but no matter how many words of encouragement I heard about how well I played, I left the park feeling defeated. I didn't want to just entertain; I wanted to be known as a guy who handled pressure. I couldn't wait to meet Artie on the court again. The way I looked at it, I was getting older and better, and he was just getting older. I wanted another chance to shut his mouth, but I had to wait.

CHAPTER 39
STREETBALL

COLONEL YOUNG AT 145TH and Lenox belonged to Chic's tournament after dusk. His name rang out in this busy, high-traffic area. The number 3 subway line and M102 bus stop were on the corner, along with the park, and a few restaurants and bars drawing people into the area. The traffic around 145th and Lenox doubled and tripled when a good game was going on, reminiscent of the Rucker Tournament heyday. People climbed out of cars or the subway or walked across the 145th Street Bridge from the South Bronx to see the action.

Chic stacked his tournament with as many high-profile players and teams as he could, and this generated even more interest. Colonel Young was well known as a sanctioned Rucker site. It was a perfect venue for featuring night games to rival other Harlem tournaments like King Towers and the RYA League near the Polo Grounds. We were the "house" team, which meant 145th was our home turf. Everyone on the street was saying Smokey's Machine was going to win it all, but we had all the local support.

Smokey's team featured Artie Green, Sam Worthen, and Kevin "Super Kev" Williams. Kev had attended a junior college before joining St. John's, along with fellow New Yorkers Chris Mullins, Billy Goodwin, and the newly acquired Walter Berry. Walt was initially playing on our squad, but then opted to play with Smokey instead. Apparently Smokey was willing to pay more for him. The explosive Fred "Disco" Brown, who was attending VCU, and Richie Adams, who was on his way to UNLV, were also on Smokey's roster. Berry and Big Ritch were usually on Chic's streetball payroll, but both broke away to play with Smokey. It was normal for the best players to exercise their free-agent status with different street sponsors for larger payoffs. Smokey's Machine was the favorite to win because they had some of the best talent on the streets.

Smokey was an old-school hustler from downtown and had been in the game for a while, longer than new-jack hustlers like Chic, LA, and Rich Porter. People said he was in business with Freddie Meyers, whose street rep was well known. With Nicky Barnes, Guy Fisher, Frank Matthews, and Frank Lucas off the streets, Meyers was the last of their era of drug operators still living the life of a millionaire.

When I heard about Smokey's squad, I wasn't scared, but I knew it was a big mountain to climb. Chic's tournament attracted all the legends in one place, where we could kill them all at once.

There were other teams in the tournament with credible talent. Easy Ed Pinckney was with the Gauchos. Scooter and Rodney McCray were on somebody's roster, as were John Salley, Olden "Big O" Polynice, Pearl Washington, and Bill "Fat" Sadler. There were no weak teams in Chic's tournament the summer of '83, and we were the youngest squad.

It was a perfect storm of high-profile athletes, and the best thing we had going for us was being the house team. Everyone venturing into 145th Street park to play us were outsiders, so we had the people on our side.

Chic's tournament would draw the kind of crowds that once dominated the corner of 155th Street in the early '70s. The scene showed a disorganized concentration of people scrambled across the sidewalk, huddled in groups, leaning against cars, fences, poles, kids hanging from fences, others settled in trees and forming settlements on the nearby bridge. It was everything I'd come to love about Harlem basketball. It was pure electricity.

Despite losing against Artie earlier in the summer, I saw nothing but opportunity for setting the city on fire and getting revenge. If I could beat even one legend, it was worth the risk. Brimming with confidence I'd cultivated in my own neighborhood, I had an enormous chip on my shoulder. I was bitter about dropping out of junior college and hardened enough to go after anyone I played against. As the summer progressed, wherever I went, people wanted to know where my next game was, and the recognition was enough to keep me pushing.

Smokey had the big names playing for him because everyone knew he took care of his players. Smokey walked the sidelines in gators, dress suits, and an occasional Fedora brim and cigar. He drove a charcoal-gray Porsche 928 before it was even out on the streets. Tom Cruise's new movie *Risky Business* may have gotten people talking about the 928, but Smokey was driving one before the movie hit theaters.

Throughout my years of playing on the playgrounds, I learned a lot about the psyche of a hustler and guys living and dependent on opportunities from hustling. They were compelled to hunt for competition in just about everything. The successful hustler pushed all limits of excess and reveled in the spoils of material wealth. In the midst of poverty, tenement slums, and corner bums, it was about materialism, fast money, and notoriety. This was the cultural mantra of a hustler's success. If no one had seen a 928 Porsche, then someone had to get one. If LA's turbo SAAB was moving and shaking up and down Seventh Avenue, and no one else had one, it put him on top of the rest.

Playground personalities ran parallel with street hustlers and their groupies. Even cats working nine to five were out fronting to be a part of the scene. Rappers and deejays were attracting groupies of females, dancers, and hip-hop heads from all over the city. People came from the Bronx, Brooklyn, Queens, New Jersey, Upstate, and other cities to hang out in Harlem's underground economy. Harlem was still the prototypical street culture for Blacks living on the East Coast. It was where you saw the latest trends, flashiest cars, and biggest events in Black pop culture. Some of the trends, by the 1990s, would find their way into mainstream society and become a part of a multibillion-dollar industry called hip-hop, driven by young people unprepared to own the culture we were creating.

I began associating with guys who didn't give a fuck about laws, school, or about finding a job. People might see me out with certain guys and assume I was hustling too, but the truth was most of the people out there weren't into that life. But "that life" was all around us. There might be ten guys on a corner, and two or three out of them might be into something. A lot of times, none of the ten were into anything heavy that involved drugs, stickups, or murder. Harlem was home to the thief, hoodlum, and the occasional murderer, but it was also home to the Good Samaritan, straight A student, and the everyday, working-class poor person.

Music, fashion, sports, art, and popular culture in Harlem changed faster than anyone bothered to measure. The '70s were gone, and the '80s ushered in a new generation coming into young adulthood. We were fueled by energy few of us knew how to harness.

CHAPTER 40
WEST VIRGINIA STATE COLLEGE

OTHER THAN A FEW calls from area junior colleges, my college options seemed to evaporate. I wasn't aware of how short my leash was and how quickly things could move on. I made it onto major scouting reports, but it was on the thinnest of threads. I seemed to have been forgotten. No one was calling, and having left Pensacola, I was impatient.

Chic was looking out when it came to money. I was keen enough not to ask, but he was generous. Still living with Ma, my only source of income was playing in his tournament. Ma was unaware why so many young boys in our building knew her name, or why people she'd never had a conversation with were quick to say, "Hi, Miss Washington." She had no idea where I was getting money or what kind of rep I had concerning basketball. Since I started playing, Ma was always around the fringes of my world but never really in my world.

Chic, with his wide-gapped teeth and freckled brown skin, was an odd dude in the drug game. He wasn't smooth, or handsome, or a trendy fashion magnet like some of the other young hustlers, but he was still well liked by a lot of ballers. He made it a point to brandish thousands of dollars in front of us, like he was giving out per-diem stipends for a road trip. He rode around with a trunk full of boxes with sneakers of all sizes like a mobile footlocker. If you were a player on the scene with skills, Chic was going to look out for you.

Even though he was one of Harlem's fast-cash moguls, no matter how many lizards and silk shirts he threw on, Chic also had his detractors, like any hustler on the streets. He had a rep for buying friends. I liked him because he loved basketball. Even when he was a corner nickel-and-dime hustler, he was out there on the courts, watching us play and sharing his observations.

I wasn't the only guy doing what Connie Hawkins was banned from college basketball for doing more than twenty years ago. Players in the ghetto accepted cash from various people willing to give it. Walter Berry, D-Mac, Dujii, Richie Adams, and plenty others were getting "ends" every now and then from Chic because he liked being around great players.

In late June, shortly before the Fourth of July, I got a call from Craig Carse, a first-year coach at West Virginia State College. I didn't know the guy and had never heard of their basketball program. He immediately started applying pressure. Cold calls didn't mean much to me anymore, but he started off telling me how great he heard I was, so I listened.

"James, we're building a top-notch program at West Virginia State, and with a player like you, I don't see any reason we can't make it to the national tournament."

"What division are you in?"

"We play in the West Virginia Conference, which is really a top-notch, competitive conference."

"What division is the conference in?"

"We're Division I NAIA."

I had never heard of a Division I NAIA conference, but I did know a little about the NAIA. When I asked around, I found out any conference outside NCAA Division I was considered Division II. Phil Walker had played for an NAIA school; so had Ted Campbell, at Coppin State. I respected these guys, and both had a lot to do with the emergence of my game, but I had no intention of following their footsteps into an NAIA school. I didn't think that could get me in the league. Even if I couldn't get into a DI school, playing in the CIAA for schools like Norfolk State, Virginia Union, and Winston-Salem, Division II institutions with a track record for producing great pro ball players, were better options. I didn't say anything to Carse, but West Virginia State didn't interest me.

"James, have you ever heard of a player named Sedale Threatt?"

"Never heard of him."

"Well, Sedale played in our conference and was drafted by the 76ers this year. From what I've heard, you may be just as talented; imagine where you'll be in two or three years. I've led two teams to the nationals from our conference and—"

"With who?"

"For the past four years I've been an assistant with Salem College, a team in our conference, and recruited two college all-Americans. James, I wouldn't be talking to you if I didn't think you could be an all-American at State. That's why you're the entire focus of my recruiting efforts at this point."

"Yeah, I understand that, but I still want to play Division I."

"James, we play in a small conference, but you're not going to find any better players six foot six and under than you'll find in the NAIA. Ron Leggett, Sedale Threatt, Daryl Pearson, these guys can flat out play. Daryl is from New York also."

"I never heard of any of those guys," I told him.

I listened to Carse's words from a distance, too far to distinguish if they made sense. My heart was set on the Big East, playing against Chris Mullins, Berry, and Georgetown. The way I saw it, the Eastern Seaboard was the future of college basketball. Willing now to entertain offers from smaller schools like Iona, Holy Cross, and Providence, I knew going small and local in the NY tri-state area was still a better option than going small and local in West Virginia. Who was going to see me in West Virginia? Two years ago, I snubbed Marshall University, a small Division I college forty minutes west of Carse's West Virginia State, and they had a bigger program than he was offering.

I was better than I was a year ago and knew I was ready for D-I. Both my mind and body had changed in a way that seemed to put everything in sync on the court. The fast-paced action of the playgrounds demanded instinctive ability and adaptive skills. I'd seen enough situations on the court and studied enough basketball to recognize certain things I could exploit quickly. This kind of training had already prepared me to play anywhere. Now it was a matter of getting onto the biggest stage in the world to show everyone what I could do.

On the streets, I was entering my prime years for a playground athlete. My individual offensive ability had progressed enough to turn any one-on-one—or in some cases, one-on-two—situations to my advantage. This was great for the playground, but I was beginning to wonder if college basketball was even for me, and if it wasn't, what was I going to do with my life?

After my first conversation with Craig Carse, I determined he was the most persistent coach I had ever talked to. Pat Kennedy was a fast talker, and so was Carnesecca when you got him going, but Carse took both speed and volume of language to a new level. If I was running the streets and happened not to be home, he was talking to Ma. She liked him. Carse was a Christian, and once he found out my mother's weak spot, he was in there with her and knew exactly what to say.

I wasn't sure if it was Carse or the prospect of getting me out of the house Ma liked more. It took a few weeks, but I finally agreed to visit West Virginia State College after meeting Carse and his assistant Jim Boone down in the Village at West Fourth Street. The two seemed overwhelmed by the density of the city, so I thought I'd cut them a break by not asking them to meet me in front of my building on 144th Street.

Ma and I were still arguing day to day, so my trip to West Virginia came at a good time. I figured I could go down for a few days, get away from Harlem, and show her I had at least one viable option for my future.

I was on borrowed time with her. She asked more and more questions about where I was getting money, and of course I couldn't tell her it came from drug dealers. And I couldn't tell her the money I received could easily double or triple if I caught a good dice game. I was gambling nearly every week. Walking around with hundreds of dollars in my pocket and bringing home new sneakers on a weekly basis convinced me I didn't need a job.

On the other hand, nearly everyone on the street, including my younger sister, Prissy, knew what Ma didn't know. I was a commodity now. Playing for Chic's summer team meant at least a couple hundred dollars after most games—almost like his personal insurance policy that I would show for every game. And Chic wasn't my only source of cash. If I ran into LA, his first words were often, "Ice, you alright? You good?" Big Smiley was also stuffing a bunch of twenties in my pocket whenever I ran across him. He and I used to go at it hard on the court, but he scaled back on ball and got deeper into the hustling, cashing in on the crack trade.

I was also playing in the Entertainer's tournament with Kool Mo Dee's crew from 123rd Street. Neil Hawk, Nappy Red, and Buda were lacing my pockets whenever I showed my face at Mount Morris Park for a game. One of the guys down there, known as Smoke, hit me off with $700 for nothing more than providing him an entertaining game. We lost and he still hit me off. He was an obvious hustler, but I didn't really know the guy. Neil Hawk told me to be careful around him, but I took the money anyway. With all my newfound hustler sponsorships, I wasn't hurting for money the summer of '83. If these guys wanted to share their fortune, I saw no reason to stop them.

Even straight nine-to-five guys like Daryl MacFadden, a McDonald's GM at the 125th Street store, hit me off with cash and free food whenever I walked into a Harlem McDonalds. If Mac wasn't in the store, a simple phone call and I could get free food. I worked for Mac back when he was one of the youngest GMs at McDonald's. He was pulling about $1,000 a week back then—not bad for a guy on the straight. He gave me my first real job in 1979. Mac loved basketball and put games together between the other Harlem restaurants on 132nd and 145th Streets. I was one of the better players working in the stores at the time, and Mac became a big fan of my game. He planned to promote me to a manager, but by the time I figured that out, I had quit to chase ball games on the streets.

I'd run into Mac at some of my games and he'd get excited, asking me what I was doing, what school I was going to, or when my next game was. We were always cool, but some guys just wanted to be around if I made it to the top, and Mac always felt like one of those.

• • •

Feeling pressure from Ma, I flew to Charleston's Yeager Airport for a visit to a college I'd never heard of and had no intention of attending. Jim Boone, a blond, skinny White guy who looked no older than me, picked me up. Thin lipped, with short, straight, brownish-blonde hair, he told me he was teaching a business course at State and was a student assistant for the team. Coach Boone had also played for State and was from a place called Winfield, about fifteen minutes away from the campus. He was friendly, but I surmised pretty quickly he didn't know much about what he was doing. I liked him a little more than Carse because he wasn't always talking.

Despite the volume of words I filtered from Carse, from time to time things he said got my attention. He mentioned recruiting Earl Jones from UDC and John Taylor, seven-foot-tall centers, to join the one he'd already signed. I'd heard of Earl Jones back when I played in the Fork Union Academy tournament. Jones was a former high school all-American who didn't like the big lights of D-I basketball. This guy was a high Division I prospect who decided to go to a Division II school, and no one could figure out why. According to Carse, he wasn't happy at UDC and was looking to leave. Jones had attended high school in West Virginia, and Carse said he was willing to play for State.

Carse also talked about Wil Rodgers, a six-foot-six guard who, like me, was a big scorer, out of Dunbar High in Washington, DC. Rather than have us dip into each other's time, he planned to play me at the point, even though he had never seen me play the point. Someone he knew or trusted must have told him I could handle the rock.

Carse made his program sound as if it was going to rival Denny Crum's at Louisville. Not many schools could land three seven-footers and put two six-foot-six backcourt players on the floor, so I wondered if it could be true.

Once I got to campus, the open space and greenery of the yard was refreshing. The smell of large trees and the sight of red-bricked buildings put my mind at ease. I thought, *This is what a college campus should feel like.* Wooden benches reinforced the walkways connecting different buildings, with one central main street splitting the campus down the middle. It wasn't a super-large campus, but it was nice.

Carse gave me the impression he didn't intend to keep any players from the previous season. He was cleaning house. Two of his new recruits were already in summer school. Wil Rodgers immediately presented himself as a person I should pay attention to. Like Donnie in Florida, Wil filled me in on everything going on in the streets of DC, from Cornell Jones to Rayful Edmonds.

The other recruit was Al Woods, a Virginia Beach native who seemed fairly accustomed to life at State, though he had only been there a month. He already had a girlfriend, Tina Collier, a local girl, and Wil let me know Al spent most of his time with her. Al and I said a few words and kept it moving. Unlike Wil, the guy didn't seem too friendly, and neither was I, so we didn't have much to say. Both these guys had attended other schools. Wil transferred from Taft College in California, and Al had attended several community colleges over a course of three or four years. Despite being classified as a sophomore, Al was already twenty-three years old.

I was scheduled to stay in West Virginia two days but got the impression Carse would keep me for weeks if he could. The more he talked, the more I withdrew. He was constantly probing for things he thought might appeal to me, like the point guard idea. Playing point was a challenge I was up for. I was a natural wing player, a scorer, but playing point was something I'd never tried and would push my boundaries.

Carse wanted to see what I had, so he had us work out for a few hours. The gym, known as "The Pit," had an odd-looking setup. The stands were three-quarters of the way around the court, but none of the seats were positioned behind the team bench area. It looked like it couldn't hold more than a couple thousand fans, waning in comparison to the gymnasiums at St. John's, Villanova, or even Iona's gym, which could hold 8,000. As for the

Carrier Dome, I tried not to think about it.

Wil was not only good in our workouts, he was exceptional. The guy was a shooter. He had a natural touch that reminded me of Chris Mullins. Wil also had a deceptive high dribble—not as good as Kenny Hutchinson's but still very good. I was impressed not only with the percentage of shots he made, but also by the level of precision. His shots weren't even hitting rim. I thought he was a legit D-I recruit.

Al was not as skilled and looked like a developmental player. He was more intense than Wil and seemed to work harder, but he reminded me of a guy learning to play again after a tragic accident. And he was pretty old to be in his second year of college, something that had me wondering what happened with his career. Whatever happened with Al, his confidence must have suffered. He was developing a hook shot, and Wil started calling him "Hook Dunker." But I could see this guy needed more development as a player to get to the level I thought I was already playing at.

I left State thinking it wasn't a bad place, just not the place for me. Even with Carse and Wil talking about Earl Jones and making it to the national tournament and how I would be drafted like Sedale Threatt, I didn't trust it. Coach Carse was saying so many things that they couldn't possibly all be true.

On the morning I was scheduled to go back to New York, I was in Prillerman Hall, and Carse had been over most of the morning. I walked into the kitchen to grab my orange juice out of the fridge and found several pieces of notebook paper on the small table with scribbled notations: "James is a great person," "This institution needs people like James," "We are blessed to have met this outstanding young man." There must have been ten affirming notes spread out over the table. He seemed to be feigning sleep. Wil told me Carse had a psychology degree, so I guess he was using what he thought he knew.

His intent was so obvious it was insulting. He suddenly "woke up" and hurriedly gathered his notes, as if he hadn't left them there for me to see. After this stunt, I couldn't muster a word to say to him. The entire way back to Yeager Airport, I was quiet. I thought Carse might have a mental problem. What normal person did shit like that? Did he think ghetto kids were that stupid or emotionally inept? Or did he think a guy who lost a father and grandmother in the last two years and was the product of a single mother could benefit from a reaffirming boost to his self-esteem?

Whatever he was trying to do, it hadn't worked. Coming off my situation with Boes in Florida, I left Charleston with an even greater sense of distrust.

CHAPTER 41
YOUNG BOYS MAKE NOISE

ONCE BACK FROM WEST Virginia, I attacked my games with a renewed purpose. The visit to State was an insurance policy I planned never to cash in. I was happy to get back to Chic's tournament, and to Harlem.

Chic's tournament and King Towers weren't sanctioned leagues; they were strictly for street cred and putting on a show. The matter was as simple as someone getting a park permit and putting the tournament together. The unrestricted nature of these leagues made them successful. A young guy like me, one possibly headed to college, could play against pro vets and not be penalized for playing in a pro league. Playing in these tournaments kept us from sacrificing our amateur status but gave us an opportunity to test our skills against legitimate college and veteran pro players.

Our team was comprised of first- and second-year college guys. Mario Ellie was at American University, D-Mac at Westchester Community, and Rodney Murray was in Florida at Daytona Beach Community College. Craig Willis, Craig Ware, and Ed Boone were all at small schools in the Northeast. We were the only guys without a big-name superstar, but when we began beating people, the local area packed the stands to support us.

We were the giant killers, the home-team favorites looking to smash the big names. Midway through the season I knew we had something special, and figuring it out along the way was fun. We were playing together as a unit, and everyone accepted their roles without bitching about it. Mario could score, but he didn't mind being a second or third option. D-Mac was a slasher with an entertaining style who could also score, but he and I never contested the spotlight, even though our abilities were similar. Ike ran the point and delivered the ball; Boone and Willis hit the boards, played good defense and filled scoring gaps when the option was there. Craig Ware and Rodney Murray easily gave us ten or fifteen coming off the bench, and if one of the main guys was off our game, either could drop twenty-five or thirty.

We were modular and interdependent, one always playing off the other. I was doing some impressive stuff out on the break and was considered our "zone buster" as the team's most deadly outside threat. I could bomb from medium or long range and was known for floaters coming across the middle, shooting off the wrong foot. Ed Boone could hit from the deep corner and was a nightmare for a zone as well. Against Harlem World, I hit five shots in a row from the outside, forcing them to abandon their zone press defense. I was also one of the best ball handlers on our team, and so was D-Mac, and we consistently snatched rebounds to initiate the break.

On another team a point guard might have had a problem with me or Mac taking off like that. With Ike, it was all about winning. He had no problem getting out on the wing if I was running the break from the center of the court. At any given time, we had a speed advantage in every position. We helped each other on defense, and anyone who came into the game ran the court and filled the lane.

Soon everyone was talking about the Young Boys Make Noise. My popularity was higher than it ever had been. It felt like all of Harlem knew who I was. Everywhere I happened to be, I saw a friendly face, an admirer, or someone who'd heard of me. I felt people's eyes on me, and I knew it was because of what was happening in Chic's tournament. Younger players were watching me, checking out how I handled myself in the same way I watched Joe Hammond and Artie Green when I was a shorty. This time in the spotlight was what I had fantasized about all those days in the park alone, shooting, dribbling and experimenting, imagining I was a big playground star who everyone was talking about.

I may have appeared like I didn't notice, but this was exactly what I wanted to happen. It was the kind of adulation I needed, especially having nothing else to cling to. I wanted the attention, the credit, the rep, because in the end, it was all I had going for me. Too bad Ma didn't see it that way.

"James, you better take that scholarship to West Virginia."

"Ma, what are you talking about?"

"You heard me. Has anyone else offered you a scholarship to school?"

"No, not yet, but soon."

"How do you know that?"

"Because I know, Ma. I'm good."

"You too good for your own good, James, and you think you know everything. How many chances you think you gonna get? So now you don't like this coach in West Virginia either?"

"Yeah, Ma. I don't trust him."

"You didn't trust the other one either!"

"Cuz they be lyin', Ma. You expect me jus to be a fool and let everyone use me."

"You need to use yourself. You wasting time, and I ain't gon let you waste mine. You better take that offer in West Virginia."

"Ma, I ain't goin' down there."

"Well, you not staying here, not without a job, and running around these streets playing basketball."

"It's cool. I'll jus stay downtown at Aunt Margaret's then."

It was as frustrating talking to Ma as it was for her to communicate with me. She watched me blow several chances to do things the right way. I could have graduated from high school and gone to almost any college I wanted. Even the prestigious Ivy League institutions and the Air Force Academy in Colorado sent me letters of interest. These were schools people would cut off their right arms to attend. To Ma, I was as a slacker, looking for the easy road. And to some degree, deep down I suspected she might be right.

I resented her not because she pressed me on my issues. I resented her inability to understand what I believed I was born to do. Why did she think all these people were calling and sending letters? Why did so many people think I was special, but she didn't really know why? Had she taken the time to find out? I began to resent her never attending any of my games. I resented her not knowing completely who I was, or what I was capable of. The basketball court was the only place I demonstrated my talent and my unique gifts to the world. She was missing a whole lot about who her son had become and how I'd gotten to where I was. There was little chance of her getting through to me. And there was no way I was going to change her mind.

We cruised through our first playoff game against the Broncos. They had Black Juny, Rudy Outlaw, and Big Bob Jones, all from the South Bronx. They were solid college scholarship material. People were calling Bobby

Jones "Baby Saddler" after Pepperdine's Bill Saddler. All of these guys had played for Brandeis High School. Bobby was about six foot three and always on the heavy side. He looked overweight but was nimble and had a handle that shocked crowds and made him entertaining. They didn't think a big, girthy dude could move like he did. Big Bobby was the showman but wasn't the type to carry a game because he simply took too many risks on the court. When it worked, it was amazing to see. Juny was a six-foot athletic guard who could play the point or the two, and I called Rudy "Mr. Hustle" because he was always playing hard and didn't back down from anyone. He was six foot two and scored when he had to but was known more as a defensive player with heart.

The Broncos also had Olden Polynice, who was on his way to the University of Virginia. Big O was seven feet tall but was often swallowed up in a big game due to his limited offensive ability. None of that mattered because we ran over them with our fast-breaking style. D-Mac put on a show toward the end, yanking the ball like it was on a string and dazzling people with spin moves to the basket and either passing it off or flipping the ball in the basket with finger rolls.

Ike was our floor leader. He was built like a small tank. He had a thick neck and Earl Campbell thighs, so he looked like a running back. Coming off four years of high school ball at Rice, Ike knew how to play to win, and it showed in some of his decisions on the court. When teams went to the zone, he knew where to look for me. I had a nose for getting into scoring position and didn't hesitate to drill shots from anywhere on the court. Only teams who gave up even bothered playing us zone. Coming out in a zone was like saying, "We can't stop you guys, so we're going to take our chances." By the time the playoffs came, we were as in sync as any team playing in a playground tournament could be. Mario, D-Mac, and I were the highest producers on offense, but Ike was the trigger releasing the ammunition.

After beating Bobby Jones's team, it was time for our real test in the semifinal game against the Gauchos. They had quite a few name players. Those who proclaimed to know basketball were picking them to end our season even though we had beaten them one out of two games. People expected our team to fold; some guys in my own block didn't think we could beat the more established players when it all counted.

Some of these guys overlooked what basketball was really about. We were going up against great players, but during the process, we had become a very good team. We helped each other on defense because we had to. I don't know how many times I came over to block a guy's shot after he'd beaten one of my teammates. We knew instinctively that if Ed Pinckney got the ball inside on Ed Boone or Craig Willis, the weak-side wing had to double down and get the big guy to pass it to someone else. When that didn't work, we pressured the passer to make it difficult to get it in to him.

Jeff emphasized the rebound. Even when in at point, I knew I had to hit the boards and not always take off on the break. Any of us could get the rebound and initiate a fast break, and it was rarely reckless or unbalanced. We had finishers.

I'd never played better basketball than this summer of 1983. I also had never played with a better group of players, or against better competition. It took these three things to elevate my game. It was a perfect storm of basketball. I was hitting the deep jumper consistently and creating shots off the break in spectacular fashion. My athletic ability was maturing but left enough ceiling to improve. I was attacking the basket more, and as a result, I was dunking on guys a lot more than I ever had. Mario was probably our hardest dunker, and Craig Ware, who we called "Sky," was our most stylish dunker, but I wasn't far behind.

We beat the Gauchos in the semifinals despite facing off against Fat Saddler, Pearl, Big Ed Pinckney and Little Joe. People were saying Rodney McCray, from Mount Vernon, was going to play. He would have been a problem but didn't show. Little Joe was a good player, but his time had come and gone. Pearl was a little late to our game, and it felt like he brought additional fans with him. By 1983, he was a phenomenon in Harlem and everywhere else in New York. Everyone wanted to see this guy play. He was playing at King Towers, and when the crowd heard he had another game at 145th Street, they followed him there from 116th.

I played big games against Harlem World, the Broncos, and Gauchos. The bigger the game, the better my performances. On one play, Little Joe was out on the break after a turnover, going up for what he thought was an easy layup. I was out on the wing and quick on the pursuit on defense. Joe couldn't dunk and went up for his shot, but I timed him perfectly, sticking the ball to the metal backboard and holding it there, a Harlem playground custom, before bringing it down. The crowd went crazy.

Chic's tournament was my second time going up against Pearl. The first was in the Governor's Cup tournament in 1981 at River Park Towers. After observing him, I really wanted to play with this guy. For the second time, I came out on top.

Pearl was so popular that I doubt he noticed. I wanted to reach out to him, get a feel for what kind of guy he was, and maybe even ask him to talk to Brendan Malone for me. I wanted to share the story about the kid down in Virginia who mistook my name for his. But Pearl was always surrounded by an entourage of fans, admirers, and gawkers, even in Harlem. It must have really been crazy for him in his native Brooklyn. I decided in that moment to resign myself to the "entourage" gravitating toward me. We beat his team despite his killer crossover.

Our next hurdle was the championship game against Smokey's Machine. All summer, Artie's words about my missing the final shot to win the neighborhood game back in June resonated in my head. Now I had a chance to vindicate myself—to set something straight in my mind and his. Before the championship game, he was going around saying we weren't ready, talking shit, beating the drums he knew we would eventually hear. He said D-Mac and I were too skinny, that we needed to be in the weight room, and how he was going to take it to us and make us quit, like bitches. At least, that was the word I got from some of the cats I knew from 149th Street.

Artie lived around 149th Street, D-Mac on 146th, and I on 144th, so word traveled quickly. It traveled even quicker through our promoter, GM, and sponsor, Chic himself. Somewhere in the back of my mind, Artie was still a legend. But he was the enemy now, out to ruin my thing, distort my rep, something I was working hard to build. The only way to reach his stature was to bust his ass and shut his fucking mouth. But Artie wasn't the only cat we had to worry about on Smokey's team.

Kevin Williams was not quite six foot four, but he was tough and aggressive. People thought he was going to shut us down, specifically me. I respected Artie, but mostly I respected his entertainment value. Legend or not, I didn't think he could stop me. "Super Kev" was more aggressive and better defensively. Kev hadn't showed up for most of the games, but this was a non-sanctioned tournament with few regulations, and therefore no minimum number of games was required to be eligible to play in the championship game. In most other leagues, Williams wouldn't be eligible because he missed too many games. Similarly, Walter Berry, Richie Adams, Sam Worthen, and Fred "Disco" Brown didn't always show up, but Smokey made sure they showed for the championship.

This game was going to be played before a prime-time audience. For all of our games, the crowds were thick, vibrant, and overflowing. Every player wanted to play on a Harlem stage; it was what we all dreamed about as kids.

We were prepared for Smokey and his crew of all-stars. He had so many players with big reps that somebody was going to have to sit down. Smokey thought he could throw a bunch of superstars together and win. Fred "Disco" Brown would start or be the star on almost any other team, but with a team that had Artie, Sam Worthen, and Kevin Williams, you could anticipate somebody was going to sit more than they wanted to. Something else working against them was Smokey himself, who wanted to be a coach. Guys respected Smokey's rep on the streets, but really, he had no idea what to do with a team of stacked superstars, or how to manage their time and keep things organized. All he knew was that he wanted to win. Sam Worthen, who was like a coach on the floor in almost any game, influenced and made the decisions when Smokey wasn't interfering.

Chic, on the other hand, played the background on our bench. He knew the game, but he was more of the enthusiastic GM who understood not to try and coach us. Jeff was a better strategist. He made the subs, designed the plays, and did most of the talking, and Ike backed him up as our floor leader and captain. This all factored into the championship game against Smokey's Machine.

I had enormous incentives to play well. LA bet ten Gs on us to win. It was just another night of gambling for him. He hit me off with $300 before the game even started. I immediately handed the money to my protégé, Ant Poole. I'd get seven more stacks if we won, maybe more if I managed to get the MVP. Chic also had a big bet with Smokey. Some said he put up twenty-five Gs, others said it was fifty, but I didn't need to know. I wasn't out there for the money.

The game didn't start until nine that night, and I spent all that day thinking about it. I couldn't relax. My thoughts were consumed with how I'd opened a lot of people's eyes over the summer. In a game at RYA on 159th Street, I shook someone with a crossover dribble and took off one step inside the foul line for a dunk that still sent chills over my body when I remembered how the crowd reacted. I felt like any woman in the stands could have been mine that night.

Leading up to the showdown, I pictured plays and games as if they had just happened. I thought about the game where I feinted one way before breaking back toward the ball to receive a pass from D-Mac. I was nearly two feet beyond the key when I caught the ball, turned in one fluid motion, and launched a shot with the game tied. I was out in deep waters, but my shot was deliberate, no hesitation, with the defense caught off guard, and with complete confidence I extended my follow-through, hitting nothing but the bottom as the ball sank through the net. No rim. The crowd aahed. I still felt the surge of adrenaline and reveled internally at how helpless my defender looked. How could you stop anyone with that kind of confidence?

Walking down 144th Street toward Lenox Avenue the night of the championship game brought all those good thoughts back. It was a Saturday night, still the best of all Harlem nights. People were hanging out in front of my building on Eighth Avenue and in the nearby tenements up and down the block of 144th Street. Mr. Levy was just closing up his candy store. A few shorties caught a glimpse of me walking toward Lenox and got excited. They were nine and ten, and even though some of our games didn't end until midnight, they followed me down the block, asking questions.

My crew was going to be there, and so would the other players who had been eliminated, all blended in with the hustlers taking big bets. I was calm now. At least, I thought I was. Traffic was crazy, people were double-parked, and in front of the park the entire sidewalk from 145 to 144th Street was covered with people. The small crew of young followers I accumulated on my way to the park were insignificant compared to this mob. They began climbing fences to get a good viewing spot. The 145th Street Bridge was covered with people sitting on the railings. A few police were posted near the subway stop on 145th, and people driving by peered through their car windows, looking at the spectacle. The stands, fences, and wooden benches inside and outside the court vicinity were condensed with bodies. It was a frenzied atmosphere.

I waded through wall-to-wall bodies to get to the court as people who recognized me tried to move aside. I pressed my way through, particularly through select females who caught my eye. People I knew spoke and nodded as I gave a smile or an acknowledgment. I saw faces I'd never seen before but more than enough I recognized. Steve Burtt was there, and so was Gary Springer, guys I made sure to speak to. Mike Rich, Imp, and Wendell—guys I respected from the block—were there. A lot of people I looked up to were going to be watching me. All of these guys had seen me play, but never when it all counted, never when the spotlight was so large. In a game like this, all the people came out—the hottest players, the hottest hustlers, the sexiest girls. Everyone came to watch and to be seen. If you failed in this moment, you might never live it down.

Finally, I made it through the crowd and to my team's bench, which was as crowded as the rest of the park. We were all excited about being on center stage. The mayhem was overwhelming.

The game announcer went to work and could be heard above all the chatter from the hundreds of milling people. As players entered the park and became visible, he made his informal introductions. "Uh-oh, there he is; entering the park, it's James Ice. It's about to get heated in here. Don't leave your seats, ladies and gentlemen. You don't want to miss this one."

He highlighted everyone with a street persona: Mario E-lie, D-Mac, Walter Berry "The Jedi," Sam "The Man" Worthen, and Big Ritch "The Animal." I didn't know who our announcer was, but he knew all the players on the scene.

By the start of the game, I was determined to do my thing but was more nervous than I had ever been for any game. A lot was at stake. Smokey managed to send a few playful, disparaging remarks my way as I pretended to ignore him. "You ain't ready for this kind of game, son. Kev gon lock yo ass up."

I smiled and continued my layup line warmups. I noticed my uncle Mosley, who was also Kenny Smith's uncle, in the crowd. I stopped and went over to say a few words. He had watched a few of our games and started following our team. He told me Kenny was on his way to UNC, and he was driving him to Chapel Hill in his Cadillac. When he told me about Jet, I felt bad I couldn't tell him I was going to school somewhere. UNC was one of the few schools I didn't get a letter from.

After watching me play all summer, Uncle Mo insisted I was more talented than his other, "Tarheel-bound" nephew, saying I should be playing on TV soon. Like Lorch, he thought Kenny was a better fundamental player but that I had more natural talent and potentially a higher ceiling than Jet. I was going to need all that natural talent against Smokey's Machine.

During the game, as expected, Kevin Williams played me like I stole something from him. He started out aggressively, evaluating my reaction. I was targeted, and so I had to deal with Super Kev as best I could. I held back starting out, creating a false illusion I wasn't going to be an offensive factor in the game. I was taller and longer than Kev and knew I could get my shot off, but I had to be smart about it and not force it. I didn't think we could win unless I had a good game. Disappearing offensively meant our chances of winning would probably disappear too. I didn't want to hear Artie Green's mouth again if I came up short. In a game surrounded by so much hype, it was easy to lose focus.

The entire first half, I pushed the fast break every chance I got and crashed the offensive boards on every shot. On one play, I caught the offensive rebound without bringing it back down and dunked it over the outstretched hands of Walter Berry and Big Richie Adams, two of the biggest, baddest dunking motherfuckas on the street. It was perfectly timed, and one of the most spectacular moves of the game. I was on another level after that dunk. Going over Berry's back for the "tap-dunk" erupted the large crowd. Walt was dunking on everyone, so I guess it was his turn.

I got comfortable in the game and heated up offensively. Initially Kevin's aggression made my guys unsure of how and where to get me the ball, so I took gambles on defense. I blocked shots from the weak side and initiated fast breaks and managed to get another high-flying dunk. By the second half I was back to scoring on my patented spin move and hitting jump shots from anywhere I could get free. Kev blocked one of my shots clean and was called for a foul. He complained to the ref and got a technical. It was a clean block, but Williams could be a hothead and seemed to pull back after that.

By the end of the game, the score wasn't close. Smokey's team of legends never got it together. They were confused over strategy, and that's all we needed. Was Walter going to get the ball or Artie? What about the tallest man on the floor, Richie Adams? Kevin also needed to get his shots. What about Fred Brown? He had to get his. This was the biggest stage in Harlem, and everyone wanted to shine. The only player with a cooperative style that made other players better was Sam Worthen. Sam was a magical point guard but couldn't salvage this one. Adding to their frustration was the fact our team was so young. They thought we would blink, but the whole park was behind us when we stepped up to the challenge. The Young Boys Make Noise did something I had never seen guys as young as us do: we beat a team of street legends.

We set a precedent that would be repeated over and over again in the '80s and '90s, where young, unproven street stars captured everyone's imagination and stepped up to beat college, pro, and veteran playground legends.

I played the entire game and hit the final shot of the tournament from half court at the buzzer to close it out. It was a perfect storybook ending to my summer. The crowd collapsed onto the court and mobbed me, hugging and pushing. I tried to keep my eye on Artie but lost sight of him. I didn't want to brag; I just wanted to see his face. I wanted to see his eyes and gauge what he thought now. I remembered Smokey's last words as time was winding down on the clock: "Boy, you one bad young mothafucka."

We won, and I was selected as the championship-game MVP. When they called my name to get my trophy, the large crowd let me know I deserved it.

I noticed a few girls I didn't know yelling my name. Then, pushing through the crowd like Moses parting the Red Sea, Uncle Mosley came toward me, letting everyone know I was his nephew. With him clinging to me around my neck, we walked out of the park together toward 142nd Street where he lived. I didn't have a chance to get my payoff from LA or Chic.

Uncle Mo was as proud as anyone out there. I guess I was moved by his praise, so much so I gave him my MVP trophy, even though it was the best-looking trophy I'd ever seen or won. Giving away trophies was a trend that would stick with me throughout my career. I gave away a lot of trophies but was always surprised at how quickly and easily people accepted them.

Harlem opened and embraced me like never before. Today, I was a champion among some of the best in the city, a playground hero who had gone up against playground legends and come out on top. It made up for all those years I played in virtual obscurity. I never suspected I'd never see the streets of Harlem quite the same way again. What seemed to be the beginning of my Harlem playground-legend legacy was actually the beginning of the end of it.

CHAPTER 42
LAFAYETTE GARDENS

LATE AUGUST WAS AROUND the corner, and my friends and peers were preparing to go back to school. Berry, Kevin Williams, and Mark Jackson were going to St. John's. Alvin Lott was at St. Bonaventure in the Atlantic 10, and Hutch was on his way to Sid Moncrief's Arkansas. Kenny Smith, my cousin, was headed to UNC, and Pearl to Syracuse. It looked like I would join the ranks of dead-end talents. I'd gotten my revenge in the biggest way against Artie Green, on the biggest stage imaginable before a Joe Hammond–like crowd. I was the MVP in the hottest tournament running uptown, and I had proved myself against the likes of Walter Berry, Richie Adams, and Kevin Williams, leading a young team to victory against all odds, but now what? What was I going to do once the summer was over?

After Chic's tournament, the reality of my long-term career came into focus. Fall and winter were coming, and I didn't have a school lined up. How was I going to make money? Going back to work at McDonald's was out of the question. After a summer of easy money and great basketball, working the grill at the 125th Street Mickey D's wasn't going to cut it for me.

Despite out-dueling some of the biggest names in New York basketball, I had few options. Howie Landa at Mercer Community in Trenton asked me to sign there, and I knew I could probably get on at Westchester Community, where Andre Slick and D-Mac were two of several guys I knew playing, but

I didn't want to go to either one. Going to another JC was the last thing I wanted to do. Schools like Indian River, Daytona Beach, and San Jacinto had called or sent letters, but I wasn't interested.

I preferred to play the wait-and-see game. At Pensacola, I had a 3.2 grade point average at the end of the semester, so I was in good academic standing. I could go anywhere. I had a monster summer, the biggest summer anyone from my neighborhood ever had. I figured the summer of 1984 was only going to be better. I just had to be patient. I built my rep in high school from the playgrounds and didn't see anything stopping me from beating the same drums again to renew interest from the big colleges.

The problem was trying to live another year with Ma. I might not last until next summer. Home didn't feel like home anymore. I asked around to see if anyone else was venturing out on their own and needed a roommate. I was smart enough to know I wasn't a hustler, at least not yet. The only hustle I had was basketball. While I was plotting my next move, I had one more money game to wrap up my summer season.

Lafayette Gardens was known as LG in Brooklyn. My cousin Gina and her family lived in LG projects before they moved to Amityville in Long Island. I had visited a few times but never played a game there. Other than the job I briefly held at Woolworth's on Fulton and Nostrand in Bed Sty, or the summer I worked two days in Greenpoint near the Williamsburg Bridge, I spent very little time in Brooklyn. I had a lot of respect for players coming out of Brooklyn, like Pearl, Sam Worthen, Fly Williams, World Free, and Cosell Brown. Unfortunately, none of that admiration was going to help me at Lafayette Gardens.

After getting the championship and MVP in Chic's tournament, my next game was a challenge game in Brooklyn not associated with any tournament. I was playing with Andre Baker, Bumpy-Face Rich, Big Al Brown, and Bobby Jones from the Bronx. We were playing against some Brooklyn cats out of Bed Sty, but one of their players was from Fort Green.

Someone put the word out that I could play and was probably the best guy on our squad. People in the crowd were asking, "This the nigga who's 'pose to be better than Jerry Ice?" I never thought I was better than Jerry Reynolds, but whatever; I wasn't backtracking from people thinking it. Especially since Jerry couldn't shoot. Better to be underestimated.

Bobby put the game together through his cousin from Bed Sty. The cousin got some of his boys from Brooklyn, and Bobby brought us from uptown. Only, it seemed like Bobby's cousin had a full crew and entourage, and they were all agitated before the game got going. It definitely wasn't a neutral venue.

One of the guys from the other team got rough with me right from the jump. His plan must have been to punk me. If he took me out of the game, we could lose. He wasn't much of a player, nothing near the caliber of a Kevin Williams. But the guy was as tall as I was and an athlete, looking to bend the rules any way he could to take my heart. I hadn't been in a fight since coming back from Pensacola and would have decked him quicker if closer to home, but I was conscious of where we were, and we were a long way from home.

This cat wouldn't back up. He was an ugly fucker, too. His breath smelled worse than any morning breath I ever smelled. He started jabbing me with his elbow even when I was off the ball. I had no choice, so I reacted. The next elbow he directed at me was going to be his last. I squared up and drilled the guy with a right hand, catching him on the side of his jaw. He swung on reflex, I slipped his swing and followed with a left hook/uppercut and another right, and both connected. The combination buckled his knees, but he didn't go down. He was dazed as I moved in for the kill.

All hell broke loose. People were grabbing and pulling me, some from my team and others from his. Bobby's cousin managed to get things settled, using a few of the guys from the sidelines. I was convinced we were going to get fucked up.

This was a neighborhood event, so of course I wasn't thrown out of the game. Bobby's cousin wanted to continue, and since he was paying the refs, the show went on. My elbow-happy defender was restrained to the sidelines, making a lot of noise about how he was going to kill me. Bobby's cousin, who didn't seem to like the guy I touched up, wanted to finish the game and apparently outranked anyone there. My better mind said, *Leave.* We were in Brooklyn; anything could happen. But Bobby kept talking about the bet and the money I could get, so I stuck around. It was a mistake.

Not ten minutes later, my antagonist was on the sidelines with an army of goons and a bruised face. The crowd grew. People were here now not just to see the game but to see the violence that would go down when it was over. The game became less important, and everyone on my team was being threatened. Guys were in the crowd now who didn't even know Bobby's cousin from Bed Sty. We all felt like we weren't going to make it out of the park in one piece.

"We gon cap that nigga after the game."

"Yeah, he gon git his. We got his ass. That nigga betta score all the points he can now; he ain't gon be scorin' no more after tonight."

My eyes flashed in the direction of the antagonist's comments.

"Yeah, I'm talking to you, bitch. We gon fuck you up!"

The guy threatening me had a gold tooth. He was dark, but I looked past him and into my future. *Is this what I want to do with my career? To play on the streets until I get hurt, maybe killed?*

I was stoic as we played, but this game had little to do with basketball anymore. The guy I fucked up had street soldiers posted everywhere. There was nowhere to run. And even if I ran, I had no idea where I was running to. I did the only thing I could do in this situation: I played basketball.

If it was going to be my last game, I wanted to play like it. Rich, Andre, and even Big Bobby were all scared to death of the menacing crowd. Everyone started playing tentatively. I was scared too but acted the opposite. I started snatching rebounds and flying up court, darting, shaking, spinning, and dropping baskets. After a while, the hostile crowd took notice. At one point I scored six or seven baskets in a row, three from long range, and two on forceful dunks that rattled the nets and wooed the crowd. The dunks were impressive because on a play before that, one of their guys tried to take me out by undercutting me when I went up for a shot. After spinning away from a guy, I attacked the baseline and dunked on two players from the Brooklyn squad, simultaneously. I was leaning sideways, but it was a hard dunk, probably better than the one I got over Big Ritch and Berry. The crowd got more frantic. People were pointing at me, watching my every move, and wondering, *Who the fuck is this kid?*

"Yo, who homeboy play for?"

I looked in the crowd for my earlier tormentor and didn't see his face. *Did he leave? Is there a chance I might get out of here alive?* Another spin move, followed by a between-the-legs dribble, left two opposing players disoriented. I immediately pulled up from the wing and hit a jumper off the board. The crowd roared so loud it drowned out the whistle blown for the and one as they hit me on the arm. I completely took over the game. If I was going to die, I wanted them to know they were killing someone special.

People starting inquiring, "Yo, how much Money got?" "He got forty-five—no he got fifty." The points were piling up, and so was the acceptance. By the time the game was over, everyone from the opposing team was shaking my hand, even though I had knocked out one of their teammates. They kept playing me hard, some of them still tried to hurt me, but I won them over on talent alone.

When the game was over, I got word that the guy I had the beef with was at the outer fringes of the park, the only exit, milling with his posse. But I wasn't being rushed; most of the people were still talking about what they saw on the court. Some wanted to talk to me.

"Yo, Money, who you play for?"

"Yo, where you from? I ain't never seen no shit like that. Yo, son, you nice!"

I took it all in, but my main concern was getting the fuck out of Brooklyn.

Bobby's cousin was smart. He had a friend call the housing police while we were still playing. They arrived a few minutes after the game. It was the first time I was glad to see the guys in blue. They came into the park, and we made our way to the street and flagged a cab. No doubt the disgruntled were setting us up for a serious beatdown. Maybe they were going to catch us in the train station. It wasn't the first time I tangled with the streets and made it out to smile about it. We were all relieved about the situation, even Bobby's cousin, who lost money on the game.

"Damn, Ice, you scored fifty-five points, B. You a bad mothafucka! How the fuck you do that shit?! Yo, I got a game set up 'in the hole' in a few weeks. You wanna play?"

"Na, B, I'm done wit Brooklyn. I got some things I need to do."

The hole was Brooklyn's famous "Soul in the Hole," their version of the Rucker Tournament. I had no desire to play in any street-money games for a while. Even though I wasn't in school, I felt like I should be playing somewhere else. I wasn't Joe Hammond or Pee Wee Kirkland. I wasn't prepared to live off the streets.

When I got home, it was after midnight and quiet. Ma and Prissy were asleep, but Ma heard me coming through the door. As usual, the kitchen light was on, and there were leftover salmon cakes on the stove, but I wasn't hungry.

"James?"

"Yeah, Ma."

"Coach Carse called you tonight."

"Okay."

"His number is on the table."

Ma's suggestion that maybe I should call him back was obvious. For the first time in the two months since Coach Craig Carse came into my life, I picked up the phone and dialed the 304 area code. It was late, but after pondering my recent experience in Brooklyn, I couldn't help myself and decided to act on emotion. This was something I couldn't get out of my mind.

"Hello. Coach?"

"Hello."

"This is James."

"I know who it is. How're you doing, James?"

"I'm good. Can you send me a ticket? I'm ready to come to State."

• • •

CPSIA information can be obtained
at www.ICGtesting.com
Printed in the USA
BVHW030011291121
622757BV00001B/33